# A Field Guide to
# 50 Drum Rudiments

## Ryan Alexander Bloom
## James A. Musser

Ruffe Dragg Press

ISBN: 979-8-9923262-0-8

# Table of Contents

## Flam Rudiments

## Hybrid Rudiments

# Introduction

Rudiments underly all the percussive arts. They are the fundamental building blocks of stick technique, some of the most basic pedagogical exercises, and an organizational system for the artform. Rudiments and rudimental drumming can be defined in several ways. Claus Hesler defines rudiments in his *Camp Duty Update* as having "defined rhythm, defined dynamic structure, defined sticking, defined nomenclature." John Pratt once said, "Drum rudiments are exercises. The rudiments of drumming are strokes," in reference to the Four Basic Strokes, which will later be explained in detail in this book. In *Encyclopedia Rudimentia*, I fleshed out Pratt's idea as, "Using Pratt's logic, almost any short pattern of strokes could be a useful rudiment," because, of course, all of the rudiments are just short patterns constructed from the basic strokes. Rudiments can be seen several ways: as tools to practice basic strokes, as functional building blocks for playing military signals (from which the oldest and most traditional rudimental patterns were originally derived), as the substitute for scales and arpeggios of non-pitched percussion, or as metaphorical "words" – where notes are letters, rudiments are words, and grooves or fills are sentences. In any case, you cannot escape the playing of rudiments – even if you wanted to.

Many drummers have tried to boil rudiments down to a basic level, to limit the number of necessary patterns to learn. There are websites, books, videos, articles, and teachers who talk about the seven basic rudiments, or the five basic rudiments, the three basic rudiments, or some other relatively arbitrary number. There is no inherently correct number of rudiments to learn (all numbers are arbitrary). Striving for the lowest possible number, is as foolish as thinking you could ever know them all by heart. There are, at least, somewhere around 1000 named rudiments (possibly many more if you include variations and grids), between the many worldwide rudimental traditions that have existed over the past several hundred years. The Percussive Arts Society (PAS) currently recommends 40 rudiments, 26 of which are the National Association of Rudimental Drummers (NARD) standards from the 1930s. Michael Eagle's "The Scottish Drumming Rudiments" lists 46 patterns, while the Percussion Creativ [sic] "Rudimental Codex" recommends 42 patterns. Several of the rudiments on these various sheets overlap, but many others do not. Outside of any of these, there are hundreds upon hundreds of Hybrid rudiments in the drum corps repertoire, and further unique rudiments in many of the individual rudimental traditions of various countries or regions. Almost anything playable on the drums can be expressed as a combination of rudiments. Whether the player knows the names, or intends to play those rudiments, is irrelevant to their existence in the playing.

In general, any drumming is made up of single strokes, double strokes, triple strokes, quadruple strokes, multiple bounce strokes (vaguely, anything above doubles), accents, taps, up strokes, and down strokes. This is an extremely limited pallet of independent motions. If there was a minimum number of skills, it would be these – and several of these are known as rudiments, already. But as soon as you practice these in combination, you stumble upon further previously named rudiments. If you took these basic elements and made up, from scratch, a list of relevant combinations that might be helpful to learn the drums, you would accidentally recreate many standard rudiments. Why bother? Standard rudiments already exist! Using extant rudiment names will ultimately be much more useful in communicating with other percussionists and drummers, than your own recreated pattern list. In other words, we use rudiments for everything – we might as well know what they are called, and how everyone else plays them.

Why this book exists:

This book primarily exists because my collaborator, James Musser, and I feel that no single previous book adequately presents a reasonable number of rudiments, in a reasonable amount of detail, with enough consistency to preclude interpretation by a teacher or other outside media. There have been many, many rudiment books published prior to this one, by authors with much more impressive names and resumes (more degrees, more championships, and/or more famous students). Unfortunately, a huge proportion of those books rely almost solely on etudes or solos, with no attempt to teach the basic information. Others try, but still fail to consistently provide basic information such as counting syllables, common alternative rhythms, sticking, or the rhythms underlying rolls or grace note figures. Some good books on the subject do exist, but many of these are only concerned with the NARD 26 rudiments, or are very outdated in their interpretations and notation styles. They do not hold up very well under a modern lens.

What we wanted was a book that taught a slightly larger and more curated list than the NARD 26 or the PAS 40, but not so many rudiments as to overwhelm the user. Here we recommend a nominal 50 rudiments for study. There are several more named rudiments slipped in, along with several variations for some of the standards, making the list quite a bit longer than 50, realistically. As stated above, there is no inherently correct number to learn. The round number 50 sounds good on the cover, though. These rudiments have been chosen based on general historical precedent, usefulness, international popularity, and sometimes to fill a perceived hole in the common pedagogical series.

We also wanted a book that helps the user **truly understand the rudiment**, rather than waiting for a teacher's clarification or relying on the perils of the internet to explain what we had written. To that end, we included: a large amount of detailed sticking, obvious counting numbers or syllables on most exercises, indications for the Basic Strokes, explanations for any other needed stick techniques, multiple notation examples in different time signatures or note values, examples of alternative usage or common variations, breakdowns of the skills with a single hand, buildups of the skills with both hands, text descriptions of the rudiments, selected audio examples, and interesting background information where available.

What we *do not* include are artistic etudes or solos. Many educational authors before us have padded out their publications with what were certainly painstakingly constructed original compositions that were meant to help the user understand the rudiments. If the user does not grasp the fundamental concept of the rudiment first, however, the etudes are relatively useless. Simply showing the standard PAS or NARD notation and then presenting an etude, however amazing, does not necessarily explain or teach the rudiment to a novice player. It only shows the user that the rudiment exists, and what it looks like in a limited context. It is then incumbent on the student to seek out additional information, if they do not immediately understand. Our goal here is simply to provide extremely basic information, so that users may later expand to performable musical repertoire with confidence. There is nothing wrong with a good etude, but it does not replace teaching basic information about the rudiment in a clear way. We also have not written a complete beginner method, such as would focus on rhythm reading and general musical knowledge. A great place to start would be my book *Subdivide and Conquer*, but there are also many other great manuals on the mechanics of music reading and general percussion playing.

Practice recommendations:

We recommend practice to achieve your goals, of course. This book is structured mostly such that playing through it in order is logical. You can skip around if you'd like, but learning Hybrid rudiments before the simpler patterns that they're combining, for example, would not make very much sense. More basic information is generally included for the first rudiment in a related group than later patterns. So, starting the general Flam rudiment group, with the first Flam (32) rudiment, would be more helpful than skipping to the later Flamacue (37) section, and missing out on a lot of essential Flam-related information. Use of a metronome is critical for both general time and the accuracy of each note. The metronome can be used in quarter notes at first, building from slow to fast, as needed. Then, try using relevant faster subdivisions like 8th notes, 16th notes, or triplets, to ensure that every stroke is precisely placed within each beat, for maximum cleanliness. Later, try backing off the clicks to half notes, or even just two successive 8th note clicks "+1" at the end/beginning of each measure. This will help your ability to keep time without the metronome, in a real performance situation. The old saying, "practice makes perfect," is not really true. A better saying is, "practice makes permanent," so make sure that attention is paid to details. Another common, yet erroneous, belief is that you must practice until you get it right, but to achieve success, you must actually practice *until you cannot get it wrong*. The repeat signs on most of the exercises are there to remind you that many repetitions are needed to really become proficient.

With the essential information about common rudiments and targeted exercises in hand, moving forward with any type of drumming – rudimental, classical, drum kit, or world percussion – should be easier and less fraught with uncertainty. There need be no mystery surrounding the rudimental drumming paradigm. Armed with the appropriate education, anything is possible.

–Ryan Alexander Bloom

**Audio Examples**

Examples of each of the 50 rudiments have been provided at the following links below. Each example will be played at 50 bpm and also at 100 bpm. While there are multiple interpretations for each, the audio will cover the Percussive Arts Society (PAS) interpretation, where applicable.

https://tinyurl.com/2s46uw48

https://drive.google.com/drive/folders/15fVR76Ws6EG8sDRngFH6tmD8EWgxFtw6

Drum Kit Notation Key

| Kick | F.Tom | Snare | Rack1 | Rack2 | Ride | Hats | Crash1 | Crash2 | China |

# Basic Strokes

There are several different ways of organizing the simplest principles of drumming, but one common method is to break drumming down into Four Basic Strokes: *Full, Down, Tap, Up*. This book will use the letters F, D, T, and U to abbreviate these strokes, which will be explained further below.

A long-held misconception among percussionists and drummers outside of the purely rudimental arena, is that rudiments are taught only so that they can be played back verbatim, in a musical context. When a drum kit player cannot think of a practical need for a specific rudimental pattern on the drum kit, in his or her preferred style of music, it is sometimes assumed that this rudiment is useless or unnecessary. "Without a direct drum kit application, how could the rudiment be relevant?" Classical percussionists have fallen into this logical trap, as well. "If it does not appear in the orchestral canon, why learn it?" These are poor assumptions based on a limited understanding of the modern use of rudiments as pedagogical tools.

The celebrated rudimental drummer, teacher, and author John S. "Jack" Pratt has been quoted as saying, "Drum rudiments are exercises. The rudiments of drumming are strokes." He is essentially saying that Basic Strokes are more fundamental than the rudiments, and are therefore necessary to play both rudiments, and non-rudimental patterns, correctly. This quote also seems to imply that rudiments are simply a way to practice the Basic Strokes, above any other benefits they may also provide to drummers.

With Pratt's reasoning, the point of learning rudiments is not only to play rudiments later, but also (and more importantly) to develop the Basic Strokes. These strokes apply to any type of playing in any musical genre or context, with or without the rudiments. A rudiment that helps develop a player's understanding of the Basic Strokes is therefore useful, even if that pattern is never directly played in a musical context.

## We learn rudiments to develop the Basic Strokes.

Any other benefit, such as actually using the rudiments in a musical context, or developing sticking pattern control, is in addition to the development of the Four Basic Strokes. Some rudiments absolutely occur in every style of music, and in every musical situation. Some are less common. Some may never be seen, depending on a player's personal musical journey. The act of learning the rudiment, and its pattern of strokes, is the main point, and is beneficial to all players.

The Basic Strokes essentially govern the height of the stick before and after each note played on the drum, enabling fluid movement between accented and unaccented notes. They are both a way to play a note correctly, and *also* to set up for the next note on that same hand efficiently. Correctly executing one accent requires a combination of different strokes in the context of a passage containing multiple notes. Most musical phrases do, of course, contain multiple notes.

It is worth noting that stick height will naturally vary with dynamic level, and this should not be confused with the differing heights of the Basic Strokes. The stroke heights indicated below will stay the same, *relative to one another,* but the actual definite height will change – all heights being smaller during piano and larger during forte, for example.

**Full Strokes (F)** start high and end high. They are used when the same hand will play multiple loud/accented strokes, successively. Also called Legato.

**Down Strokes (D)** start high and end low. They rebound from the head, but not as high as they started. They are used when a quieter/unaccented note will follow a loud/accented note, on that same hand. Also called Control or Staccato.

**Tap Strokes (T)** start low and end low. They are used when the same hand will play quiet/unaccented notes, successively.

**Up Strokes (U)** start low and end high. The upward motion of the stroke happens after the note has been played. They are used when a louder/accented note will follow a quieter/unaccented note, on the same hand. Also called Tap-up, Pull-up, or Pull-out.

The following exercises should help clarify when each stroke is appropriate.

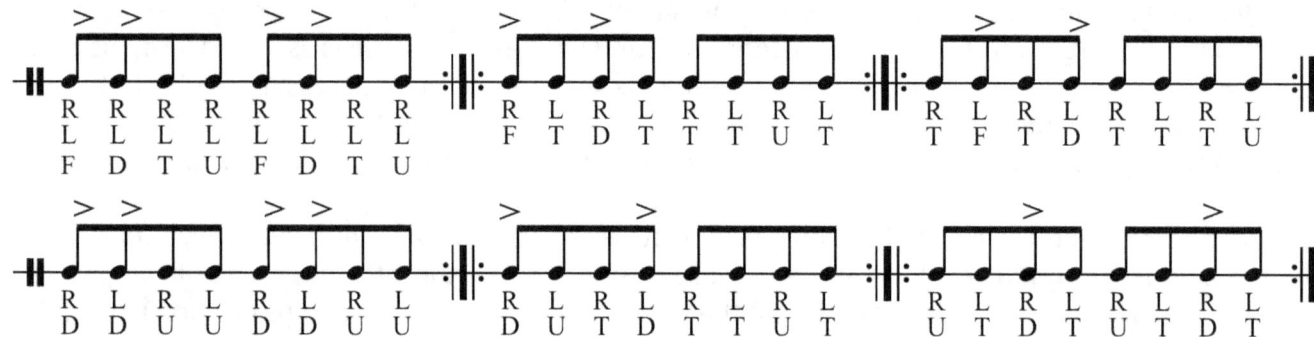

Not every pattern of accents requires all Four Basic Strokes, but more than one stroke is required when any combination of accents and taps are present. Rudiments or other patterns with double strokes, triple strokes, and buzzes will require a slight extension of these strokes to produce the correct motions, but the idea will still be the same. Flams (32) have an inherent high and low stick, and these same Basic Strokes govern the motion of Flams, as well (as shown on the Flam rudiment page).

Note: there are many sets of percussion terminology to describe these same four stroke motions; FDTU is but one set of names for these strokes. The words Legato and Staccato here, are mentioned as part of another set of stroke names, and have nothing whatsoever to do with the length or articulation of the actual notes. They are borrowed and repurposed to be a completely different concept.

# Grace Notes

In the past, rudimental drumming was written a number of different ways. The notation from one era is often illegible to drummers from another. One thing that has been fairly common for more than a century is the use of grace notes for the indication of various types of Ruffs, Drags, and even short Rolls. Grace notes are notes that fundamentally have no time. They are written smaller than the standard, or primary, notes around them. Grace notes are often, but not always, tied to the primary note they embellish. They are sometimes, but not always, struck through with a line to further indicate their lack of counted time. This strike through is more common on single grace notes than groups of grace notes but can sometimes occur on any grace note combination.

Rudimental drumming is an exact science – or at least it is supposed to be. Grace notes are, unfortunately, open to some level of interpretation. Notes without a definite place in metronomic time are antithetical to the theoretical precision of rudimental drumming. Somehow, counterintuitively, the use of grace notes is near ubiquitous in many eras and styles of drumming.

Several different styles of notating one or two grace notes in percussion music are shown below.

In American rudimental drumming, single grace notes should be interpreted as Flams (32), while any double grace note figure could represent a Drag (23) or a Ruff (24). In some European systems, depending on the composer or era, these different writing styles are not always synonymous. The slash through the notes sometimes has definite meaning, as does the tied or untied state of the grace notes to the primary note. For example, in some French notation the non-slashed grace note implies a Flam while the slashed note implies an Inverted Flam Tap (43), a completely different rudiment with a different number of notes. In late era Prussia and early incarnations of Germany, for another example, an 8th grace note was intended to be a right-handed Flam and a 16th grace note a left-handed Flam. There is no other indication of sticking, so careful attention must be paid to the tiny grace note flags. While these instances may never come up in modern American rudimental drumming, it is interesting how grace notes are used in other rudimental cultures and how small details can sometimes be very important.

Grace notes in drumming originate in the Baroque period's use of improvisation around the written notes on melodic instruments. Composers would indicate possible embellishments, such as appoggiatura or acciaccatura, with grace notes. This is fine for music with a flexible interpretive nature, but when the grace notes are intended to represent a repeatable, exacting rhythm that must be adhered to as canonical absolute, especially in a group setting, they do not do the job well.

The opposed ideals of interpretable notes without time and the rigidity of rudimental drumming ought not be connected, but they are very commonly intertwined. This leaves drummers in an awkward place when trying to play from music that they have never heard before. How ought a given set of grace notes be played? Sometimes that answer is fairly clear and other times it is anyone's guess. The Flam is fairly easy. It has just one grace note, and it is generally agreed upon in modern American drumming how a Flam should sound at any speed or in any context. In the past, briefly, there were both Open Flams and Close Flams, but that distinction has become obsolete. Today, Flams are still notated with grace notes because now there is only one correct Flam sound and one correct Flam execution. Drags, for a counterexample, are largely *not* notated with grace notes in the current marching percussion paradigm. Grace notes were abandoned for Drags specifically because two grace notes can be spaced in a number of ways compared to the associated primary note and this ambiguity is undesirable.

Vague writing is rarely tolerated in the 21st century. In modern rudimental writing, the exact note values are indicated in primary notes, not in grace notes. Double strokes, as in a Drag, are typically indicated with a tremolo slash through a primary note with exact metronomic time. If two 32$^{nd}$ notes are needed for a Drag figure, a primary 16$^{th}$ note with a tremolo slash through the stem will be written and all players will interpret that information exactly the same way. No arguments possible.

The example below shows potentially the same basic Drag rhythm as the notated example above, but this can only be interpreted one way – as 32$^{nd}$ notes preceding the downbeats.

I recommend using this tremolo slash system when writing your own music, as it is unambiguous. Prior to the past two or three decades, grace notes could still be found abundantly in rudimental writing, which forced the player to make a decision on the timing of the grace notes. It wasn't inherent to the notation.

Drags and Ruffs (two completely separate rudiments as will be explained in the relevant sections later) are both notated the exact same way in older writing styles: two grace notes before a primary note. How is one to know the difference? Untold numbers of drummers do not know that Drags and Ruffs are actually separate rudiments precisely because of grace notes and their inaccurate representation of the intended rhythms. Their conflation into the same rudiment is almost entirely based on the poor notation practices of the past.

It would be fantastic if there was a rule of thumb that could be printed here to explain how to interpret two grace notes, three grace notes, four, etc., but the reality is that it is impossible to make any sweeping statement on the subject that will hold true in all cases. The rudiments listed later in this book that are commonly notated with grace notes, notably the Drag rudiment section, will have some interpretation hints for each specific rudiment. Still, these cannot be applied universally.

**What are we to do?**

Firstly, stop writing grace notes in rudimental percussion music. If you compose rudimental music, do not use grace notes for anything but Flams. All other figures can be written out in precise metronomic time using primary notes. Write precisely and unambiguously the rhythm you intend without the use of grace notes. Secondly, you must decide what rudiment you are trying to play, with any given set of grace notes found in a piece of music. There are accepted rhythmic interpretations for different rudiments that can be applied to the grace notes, if you know what rudiment the grace notes are contained within. If the grace notes are clearly part of a Drag Paradiddle No. 2 (29), that can inform the necessary timing. Thirdly, if in doubt, look at the space that the grace notes occupy, then try to fill the space neatly. If you have two grace notes between successive primary 16$^{th}$ notes, the rhythm will necessarily be faster than if they are between two successive primary 8$^{th}$ notes. Keeping the speed of Drags consistent throughout a piece of music is a good place to start. Figure out how fast the fastest Drag needs to be to fit in the smallest given space, then play the rest of the Drags at the same note value, for consistency. The composer most likely intended one sound for all cases.

This explanation is likely unsatisfactory for the beginner rudimental drummer. It makes no definitive statement. Unfortunately, the more concrete an answer sounds on a topic such as grace note timing, the less likely it is that the source is well informed. The more you know, the more you realize that concrete answers are few and far between. Any precise definition of the timing for grace notes is only relevant to a given piece of music, a specific composer, or a definite time and place in musical history. There is no correct answer that spans all of rudimental drumming. When playing rudimental music from any era before the use of tremolo slashes for double strokes became common, there is room for debate on any given Drag or Ruff figure. Honestly, there is sometimes room for debate on the primary notes, as well. Many times one must play the rudiment, not the rhythm, which is the opposite of today's mantra.

# 1. Single Stroke Roll

**PAS:** *#1*
**NARD:** *#14*
**Other Names:** *Einfacherstreich, Einerstreich, Tan, Tau, Tao, Enkelslag, Colpo, Battuta Semplice, Frisés, Coup Simples, Bâton Rond, Tapatapa, Golpes, Enkeltslags, Patapata, Dagalaga*
**Alternation:** *yes*
**Origin:** *unknown, ancient*

The Single Stroke Roll is the simplest rudiment, consisting of one note per hand alternating back and forth between the hands for an indefinite duration. There are no accents or rhythmic changes, only alternated strokes. All strokes will be the same Basic Stroke type, either Taps or Full Strokes.

This rudiment can be played with a variety of hand techniques, including wrist strokes, finger strokes, arm strokes, or combinations thereof. It can also be played with or without utilizing the rebound from the head. At a basic level, the Single Stroke Roll can be produced from the wrist on any surface, regardless of rebound. This works well for slow tempos or note values on any surface, and can be done fairly fast, but with an upper limit to the speed of a wrist-only motion. Higher speeds are easier to achieve with only the fingers and/or by utilizing the rebound of the head. Much like dribbling a basketball, allowing the stick to rebound off the head and only actively being involved in the downward part of the stroke will make faster playing easier. Moving only the fingers, instead of the hand or arm, will also increase the efficiency of each stroke and make playing at higher tempos or note values easier. The fastest single strokes are often a matter of pure timing – using the fingers to "dribble" the sticks off of the head with the minimum possible input to the stick, while taking great care to produce an even stream of notes.

Single strokes entered the American rudimental practice as a formal rudiment potentially as late as 1862, probably because they were previously thought to be so obvious as to not need explanation or consideration as a rudiment. They are ubiquitous in every style of rudimental drumming and, of course, in all types of percussion.

Single Stroke Rolls can be played with any note value and for any duration, there is no specificity. The exercises below will be very basic in light of the repetitive nature of this rudiment. That said, it is perhaps the most important rudiment to master and should be practiced at a variety of tempos, note values, and dynamic levels. It can be used in rudimental contexts, drum kit applications, and classical music, including keyboard, bass drum, and timpani rolls, as well as snare drum excerpts. It is the primary skill behind 3 Stroke (2) and 4 Stroke (3) Ruffs and the Single Stroke 7 (4), and is used in Paradiddles (20-22), Flam (32-43) rudiments, Drag (23-31) rudiments, and many Hybrids (44-50).

PAS Notation

R L R L R L R L

PAS Counted

R L R L R L R L
1 e + a

## NARD Notation

## Triplet Notation

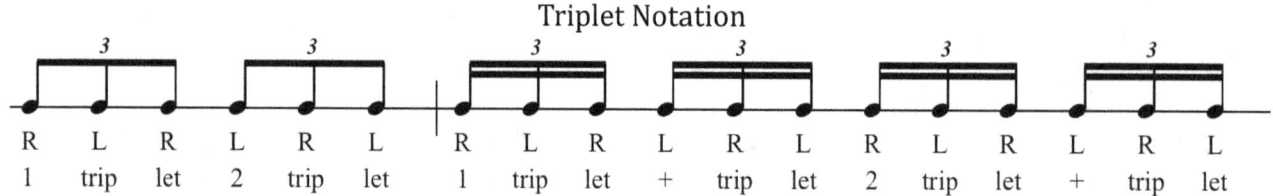

## 16th Note Timing Exercise

## Suggested Drum Kit Application

# 2. Single Stroke 3 (or 3 Stroke Ruff)

**PAS:** *n/a*
**NARD:** *n/a*
**Other Names:** *Single 3, Tap Ruff, 3 Stroke Rough, Treble Stroke, Ruff – Old Style, Single Backs, Coup Frisés de 3, Tagada, Pra, Pri*
**Alternation:** *yes*
**Origin:** *unknown, possibly British*

The 3 Stroke Ruff is essentially the same as a Drag (23), but is executed only in single strokes. Many percussionists and drummers have erroneously conflated the Drag, the Ruff (24), and the 3 Stroke Ruff as being the same rudiment. They are not – they are different rudiments, each with a different execution. The name 3 Stroke Ruff lends itself to confusion, since all three rudiments are notated with three notes. Despite this confusion, it is, unfortunately, the most common name for the single stroked pattern.

The 3 Stroke Ruff is less common than the Drag in snare drumming, but is most players' default sticking for figures with two grace notes on timpani or keyboard instruments. Similarly, it is very useful on drum set when maximum clarity is required or when playing a fast set of three notes on toms or other instruments with lesser rebound. It is extremely simple in terms of the Basic Strokes, requiring only Taps to execute. It has been listed as a rudiment in the USA since at least 1810, with a healthy record in print up to the present, though it is omitted from both the NARD and PAS sheets. Prior to its use in the USA, it could be found in British sources, though its origin is not certain, since it also appears in French and Belgian traditional drumming.

# 3. Single Stroke 4 (or 4 Stroke Ruff)

**PAS:** *#2*
**NARD:** *n/a*
**Other Names:** *Ruff, Ruffe, 4 Stroke Rough, Rau, Coup Frisés, Triplet Stroke, Full Drag, Halbe Ruf, Kortruff, Ra de 3, Französischer Ruf, Voorslag van Drie, Forschlagi iz Trek Not*
**Alternation:** *no*
**Origin:** *unknown, possibly England*

The Single Stroke 4 is a variation of the Single Stroke Roll (1) that contains exactly four notes. It is also commonly seen as a modern incarnation of the 4 Stroke Ruff, which is a set of three grace notes ahead of a primary note, usually played in single strokes in the American rudimental style. Since both the Single Stroke 4 and the 4 Stroke Ruff contain four evenly spaced single strokes, the technical execution for both variations is identical and they have been combined here onto the same page. The placement on the beat, however, is often opposing – the Single Stroke 4 is commonly played **starting** from the downbeat, while the 4 Stroke Ruff **ends** on the downbeat.

The 4 Stroke Ruff entered American drumming in the late 18th century, coming directly from the British. It was used in Britain from at least the mid-17th century, appearing in the Douce Manuscript, but possibly earlier. A pattern with three grace notes like the 4 Stroke Ruff is one of the most common rudiments worldwide, appearing in many countries' historical traditions. It is also a common classical snare figure. In other rudimental drumming styles outside of the USA, there are a number of stickings for the same sound and notation – RLLR in France, Sweden, and Switzerland, LLLR in Germany, RRLR in Russia (among other stickings, there does not appear to be just one standard), and RLRR in pipe band. Any of these could be substituted below with a similar effect.

PAS Notation 🎧

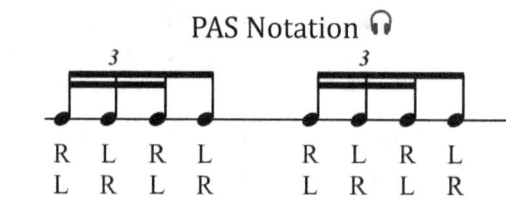

| R | L | R | L | | R | L | R | L |
| L | R | L | R | | L | R | L | R |

PAS counted – and using the name

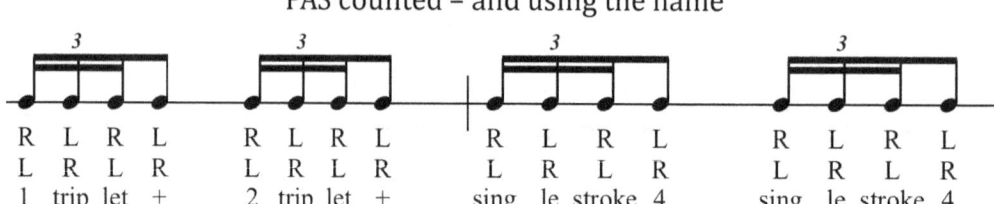

| R | L | R | L | R | L | R | L | R | L | R | L | R | L | R | L |
| L | R | L | R | L | R | L | R | L | R | L | R | L | R | L | R |
| 1 | trip | let | + | 2 | trip | let | + | sing | le | stroke | 4 | sing | le | stroke | 4 |

Four Stroke Ruff Notation 🎧

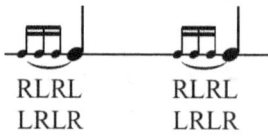

RLRL   RLRL
LRLR   LRLR

## Interpretations of the Grace Notes Open and Closed

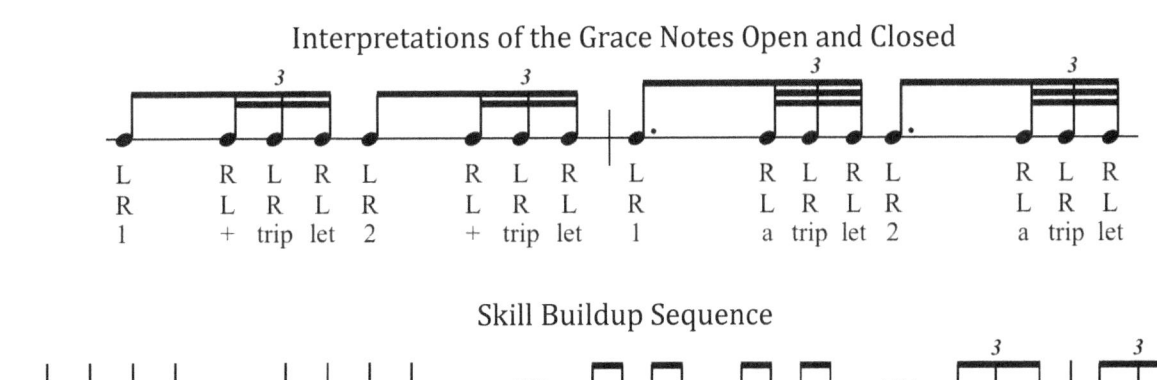

## Skill Buildup Sequence

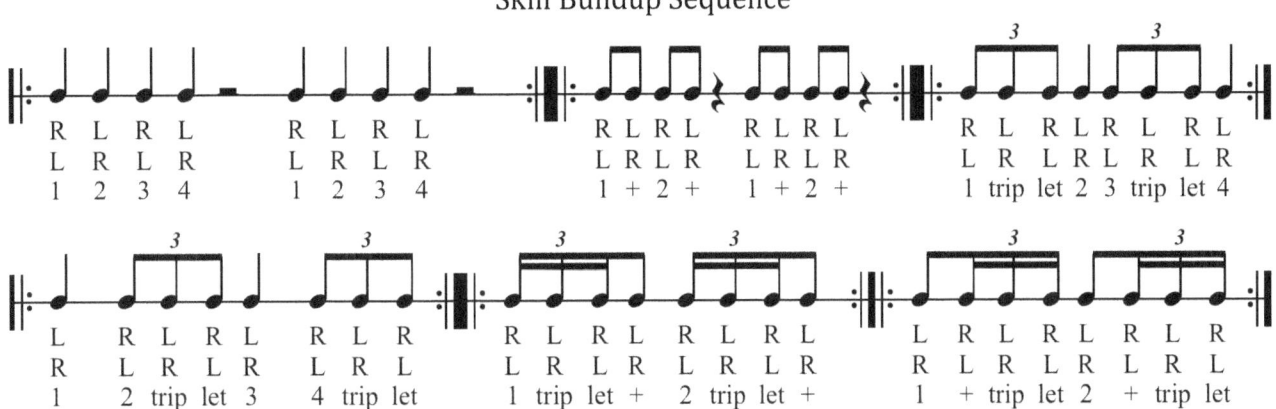

## Suggested Drum Kit Application

# 4. Single Stroke 7

**PAS:** *#3*
**NARD:** *n/a*
**Other Names:** *Frisés de 7, Triple Compound Drag Beat, Roll of 7 Single Strokes*
**Alternation:** *yes*
**Origin:** *unknown, likely France*

The Single Stroke 7 is a variation of the Single Stroke Roll (1) that contains exactly seven notes. Since there is no accent or other dynamic variation, it can be played entirely with the same Basic Stroke, Taps. This rudiment seems to have entered American playing during the Civil War when Col. H.C. Hart called it the Triple Compound Drag Beat in 1862. It is also featured in traditional French drumming. The Single Stroke 7 is often played as a sextuplet, or a group of six notes in one beat, plus one additional note on the next downbeat, though any evenly spaced group of seven notes would work.

# Tremelo Slashes and Roll Notation

Roll notation can be confusing to the beginner drummer and seasoned veteran alike. The standard convention for writing rudimental rolls has changed several times throughout history. The most modern convention, which is the least ambiguous, is common, but not universal today. Older conventions can range from slightly ambiguous to completely open to interpretation. Here we will look at two of the most common ways of notating a rudimental roll, both of which utilize tremolo slashes on the stem of notes to indicate that a roll should be executed. We will start with tremolo slashes as abbreviations first, before moving to rolls, specifically.

In the example on the next page, the "Old Style Abbreviations" refers to a fairly antiquated convention that applies to all instruments, not just percussion. Here, tremolo slashes on the stems of notes are an abbreviation for multiple notes of a smaller value. These are not necessarily rolls, when used in percussion, though this is clearly how the roll notation came to be. In this system, one slash tells the player to play $8^{th}$ notes for the duration of the note carrying the slash. In the example measure, a quarter note with one slash signifies that two $8^{th}$ notes should be played in that space. The one slash corresponds to the $8^{th}$ note's single flag or beam. If the note carrying the slash were to be a half note instead, the single slash would indicate four $8^{th}$ notes, because that adds up to the value of the note carrying the slash. Any note denomination can carry the slash, and the player must know how many $8^{th}$ notes are equivalent. Following this logic, two slashes on a quarter note would indicate four $16^{th}$ notes in the duration of the quarter note. Again, two slashes correspond to the two flags or beams on a $16^{th}$ note. Three slashes indicate eight $32^{nd}$ notes should be played in the duration of the shown quarter note. This pattern can also be applied to triplets, with the addition of the number 3 marked over the note. It requires a little bit of thought, but this abbreviation system is perfectly logical.

As mentioned above, the use of tremolo slashes to indicate rolls is directly related to these abbreviations. The three tremolo slashes, indicating $32^{nd}$ notes, is equivalent to eight strokes per quarter. This corresponds directly to the most common rudimental interpretation of a 9 Stroke Roll (10), for which eight of the nine strokes fall on the quarter note, and the final stroke is on the following downbeat. The only difference between the pure abbreviation and the 9 Stroke Roll interpretation is that rudimental drummers assume double strokes for a 9 Stroke Roll, where the pure abbreviation does not necessarily indicate sticking, by itself.

In the most modern usage of tremolo slashes, this old system is hinted at, but not followed precisely. Under "Modern Use of Stem Marks" we can see that a single slash on the stem specifically denotes a double stroke. This means that the same notation has become more specific in rudimental drumming than it was in the pure abbreviation paradigm. Instead of indicating simply two $8^{th}$ notes, a single slash on a quarter note in rudimental drumming now means precisely two $8^{th}$ notes *played with the same hand*. This holds true for other note values, where the single slash also implies two notes with the same hand, or *a double stroke*.

Three tremolo slashes on a note (without any beams or flags) indicates a roll. If the note has one or more beams or flags, such as an $8^{th}$ note or $16^{th}$ note, the number of beams/flags plus slashes will add up to three. For example, an $8^{th}$ note roll will have 2 slashes plus the single beam. A $16^{th}$ note roll will have a single slash plus the double beam. Each case adds up to three, total. In the modern concert and orchestral usage, three slashes (or beams plus slashes) mean a buzzed or Multiple Bounce Roll (17), that lasts for the value of the note. In rudimental usage, this indicates a double stroked open roll that fills the value of the note. If a Multiple Bounce roll is preferred in rudimental notation, the letter Z on the stem will replace the slashes. The place where this system could break down slightly is when a single slash appears on a 16th note. According to the rule above, a single slash should indicate a double stroke. BUT, if the composer desired a longer roll, the notation would likely still feature just a single slash (plus a numerical indicator of the roll length). This is unlikely unless the tempo was extremely slow, but it could potentially happen.

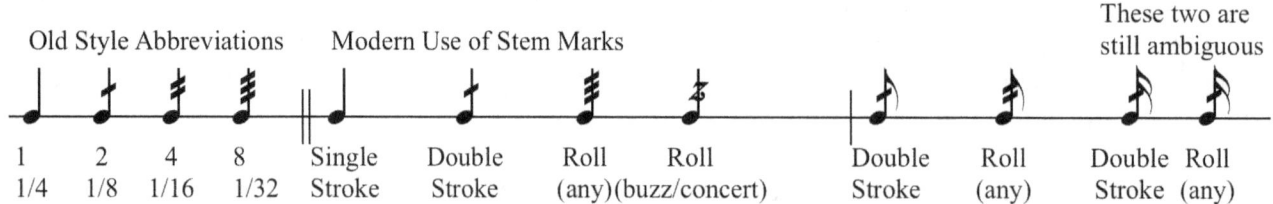

So, as confusing as that is, we have a system in place. The remaining question is, when a roll is indicated with three tremolo slashes in rudimental notation, how many strokes should that roll contain? If we were to simply following the old tremolo abbreviation method, the answer would correspond exactly the number of notes indicated by the abbreviation. This is **NOT** how it works in rudimental drumming.

All numbered rudimental rolls will have three slashes (or beams and slashes that add up to three). The number of strokes inside the roll will sometimes be unrelated to the old abbreviation system. In most, but not all rudimental examples, a number near the roll will indicate the required number of strokes. Below, the notation example shows several rolls notated with identical quarter notes, and three tremolo slashes. Each has a different number adjacent to it. This number fundamentally changes the note value of the individual roll strokes, meaning that the tremolo slashes really only indicate that some type of roll is present. The stroke number is completely independent of the note value or the tremolo slash notation. The only roll that actually corresponds to the slashes and note value exactly is the 9 Stroke Roll, as mentioned above. The 5 Stroke (6), 7 Stroke (7), and 11 Stroke (12) are all possible in this space, but feature a different denomination for the strokes of the roll, in order to fit in the space of the quarter note.

Most rudimental notation from the 20th century is written with tremolo slashes and stroke numbers. Some, for whatever reason, uses the tremolo slashes, but will not indicate stroke number anywhere. In these cases, the decision is up to the individual player (or ensemble) for how many strokes to include for each roll. The answer will depend on the skill of the player(s) and the speed of the piece.

In 21st century standard rudimental notation, the rolls are usually, but frustratingly not always, notated like the right half of each measure above. The actual rhythm of the rolls are written out exactly (as in the 5 Stroke Roll example). Or, the rhythm of the roll's skeletal meter is written out, with the single tremolo slash indicating which notes are to be played with double strokes (as in the 7 Stroke, 9 Stroke, and 11 Stroke examples, above). This method eliminates confusion, because the required number of strokes and the note values necessary to play those strokes are obvious. This is especially helpful if, like in the 11 Stroke example, the note value will be an odd value in a beat, or possibly a polymetric value over several beats.

It is strongly encouraged that drummers learn to read both types of notation above. If you are interested in writing your own rudimental music, it is strongly suggested that rolls be written explicitly, using the actual note values (like the 5 Stroke example) or the single slash indication of double (like the 9-11 Stroke examples), so that other players do not have to think, do any math, or vaguely interpret your intentions.

Below are 4 ways that a composer could write a 9 Stroke Roll. In the "Bad" example, it is unclear that the composer wants a 9 Stroke (it could be another roll). In the "OK" example, the 9 Stroke is indicated but the player must already know or figure out logically that eight 32nds are needed, to play the roll correctly. This is fine for experienced players, but could trip up a beginner or low intermediate player. The "Good" example shows all the necessary information, with no ambiguity – but, is unwieldy, and may intimidate a lower skill player by simply showing 32nds, at all. The "Best" example shows the 16th note skeletal meter of the roll, and also indicates that the notes are doubles. A beginner can count the 16th notes, and then add the doubles without much trouble, and an experienced player can see that it is a 9 Stroke Roll, without hesitation – plus, it takes up less space on the page, is easier to read quickly, and is less intimidating than the "Good" example.

In the case of an odd grouping or nonstandard note value roll (like an 11 Stroke Roll on a quarter note, as shown below), notation is even more important. Simply showing a quarter note roll (as in the first "Bad" example), will rarely cause anyone to play the 11 Stroke Roll desired by the composer. Most drummers will assume a 9 Stroke Roll, and further assume the sticking is a mistake. A small few will potentially understand that 11 Strokes are desired, but it will take undue thought to come up with the appropriate execution. In the second "Bad" example, the extra grace notes are an abnormal usage and, while it has been done this way in the past, most drummers will be confused, and again, assume a mistake has been made. In the best case, the player may play the appropriate 11 Stroke, but will be thrown off, or agitated slightly by the strangeness of the notation. The "OK" example should cause most experienced drummers to execute the roll correctly, but the fact that the 11 Stroke Roll will not utilize 16th notes, 32nd notes, or triplets of any type, will still confuse, or even completely stump inexperienced players. They may not even guess that a quintuplet is an option. In the "Good" example, the odd grouping and precise stroke number are obvious, but this is still somewhat hard to read and count. The "Best" example makes it very clear that the skeletal meter for the roll is odd, and it does not appear to be a mistake. This roll would still be tricky for a beginner, but the information necessary is clearly presented, and an experienced player would be able to execute the 11 Strokes in the required space with no hesitation.

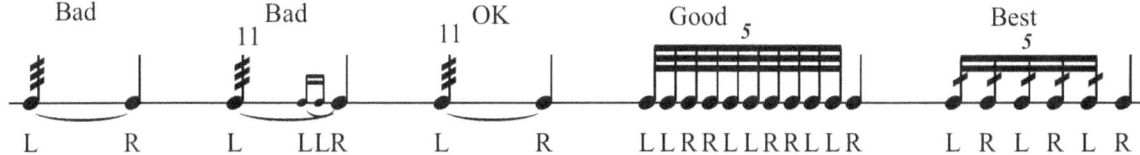

It should be noted that some composers will still utilize some of the "Bad" or "OK" practices in the 21st century. These were standard and extremely common in the 20th century, and it is still a good idea to become somewhat familiar with them.

# 5. Double Stroke Open Roll

**PAS:** *#6*
**NARD:** *#1*
**Other Names:** *Double Stroke Roll, Long Roll, Dada-Mama Roll, Daddy-Mommy Roll, Papa-Mama Roll, Open Diddles, Roulement, Rullo, Redoble, Wirbel, Hvirvel, Virvel*
**Alternation:** *yes*
**Origin:** *unknown, ancient*

The Double Stroke Open Roll consists of a smooth stream of notes played in pairs of rights and lefts, and is one of the most important rudimental skills to develop. All of the numbered rolls, the Paradiddle rudiments, the Drag rudiments, and several of the Hybrid rudiments require a competent double stroke. There are also some Flam rudiments that contain a double, and the techniques used for doubles are very similar to those used for multiple bounce strokes and triple strokes. In other words, the list of rudiments NOT requiring a good Double Stroke Roll is very, very short.

This type of roll has been present in nearly every tradition of rudimental drumming for centuries and may trace back to the origin of rudiments in medieval Europe.

A perfect Double Stroke Roll sounds identical to a Single Stroke Roll (1), but executed with a different sticking. Each note must be audible and even in time with no obvious difference between hands or between the first and second note of each hand. This roll can be played in a number of ways, depending on the desired tempo, the tuning of the drum, the sticks, the dynamic level, etc.

The simplest way to play double strokes is to play two identical, separate single strokes from the wrist with one hand, and then play two more with the other hand, in a repeating pattern – RRLLRRLL. Each note is a distinct full stroke, with its own wrist motion. This is the most precise way to the play the roll, and is also the only way to play it at extremely slow tempos or note values. The drawback to this approach is that it limits top end speed, significantly. To achieve higher speeds, a different hand technique is necessary.

There are several options for increasing the speed of double strokes. To play this rudiment open-close-open in the most rigorous manner, more than one hand technique is required within a single open-close-open sequence. No single approach to the roll will span all possible tempos, and care must be taken to switch techniques at the appropriate time, without affecting the sound of the roll.

The next easiest way to play double strokes is by fully utilizing the rebound provided by the drum. Adding additional pressure at the end of a single stroke, so as to inhibit the full return of the stick after the first note, can cause the stick to play multiple bounces for the same individual wrist motion. This is the same technique used for Multiple Bounce Rolls (17). With care, it is possible to bounce the stick exactly twice. Pressure must be released after the second note, so that further bounced notes are not produced unintentionally. Lifting the wrist can help with this. Adjusting the strength of the grip, and the amount of pressure applied toward the head, will change the speed of the bounces, making this a viable technique at a range of tempos or note values. The bounced double stroke works well at extremely fast speeds, since the wrist actively plays only half of the notes that the stick produces. This type of double can be slowed down significantly, but there is an effective limit at the slower end of the spectrum. At some point, the bounces become awkward and sound uneven when played too slowly.

A third way to play double strokes is with a push-pull, drop-catch, or open-close motion. There are a few variations on this technical approach, but the uniting theme is that one of the notes is produced with the wrist and the other with the fingers. A normal wrist stroke is played, but the rebound is interrupted by a finger stroke, and the stick returns to the head for a second note. The advantage to playing the second note of the double with the fingers is that its precise location in time, and its volume, can be adjusted independently of the first note. The extra control of a finger stroke results in a better sounding roll at slow to medium tempos, than the purely bounced double stroke, previously mentioned. It is not quite as precise as two individual wrist motions, but can be played significantly faster – though not quite as fast as the bounced double. It represents a very good middle ground between the previous two techniques, and can be used for the majority of tempos and note values. The extreme ends of the speed spectrum do require other technical approaches.

There may also be other ways to produce this roll. It is important that the roll sound good, with even strokes, regardless of the technique used. Some of the exercises, including the official NARD notation, indicate accents on the second note of each double. This is for training purposes and is rarely required for a normal Double Stroke Open Roll. It does help with the development of the roll and with playing other rudiments that have inherent accent patterns.

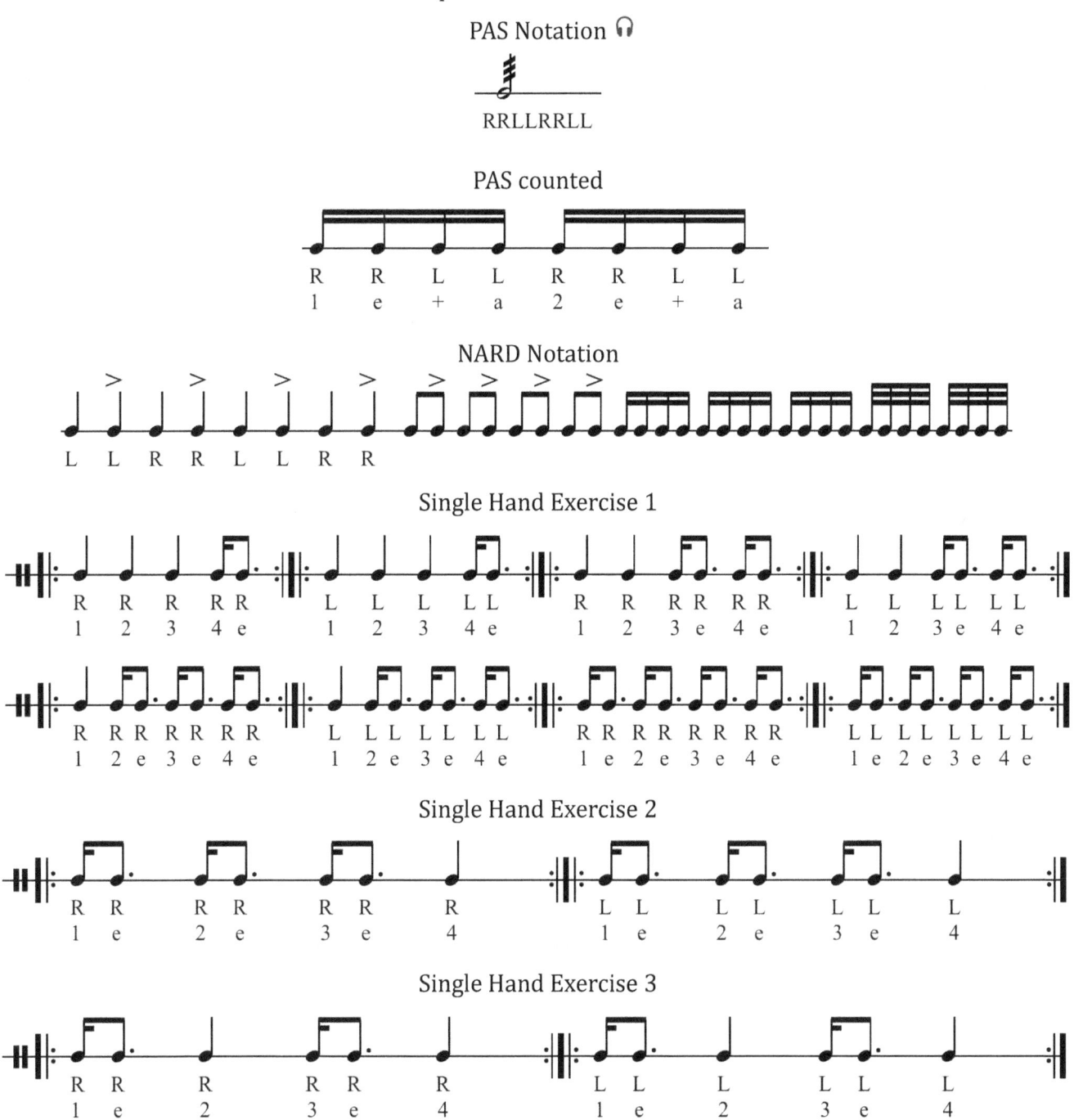

PAS Notation

RRLLRRLL

PAS counted

R R L L R R L L
1 e + a 2 e + a

NARD Notation

L L R R L L R R

Single Hand Exercise 1

Single Hand Exercise 2

Single Hand Exercise 3

## Two Hand Exercise 1

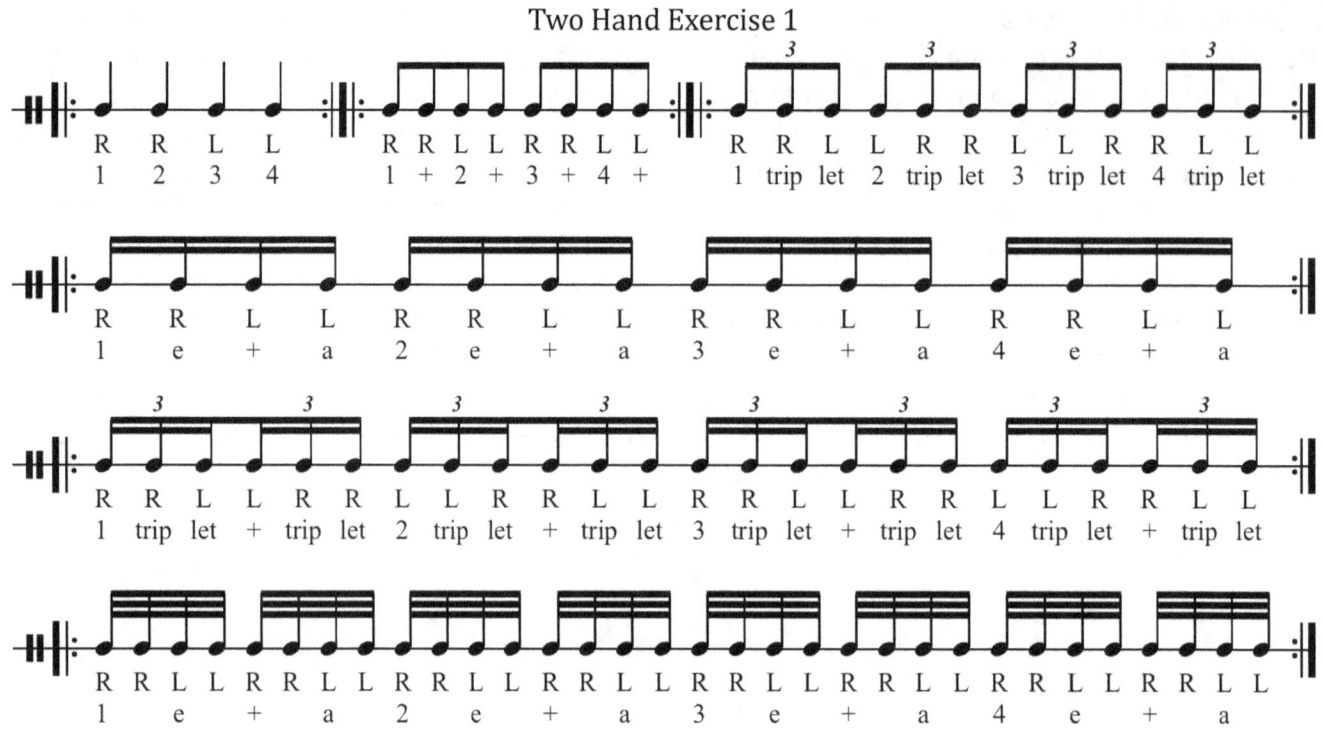

## Basic Strokes (necessary for Two Hand Exercise 2)

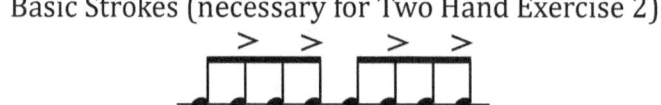

## Two Hand Exercise 2

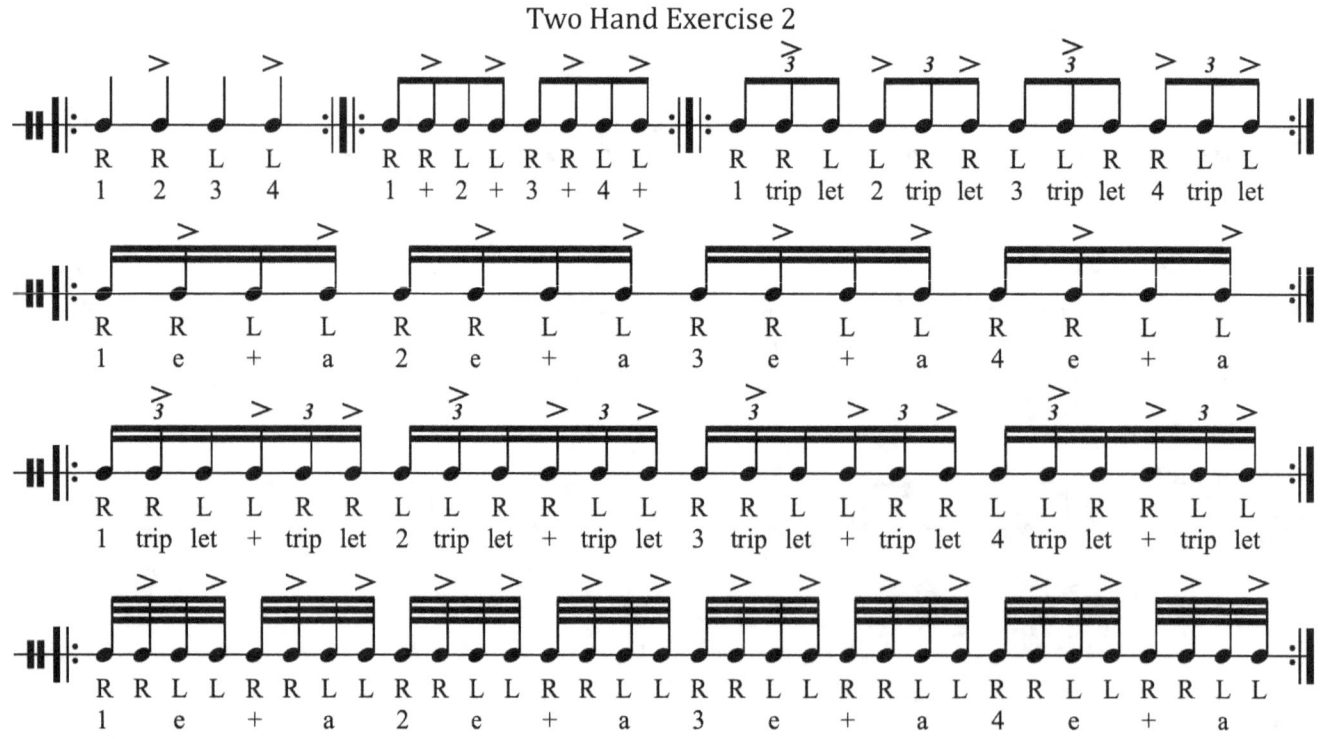

# Numbered Rolls

One point of continuous confusion among many drummers is the concept of the numbered Double Stroke Rolls. Each has several rhythmic iterations commonly found in music, but at a base level, the idea is actually very simple – The Double Stroke Open Roll (5) is played up to a given number of individual strokes, and then ceased abruptly.

The longest numbered roll could be extremely long, hundreds or thousands of strokes, though very rarely are such rolls talked about and they're never listed as rudiments. More reasonable numbers are abundant in written music. For example, a whole note played in $32^{nd}$ notes, or double strokes on $16^{th}$ notes, will end up being 33 strokes if you end the roll exactly on the downbeat, or beat 1, of the following measure. A half note roll is normally played as a 17 Stroke Roll (16), the longest roll on most rudiment sheets. Every smaller number below this down to 3 strokes can be played, and many are standardized rudimental selections.

The general pattern is easy enough to follow. For odd numbers, double strokes make up the bulk of the roll, and a single stroke is added to complete the desired number. For a 5 Stroke Roll (6), this means two double strokes, for a total of four notes, and a single stroke, for the fifth note. For even numbers, the bulk of the roll is similarly played in double strokes, but two of the notes are played as single strokes. For a 6 Stroke Roll (7), two double strokes, again adding up to four notes, plus two single strokes, for the fifth and sixth notes. These need not be played in precisely this order, but the pattern holds true for other stickings or inversions.

Again, the pattern is: one single stroke for odd numbered rolls and two single strokes for even numbered rolls, and the rest of the required notes played with double strokes. Notation below will clarify for each individual number.

The PAS 40 rudiments include rolls with 5, 6, 7, 9, 10, 11, 13, 15, and 17 strokes. The NARD 26 includes rolls with 5, 7, 9, 10, 11, 13, and 15 strokes. Despite some obvious missing rolls in these sequences, every number can be used for a Double Stroke Roll, starting from 3 strokes, at the shortest.

We call the 3 Stroke Roll a Drag (23), in most cases, but it is also a roll. Despite the special name, it follows the pattern stated above. It is an odd number, thus there is a double stroke for two of the notes and a single stroke for the third. It is the same pattern as the example 5 Stroke Roll, but with fewer total notes.

Next would be the 4 Stroke Roll, but we call this the Single Drag Tap (26). It follows the pattern of the 6 Stroke Roll above with two notes played as a double stroke, then two single strokes to bring the total number to four strokes. Even with the special name, it functions identically to an even numbered roll.

The 5, 6, and 7 Stroke rolls are all normally included on the PAS and NARD lists, but not the 8 Stroke Roll. This is odd because it was very often used throughout rudimental history, and conforms to the pattern of the 4 Stroke and 6 Stroke Rolls, outlined here. Both major lists then include 10, and 11 Strokes, while also ignoring the 12 Stroke Roll, though it has been published, and definitely exists. Then, both lists include the 13, skip the 14, include the 15, skip the 16, and the PAS 40 does include the 17 Stroke Roll. This book will feature all of these rolls later, 3-17, with the exception of the 14 Stroke Roll and the 16 Stroke Roll, which are both quite rare. They follow the pattern, and will be shown in the table of examples on page 25, but are not historically common in rudimental repertoire.

While the pattern of the numbered rolls is simple at heart, there are many different ways to use any given roll. Recognizing the roll, in context, can be somewhat challenging. In some notation, the roll number is obviously stated, but the appropriate note values to fit the roll into the space, must be inferred. In other notation, the roll will be shown without a number, so the correct number of strokes and the note values, must be inferred. In yet other places, rolls could be written with grace notes (see the section on Grace Notes on page 9), so that the number of strokes is obvious, but the note value and the space the roll should fill, must be inferred. Still other times, all the notes will be written out, with no ambiguity. Rolls can be the easiest or the hardest part of a piece to decipher, depending on the notation used by a composer.

Modern rudimental writing has trended toward writing out the skeleton of the roll, and adding tremolo slashes to indicate which strokes are doubled. This removes doubt, and the rolls are clear and obvious. In these cases, because the note values are given, and every roll stroke is accounted for, composers often do not specify the number of the roll. When there is no need to infer any of the information, playing the given rhythm and simply counting the beats in the piece of music will result in the correct roll. It can later be determined which roll is which by counting, but that information is actually secondary to the performance of the music. Practicing rolls of varying lengths is still a critical exercise in the development of the skill, despite not needing to be able to recall each roll length, and its idiosyncrasies, in the same way that was required of older notation systems.

On the following page are examples, showing the number of notes in each roll, along with the sticking. These patterns can be played in different note values, so as to fit in different rhythmic situations. They can also be inverted, so that the single strokes fall in different places, such as at the beginning of the roll. The thing that will never change is the pure number of strokes. A 5 Stroke Roll can never have more or less than five notes, regardless of the order they fall in, the note values used, the meter, or the accent pattern.

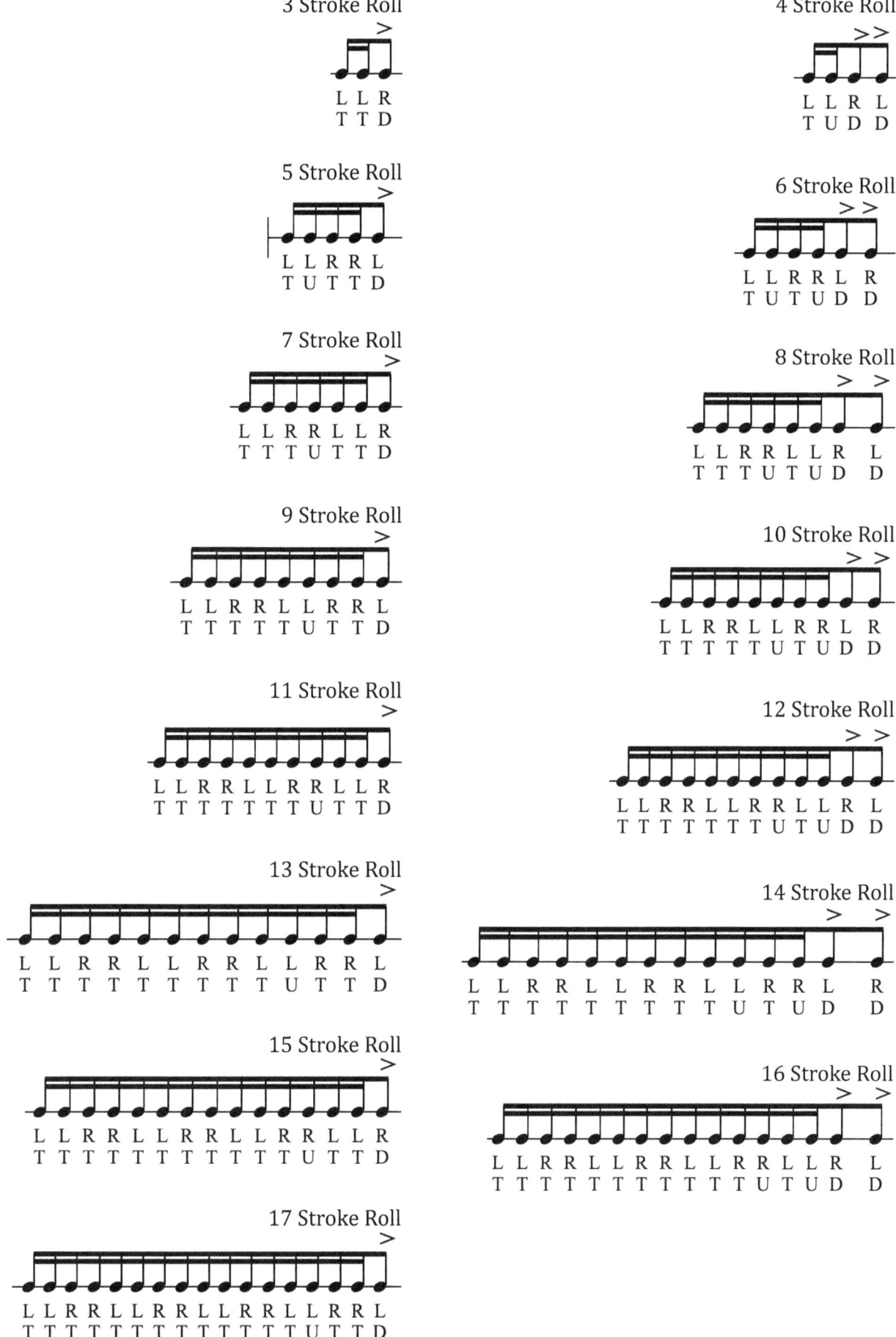

# 6. 5 Stroke Roll

**PAS:** *#7*
**NARD:** *#2*
**Other Names:** *Mother Roll, Rau da 5, Rau de Cinco, Ra de Cinq, Funfer Ruf, Du, Ran de 5, Roffel van 5*
**Alternation:** *yes*
**Origin:** *unknown, ancient*

The 5 Stroke Roll is a finite variation of the Double Stroke Open Roll (5) that contains exactly five notes. It has been called the Mother Roll in the past, and has been a part of rudimental drumming for centuries, entering the American written record in the late 18th century. It can be played in both duple and triple feel, and can be played from the downbeat or to the downbeat in either feel, yielding four main practice variations. There is also the possibility of playing it "slurred," which would be a fifth version. All odd-numbered rolls fit the pattern set up by the 5 Stroke Roll, where all the notes are grouped into doubles, except for one – which is usually (but not always) accented.

The 5 Stroke Roll is not the shortest numbered roll, but it is the shortest roll that is customarily referred to as a roll. The Drag (23) and the Single Drag Tap (26) can also be considered numbered rolls (3 Stroke and 4 Stroke Rolls, respectively), but are most often referred to by their more specific names, and categorized separately, with the other Drag rudiments. See the general page on Numbered Rolls (pg. 23), and the specific rudiment pages for Drags and Single Drag Taps, for more information. In light of this naming custom, the 5 Stroke Roll is very often the first numbered roll presented to a drummer.

It appears in many different rudimental traditions, and is one of the most common rudiments, worldwide. It is also a feature of classical music, where it is often notated as a set of four grace notes preceding a primary note, essentially as a 5 Stroke Ruff. A 5 Stroke Ruff could be played in single strokes, or another sticking pattern, but the rudimental 5 Stroke Roll is a common classical interpretation.

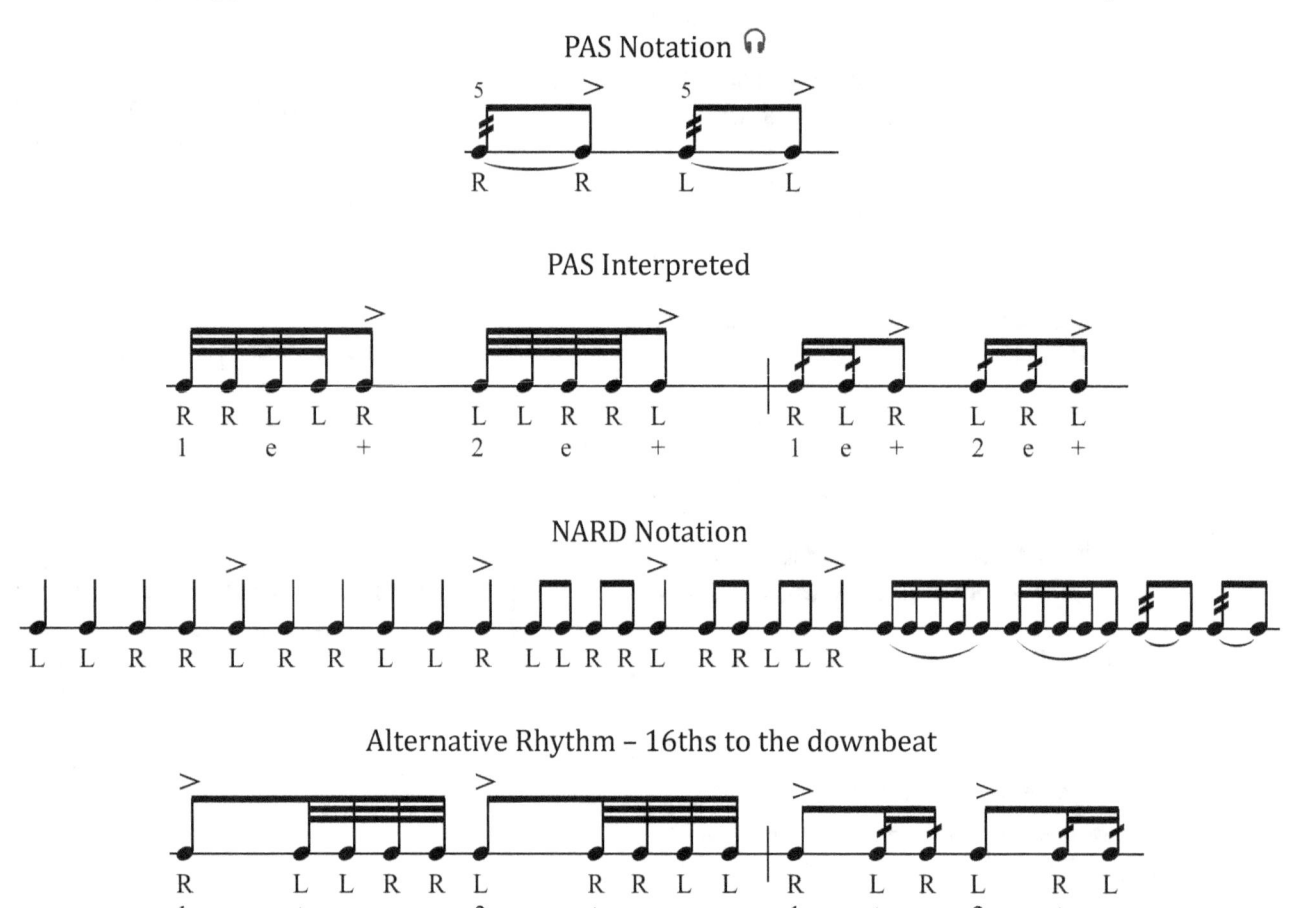

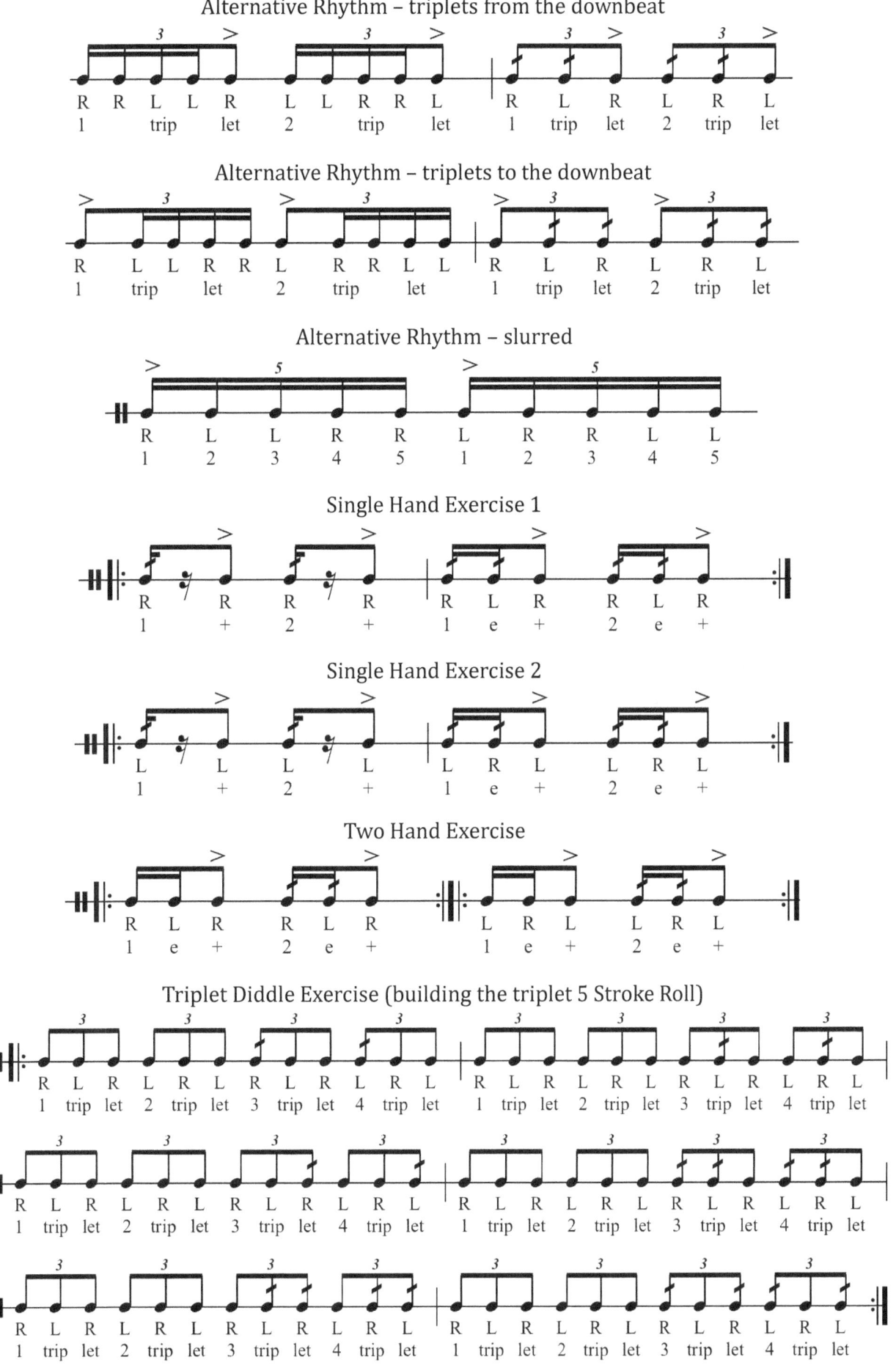

## Alternative Rhythm – triplets from the downbeat

| R | R | L | L | R | L | L | R | R | L | R | L | R | L | R | L |
|---|---|---|---|---|---|---|---|---|---|---|---|---|---|---|---|
| 1 | | trip | | let | 2 | | trip | | let | 1 | trip | let | 2 | trip | let |

## Alternative Rhythm – triplets to the downbeat

| R | L | L | R | R | L | R | R | L | L | R | L | R | L | R | L |
|---|---|---|---|---|---|---|---|---|---|---|---|---|---|---|---|
| 1 | | trip | | let | 2 | | trip | | let | 1 | trip | let | 2 | trip | let |

## Alternative Rhythm – slurred

| R | L | L | R | R | L | R | R | L | L |
|---|---|---|---|---|---|---|---|---|---|
| 1 | 2 | 3 | 4 | 5 | 1 | 2 | 3 | 4 | 5 |

## Single Hand Exercise 1

| R | R | R | R | R | L | R | R | L | R |
|---|---|---|---|---|---|---|---|---|---|
| 1 | + | 2 | + | 1 | e | + | 2 | e | + |

## Single Hand Exercise 2

| L | L | L | L | L | R | L | L | R | L |
|---|---|---|---|---|---|---|---|---|---|
| 1 | + | 2 | + | 1 | e | + | 2 | e | + |

## Two Hand Exercise

| R | L | R | R | L | R | L | R | L | L | R | L |
|---|---|---|---|---|---|---|---|---|---|---|---|
| 1 | e | + | 2 | e | + | 1 | e | + | 2 | e | + |

## Triplet Diddle Exercise (building the triplet 5 Stroke Roll)

| R | L | R | L | R | L | R | L | R | L | R | L | R | L | R | L | R | L | R | L | R | L | R | L |
|---|---|---|---|---|---|---|---|---|---|---|---|---|---|---|---|---|---|---|---|---|---|---|---|
| 1 | trip | let | 2 | trip | let | 3 | trip | let | 4 | trip | let | 1 | trip | let | 2 | trip | let | 3 | trip | let | 4 | trip | let |

| R | L | R | L | R | L | R | L | R | L | R | L | R | L | R | L | R | L | R | L | R | L | R | L |
|---|---|---|---|---|---|---|---|---|---|---|---|---|---|---|---|---|---|---|---|---|---|---|---|
| 1 | trip | let | 2 | trip | let | 3 | trip | let | 4 | trip | let | 1 | trip | let | 2 | trip | let | 3 | trip | let | 4 | trip | let |

| R | L | R | L | R | L | R | L | R | L | R | L | R | L | R | L | R | L | R | L | R | L | R | L |
|---|---|---|---|---|---|---|---|---|---|---|---|---|---|---|---|---|---|---|---|---|---|---|---|
| 1 | trip | let | 2 | trip | let | 3 | trip | let | 4 | trip | let | 1 | trip | let | 2 | trip | let | 3 | trip | let | 4 | trip | let |

# 7. 6 Stroke Roll

**PAS:** *#8*
**NARD:** *n/a*
**Other Names:** *n/a*
**Alternation:** *no*
**Origin:** *unknown*

The 6 Stroke Roll is much like the 5 Stroke Roll (6) in that it is a variation on the Double Stroke Open Roll that contains exactly six notes. It has been listed as a rudiment in the USA since 1817, when it was published by Rumrille and Holton, but is certainly an older idea. It is one of the most common even-numbered rolls in the USA. Though it does not appear on the NARD sheets, it was listed in many prominent American drum books in the era directly preceding the official selection of the NARD rudiments. The major difference between even-numbered rolls and odd-numbered rolls is that two single strokes are used in even rolls. The placement of the single strokes and the timing of the 6 Stroke Roll can vary and it is commonly seen in a few different arrangements that will be listed below.

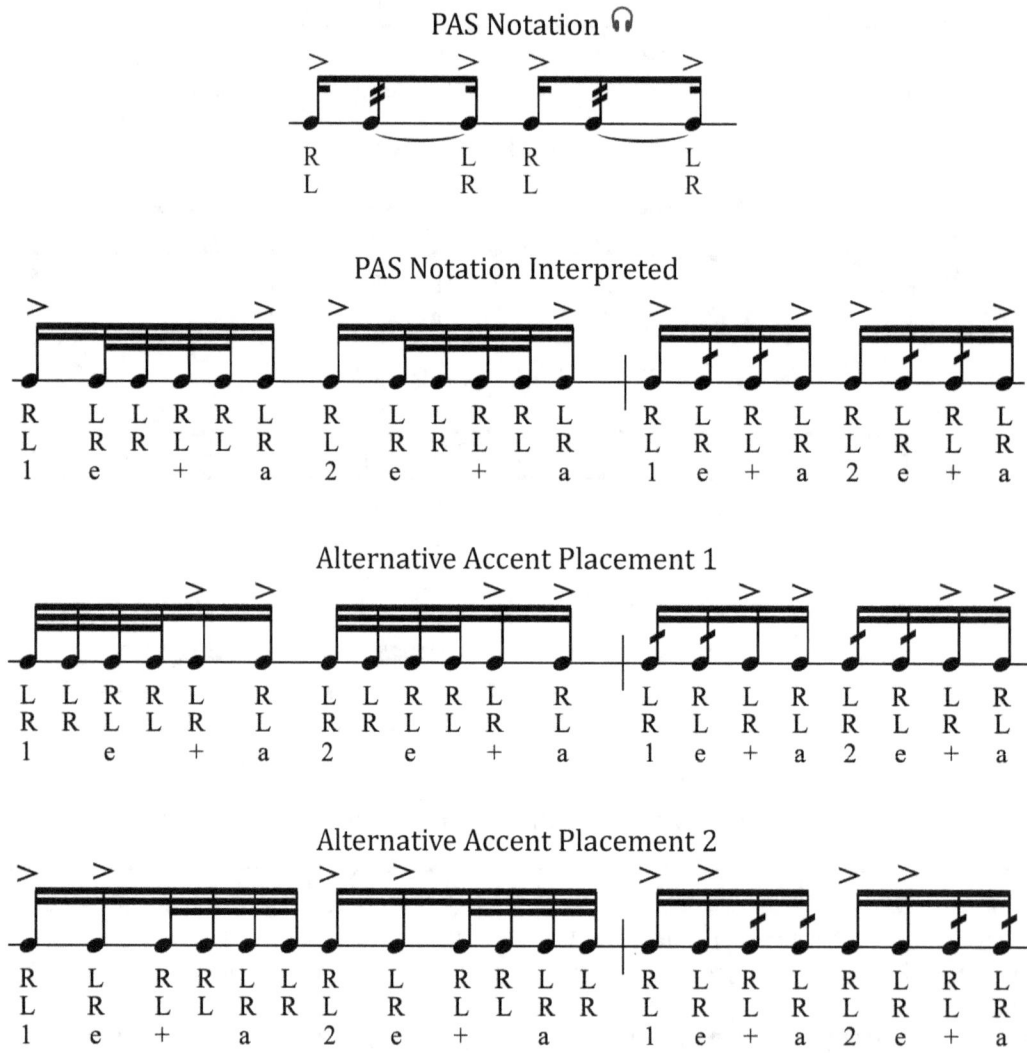

## Alternative Rhythm

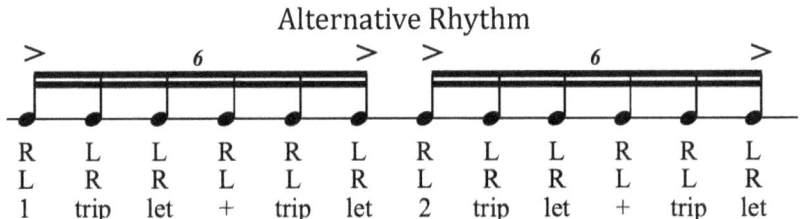

| R | L | L | R | R | L | R | L | L | R | R | L |
|---|---|---|---|---|---|---|---|---|---|---|---|
| L | R | R | L | L | R | L | R | R | L | L | R |
| 1 | trip | let | + | trip | let | 2 | trip | let | + | trip | let |

## Bounce Exercise

| R L R L R L R L | R L R L R L R L | R L R L R L R L | L R L R L R L R |
|---|---|---|---|
| L R L R L R L R | L R L R L R L R | L R L R L R L R | R L R L R L R L |
| 1 e + a 2 e + a | 1 e + a 2 e + a | 1 e + a 2 e + a | 1 e + a 2 e + a |

## Skill Buildup 1

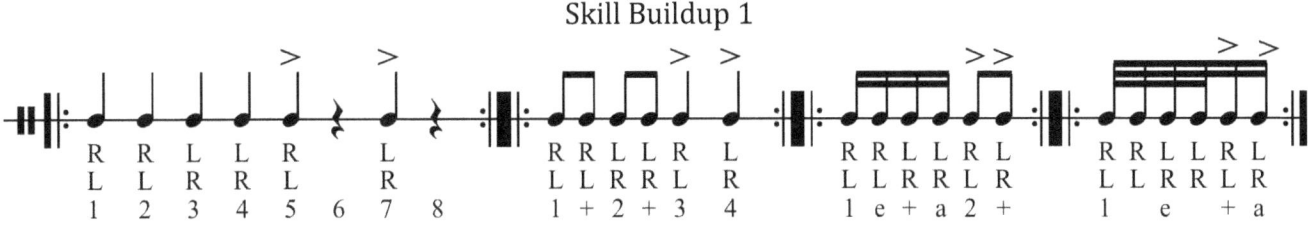

| R | R | L | L | R | | L | | R R L L R | L | R R L L R | L | R R L L R | L |
|---|---|---|---|---|---|---|---|---|---|---|---|---|---|
| L | L | R | R | L | | R | | L L R R L | R | L L R R L | R | L L R R L | R |
| 1 | 2 | 3 | 4 | 5 | 6 | 7 | 8 | 1 + 2 + 3 | 4 | 1 e + a 2 | + | 1 | e + a |

## Skill Buildup 2

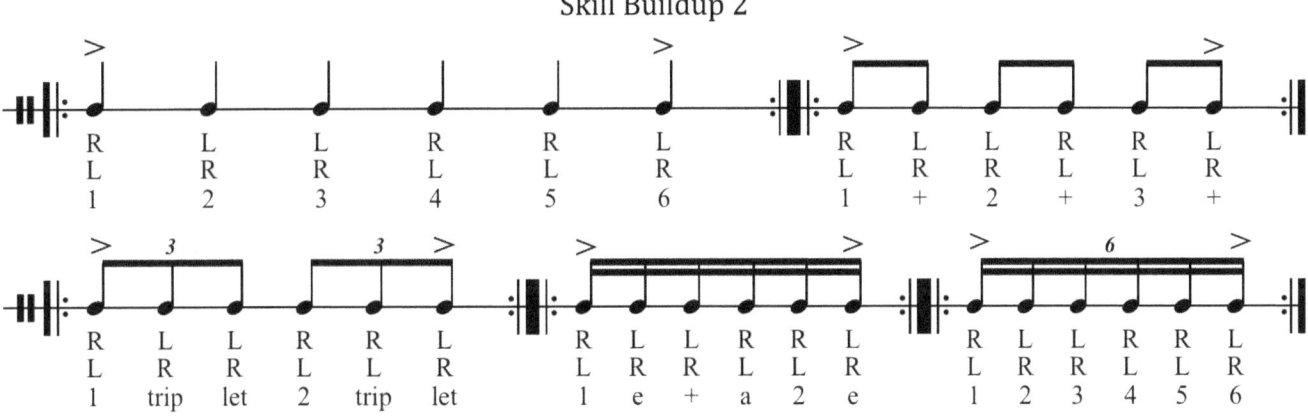

| R | L | L | R | R | L | R | L | L | R | R | L |
|---|---|---|---|---|---|---|---|---|---|---|---|
| L | R | R | L | L | R | L | R | R | L | L | R |
| 1 | 2 | 3 | 4 | 5 | 6 | 1 | + | 2 | + | 3 | + |

| R | L | L | R | R | L | R | L | L | R | R | L | R | L | L | R | R | L |
|---|---|---|---|---|---|---|---|---|---|---|---|---|---|---|---|---|---|
| L | R | R | L | L | R | L | R | R | L | L | R | L | R | R | L | L | R |
| 1 | trip | let | 2 | trip | let | 1 | e | + | a | 2 | e | 1 | 2 | 3 | 4 | 5 | 6 |

## Suggested Drum Kit Application

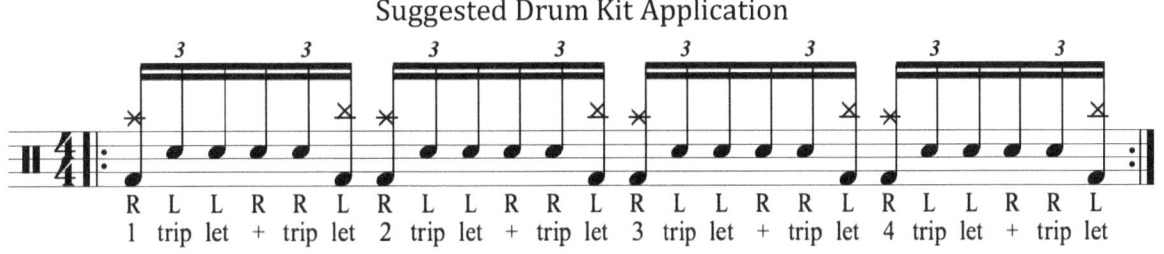

| R | L | L | R | R | L | R | L | L | R | R | L | R | L | L | R | R | L | R | L | L | R | R | L |
|---|---|---|---|---|---|---|---|---|---|---|---|---|---|---|---|---|---|---|---|---|---|---|---|
| 1 | trip | let | + | trip | let | 2 | trip | let | + | trip | let | 3 | trip | let | + | trip | let | 4 | trip | let | + | trip | let |

# 8. 7 Stroke Roll

**PAS:** #9
**NARD:** #3
**Other Names:** *Ra de 7, Rau da 7, Ran de 7, 7er Ruf, Syvslags Hvirvel, De, Roffel van 7*
**Alternation:** *no*
**Origin:** *unknown, ancient*

The 7 Stroke Roll, like the previous numbered rolls, is a variation on the Double Stroke Open Roll (5) that contains exactly seven notes. The idea for a 7 Stroke Roll is undoubtedly very ancient overall, and it has been used in American drumming since late 18th century. It can be played in various rhythmic situations, but is most commonly seen phrased as a triplet in the space of an 8th note, as a replacement for the 5 Stroke Roll (6), or as 32nd notes. The triplet version will often end on a downbeat, while the duple version will often start on a downbeat.

PAS Notation

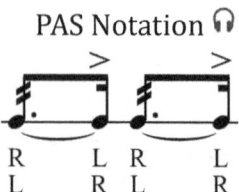

PAS Notation Interpreted

NARD Notation

Triplet Rhythm

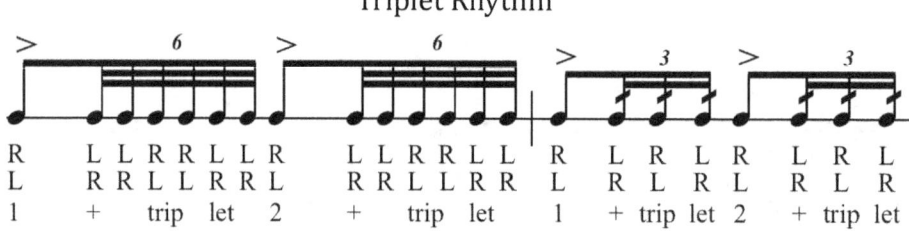

Exercise 1

## Exercise 2

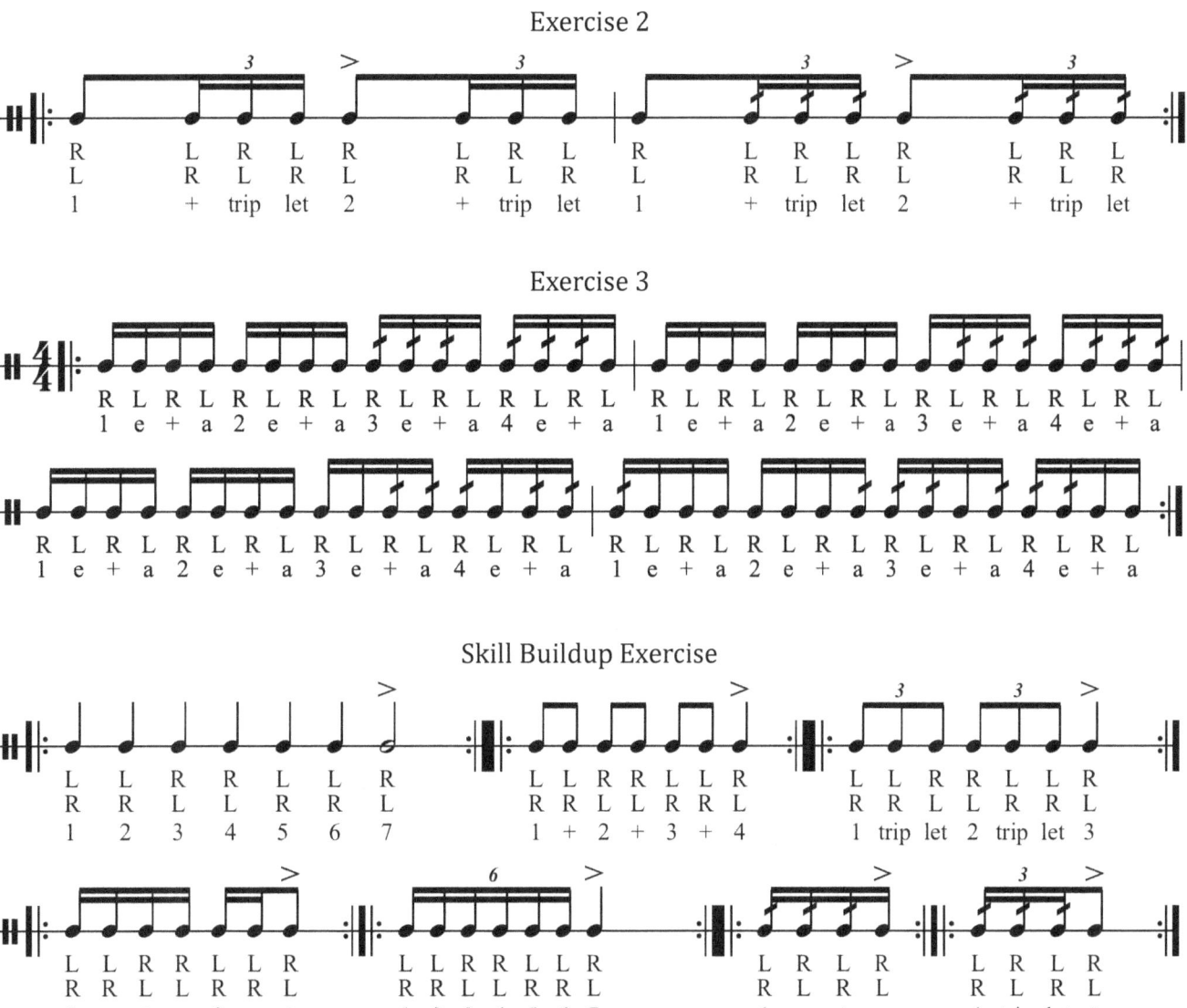

## Exercise 3

## Skill Buildup Exercise

# 9. 8 Stroke Roll

**PAS:** *n/a*
**NARD:** *n/a*
**Other Names:** *n/a*
**Alternation:** *yes*
**Origin:** *unknown*

The 8 Stroke Roll, like the previous numbered rolls, is a variation on the Double Stroke Open Roll (5) that contains exactly eight notes. It is neither a PAS rudiment nor a NARD rudiment, but it has a long history in rudimental drumming. It was first published in American drumming in 1818, by Alvan Robinson, and was a fairly standard American rudiment, into the early 20th century.

It became less common after the publication of the NARD rudiments in the 1930s, but persisted in many rudimental methods, into the 1990s. It can still be found occasionally today. It is included here to fill out the gaps in the standard set of stroked rolls – because of its historic usage, and because it is actually fun and interesting to play.

In the 19th century, the most common usage was as a replacement for a 7 Stroke Roll (8) on an 8th note. This is the hardest usage to read and comprehend. It can also be played in the space of a quarter note as 16th notes, or as a quintuplet, and in a triplet or 6/8 framework. In all cases, it uses a similar pattern to the 6 Stroke Roll (7), with two single stroke accents, and the remainder played in double strokes. Also, much like the 6 Stroke Roll, it can be played evenly – with every stroke receiving the same note value – or with the accents played slower than the doubles.

### 8th Note Rhythm

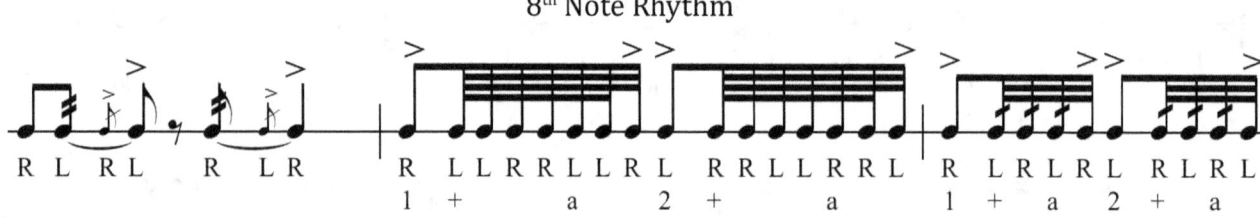

8th Note Rhythm Expanded – 64th notes are hard to read and count, so the measure below is the same basic rhythm as the 8th Note Rhythm above, but expanded to double the note values.

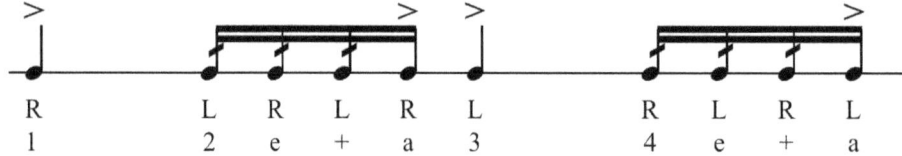

### Quarter Note Rhythm 🎧

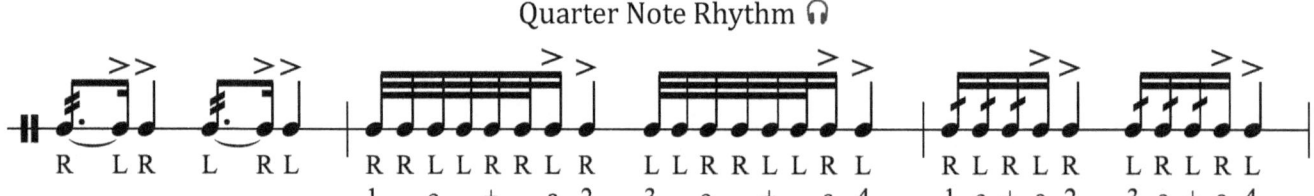

### Evenly Spaced Rhythm in 16ths or 32nds

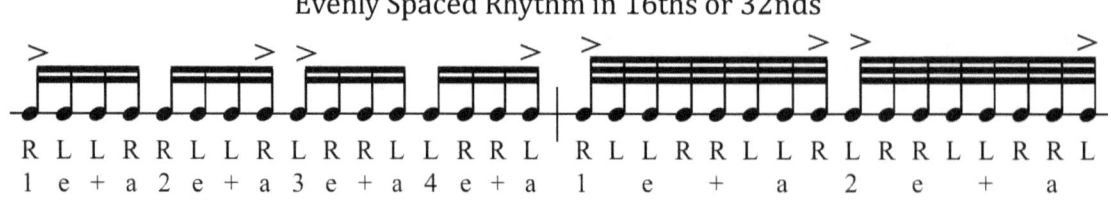

The 5 Stroke Roll (6), 8 Stroke Roll (9), 9 Stroke Roll (10), 10 Stroke Roll (11), and 11 Stroke Roll (12) all have quintuplet phrasings, as well as the Double Drag Tap (27) and Eggbeaters (49), in other sections. Quintuplets may be unfamiliar to beginner or even intermediate drummers, but they are a common feature of rudimental music. Learning to play five "16$^{th}$ notes" in a beat, with the further ability to double stroke any, or all those five 16th notes, is essential for American rudimental playing.

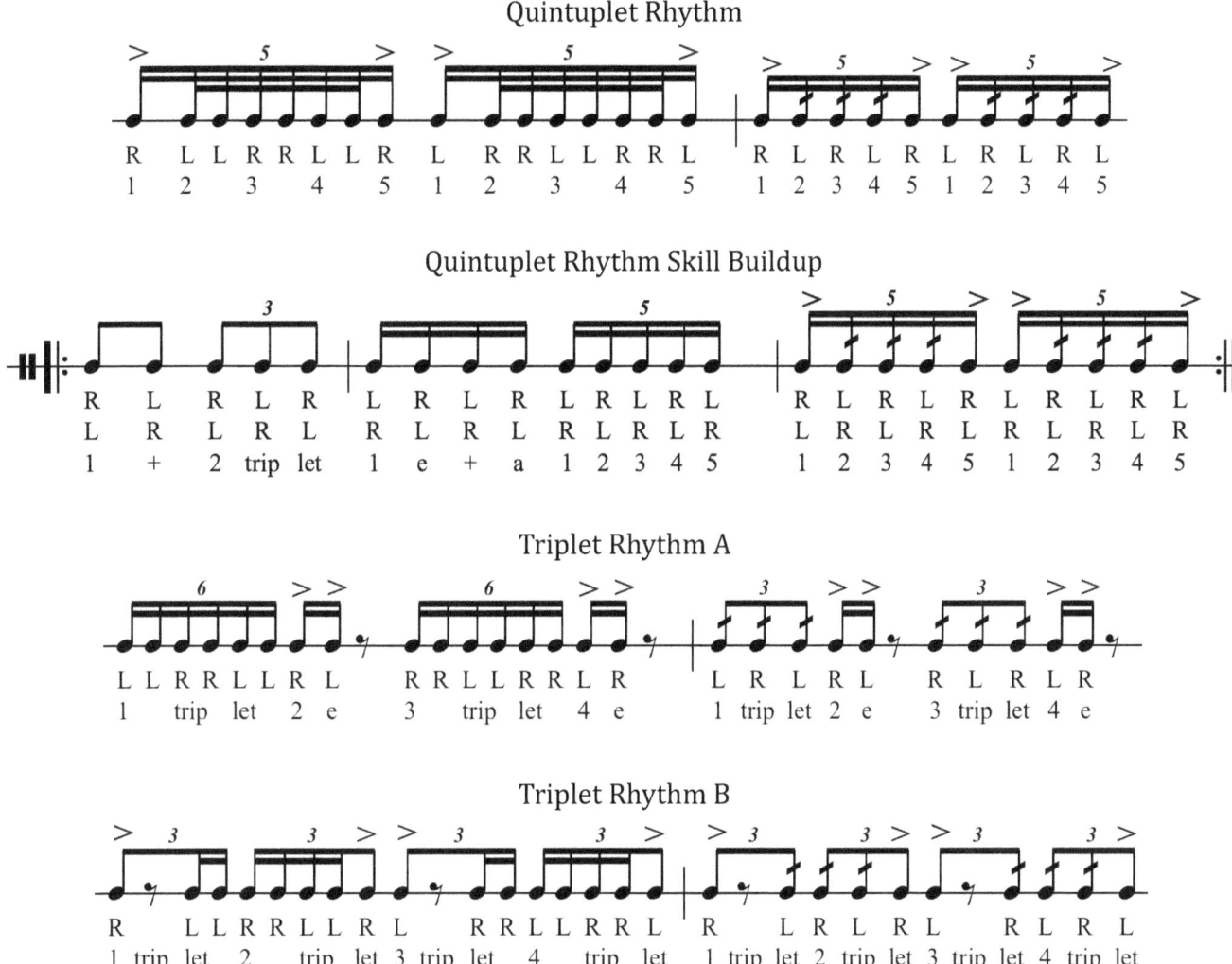

# 10. 9 Stroke Roll

**PAS:** *#10*
**NARD:** *#15*
**Other Names:** *Rau da 9, Ra de 9, Ran de 9, Roffel van 9, 9er Ruf, Do, Redoble de Negra*
**Alternation:** *yes*
**Origin:** *unknown*

The 9 Stroke Roll is a variation on the Double Stroke Open Roll (5) that contains exactly nine notes. It has been a part of American drumming since the late 18th century, and was listed in manuals by Isaac Day and Benjamin Clark. Its history in Europe goes back even further. In general, it can be said that the 9 Stroke Roll takes up one beat in 4/4 or 2/4 time. The usual modern interpretation is a quarter note, tied to another quarter note, with the roll being played in 32nd notes, or doubled 16th notes. This interpretation usually allows for two rolls to fit neatly into a 4/4 measure (as in the PAS notation example). It can also be played with a quintuplet rhythm, such that every beat contains a 9 Stroke Roll – meaning four rolls can fit into a 4/4 measure, or two rolls into a 2/4 measure. It can also be seen in 6/8 time, in both a standard triple meter (Rhythm A), or as a quadruplet over three of the beats (Rhythm B).

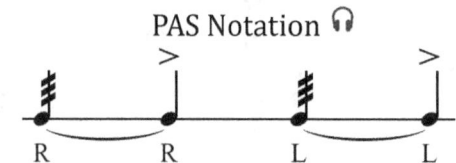

PAS Notation 🎧

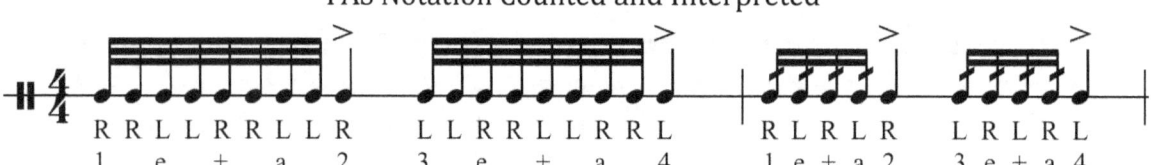

PAS Notation Counted and Interpreted

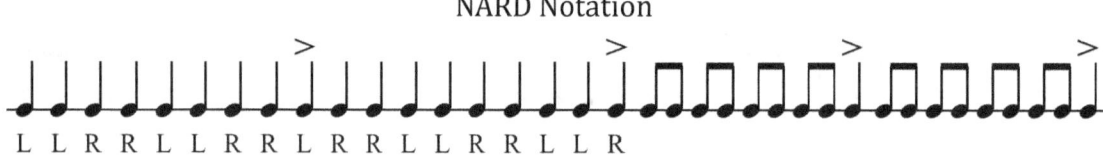

NARD Notation

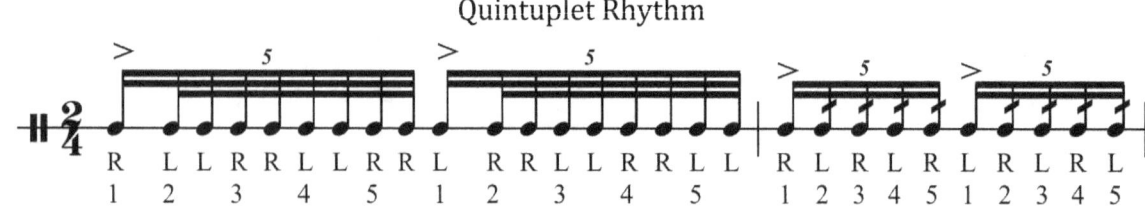

Quintuplet Rhythm

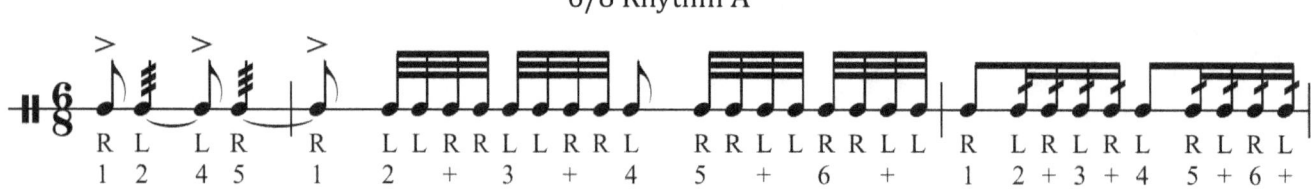

6/8 Rhythm A

## 6/8 Rhythm B

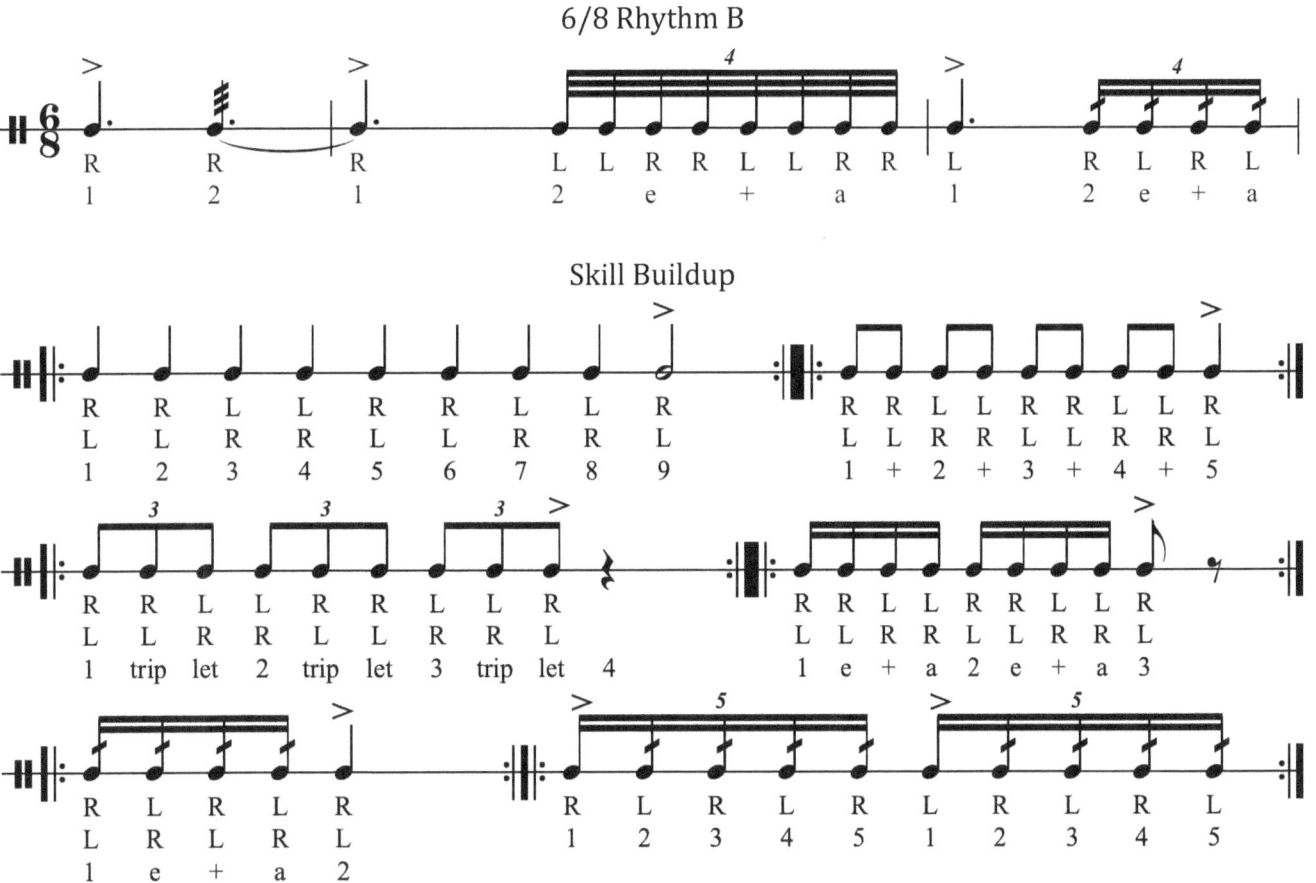

## Skill Buildup

# 11. 10 Stroke Roll

**PAS:** *#11*
**NARD:** *#16*
**Other Names:** *Ra de 10*
**Alternation:** *no*
**Origin:** *unknown, possibly France*

The 10 Stroke Roll is a variant of the Double Stroke Open Roll (5) containing exactly 10 notes. It is much like the 6 Stroke (7) and 8 Stroke (9) Rolls, in that it utilizes two single strokes, typically accented, with the remainder played in double strokes. The 10 Stroke Roll is one of the oldest rudiments explicitly mentioned in American history, being named (but not notated) in Baron de Steuben's regulations, written at Valley Forge in 1779, for General Washington's forces. It was featured in notation in several books within the first few years of the 19th century. It is the only even numbered roll on the NARD sheets. It can be played in a duple meter, but is more often seen in 6/8 time, or as triplets. It can also be played slurred, in a quintuplet rhythm.

### PAS Notation 🎧

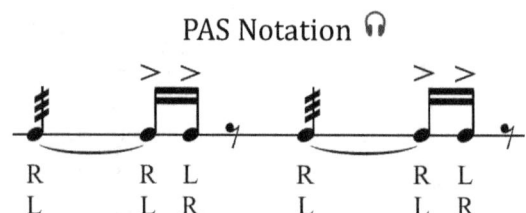

### PAS Notation Interpreted and Counted

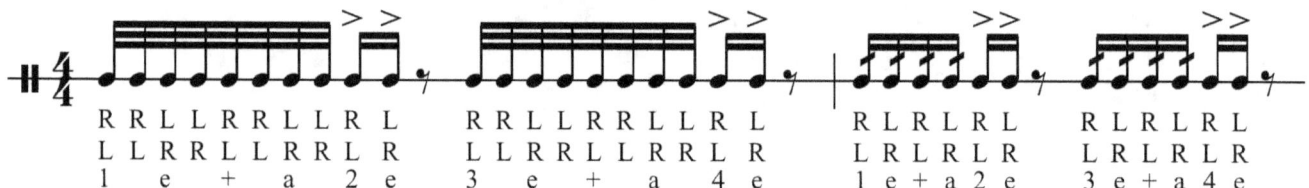

### NARD Notation

### 6/8 Rhythm

### Evenly Spaced Quintuplet Rhythm

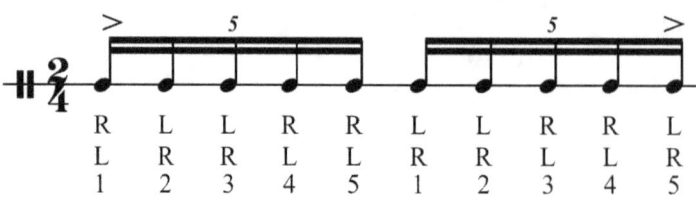

## Triplet Rhythm

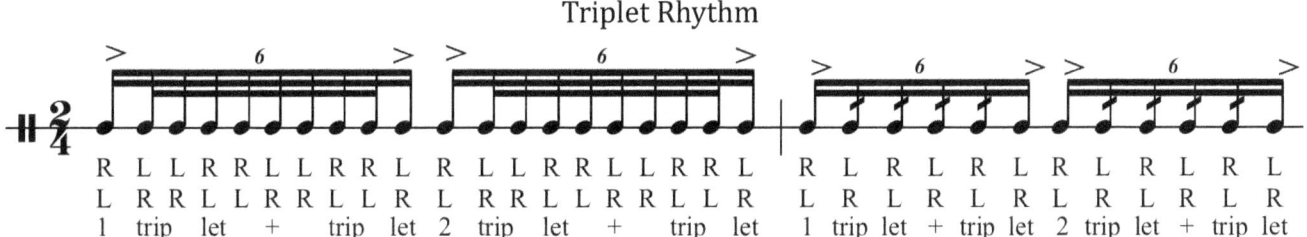

The following notation could be interpretted as counted below, or as triplets, like the previous triplet exercise, above.

## Alternative Notation Styles

## Skill Buildup

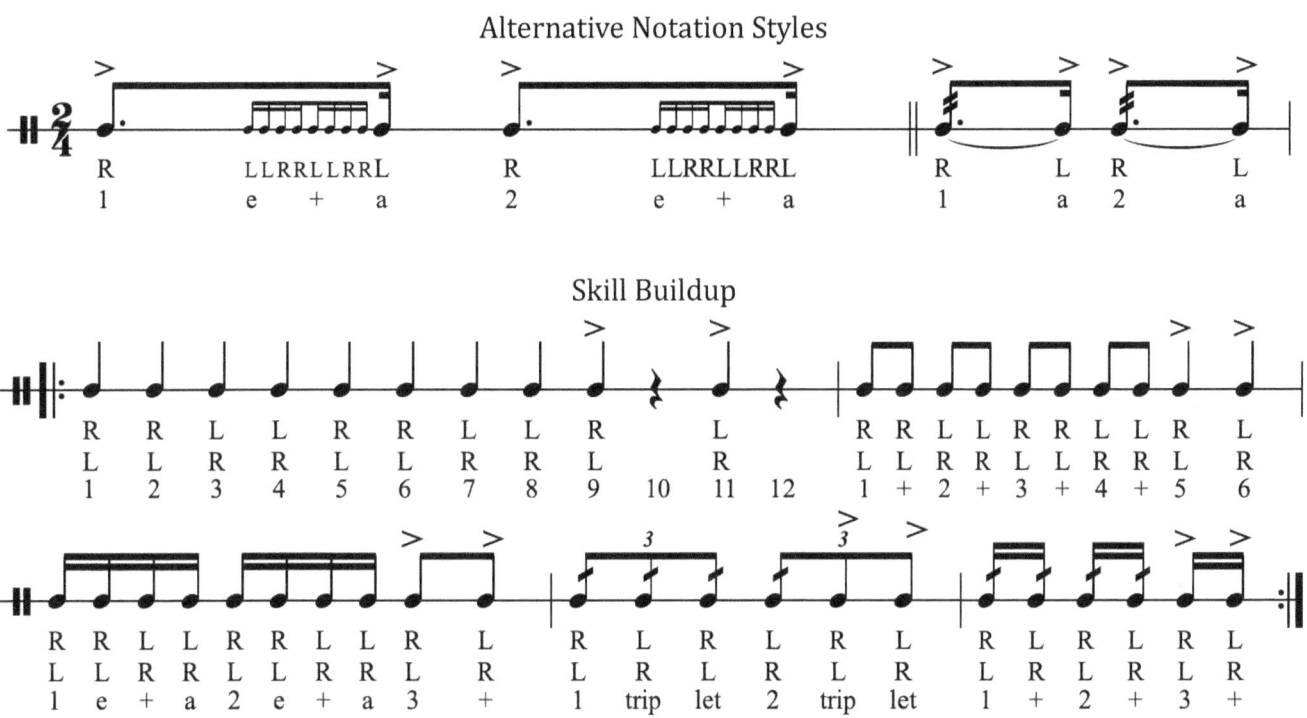

# 12. 11 Stroke Roll

**PAS:** *#12*
**NARD:** *#17*
**Other Names:** *Ra de 11, 11er Ruf, Då*
**Alternation:** *no*
**Origin:** *unknown, ancient*

The 11 Stroke Roll is a variant of the Double Stroke Open Roll (5) containing exactly 11 notes. It is much like the 5 Stroke (6) and 9 Stroke (10) Rolls, in that it utilizes one single stroke, typically accented, with the remainder played in double strokes. The 11 Stroke Roll appears in American rudimental manuals in the very early 19th century, and has been a staple rudiment for all of American drumming history. It can be played in a duple meter, but is more often seen in 6/8 time, or as triplets. It can also be played in a quintuplet rhythm where, like a 9 Stroke Roll, it is often notated in the space of a quarter note, with the final stroke landing on the following downbeat.

PAS Notation 🎧

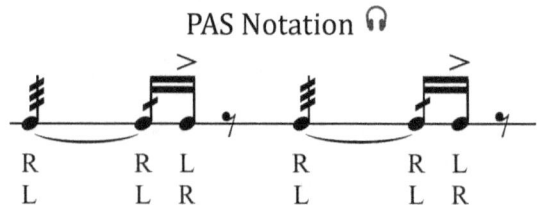

PAS Notation Interpreted and Counted

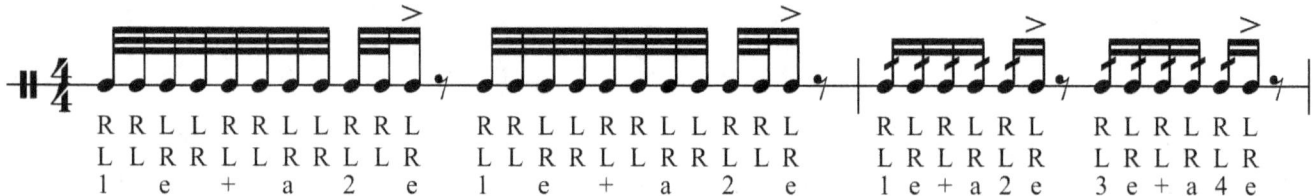

NARD Notation

Triplet Rhythm

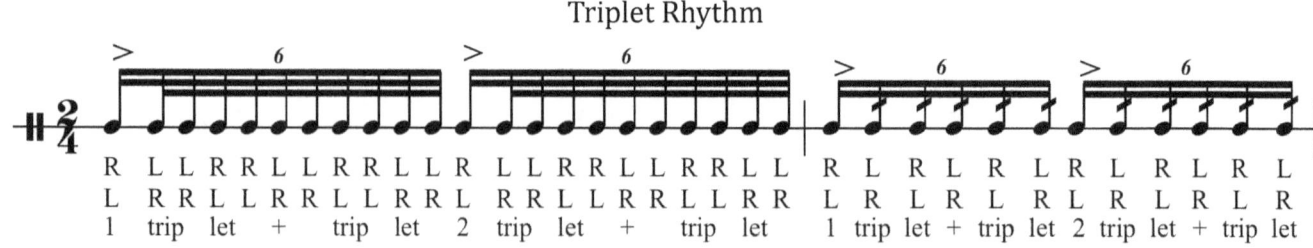

6/8 Rhythm

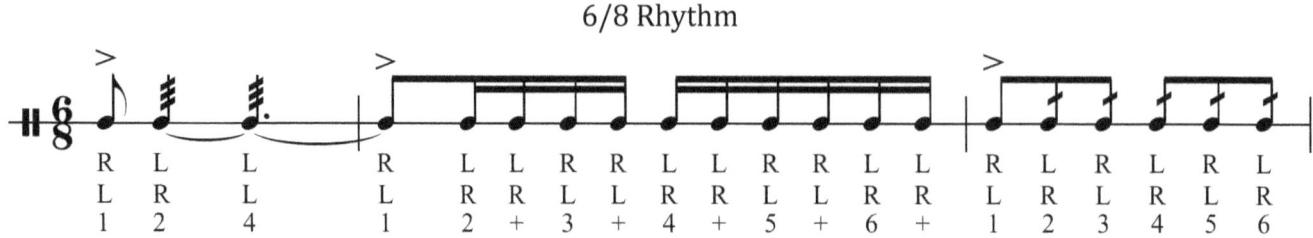

## Quintuplet Rhythm

## Alternative Notation Style for Quintuplet Rhythm

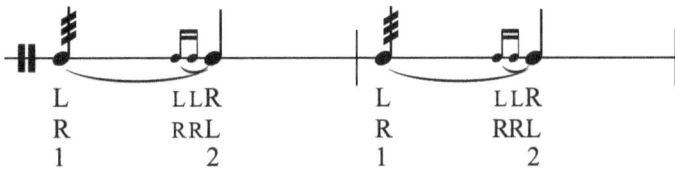

## Skill Buildup

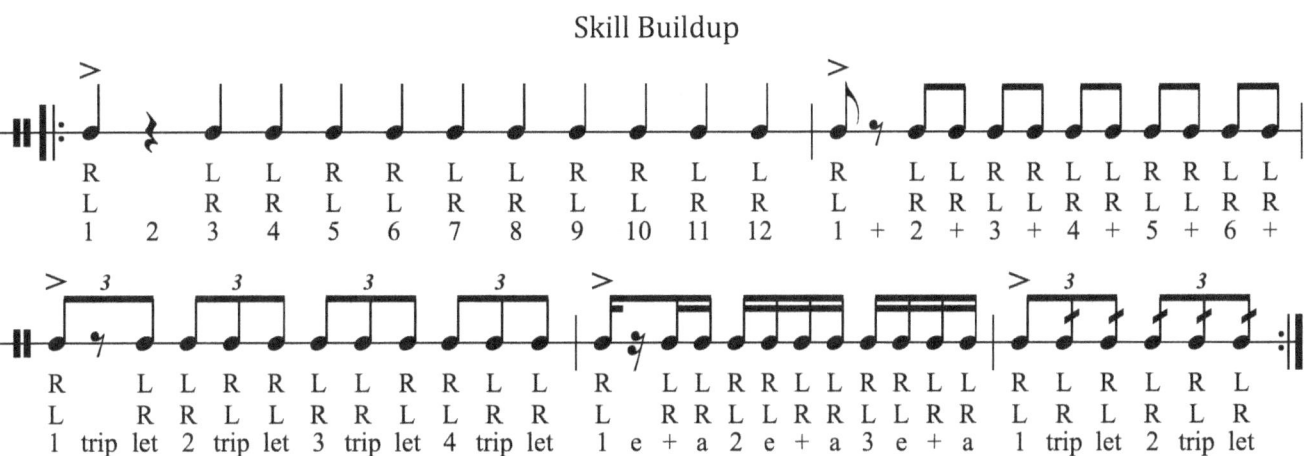

# 13. 12 Stroke Roll

**PAS:** *n/a*
**NARD:** *n/a*
**Other Names:** *n/a*
**Alternation:** *yes*
**Origin:** *unknown, possibly USA*

The 12 Stroke Roll is a variant of the Double Stroke Open Roll (5) containing exactly 12 notes. Following the pattern of the 6, 8, and 10 Stroke Rolls, it features two single strokes, with the remainder played in doubles. It appears on neither the NARD nor PAS rudiment sheets, but dates from 1804, in the USA. It was present as a variation of the 11 Stroke Roll (12), in Colonel Hart's 1862 manual, and was indicated in Wilcoxon's *All American Drummer,* in 1945, among other places. It can be played in both duple and triple meter, and can be made to fit in one beat, two beats, or even one and a half beats. The 12 Stroke Roll is the largest even numbered roll featured in this book – not because longer even numbered rolls aren't possible, but because there is almost no historical precedent for their use. 14 Stroke Rolls are nearly unknown in rudimental literature, and have rarely, or possibly never, been included in standard rudiment lists. 16 Stroke Rolls are slightly more common, but still particularly unlikely to be encountered. The extreme rarity of longer even numbered rolls, doesn't preclude their future use in music – but here, they will just be an assumed extension of the information already presented for the other even numbered rolls.

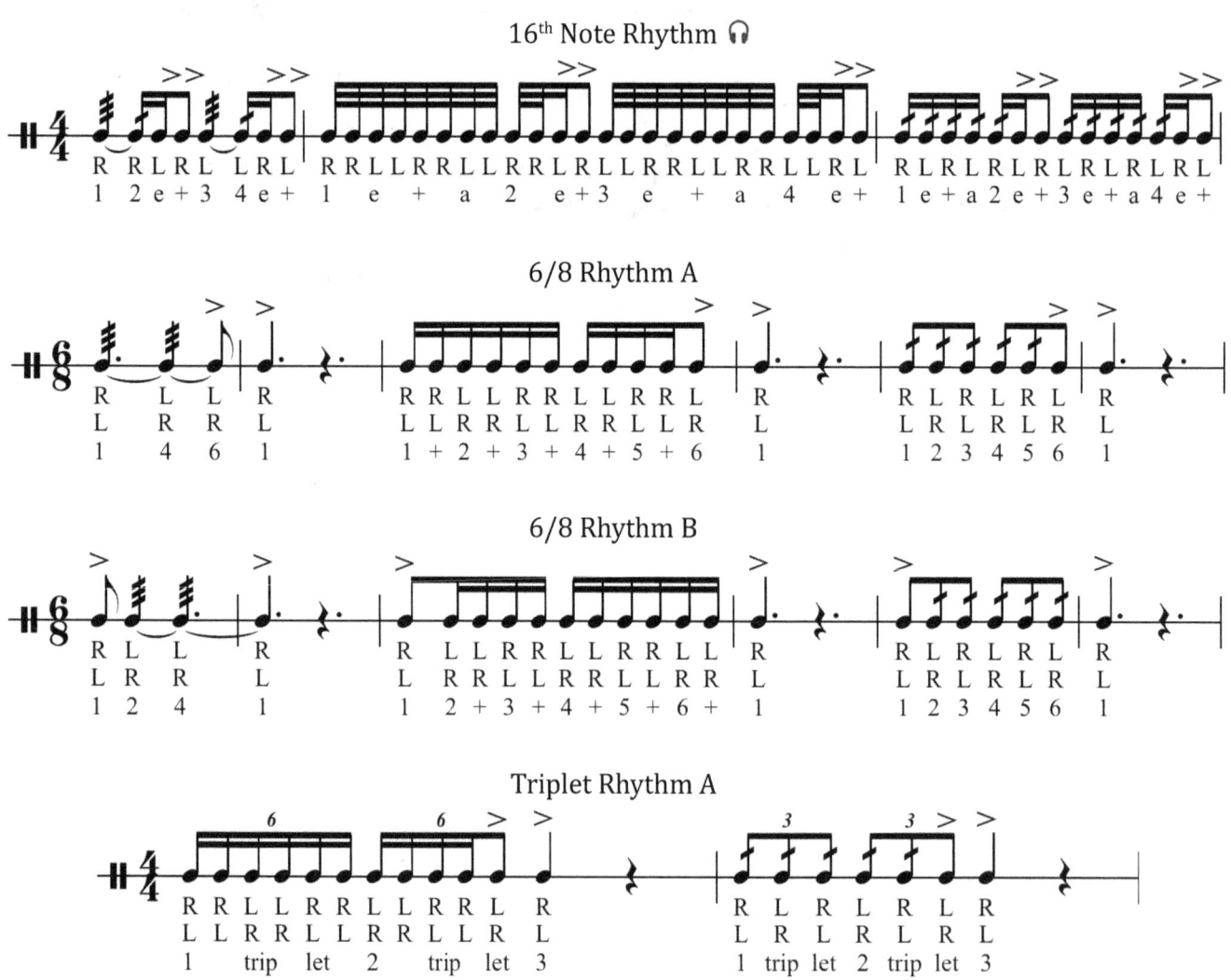

## Triplet Rhythm B

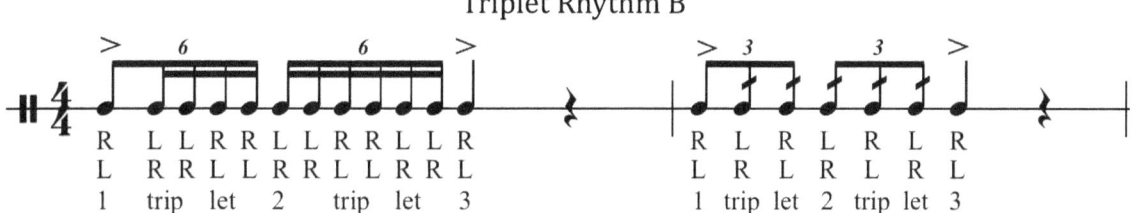

## Triplet Rhythm C

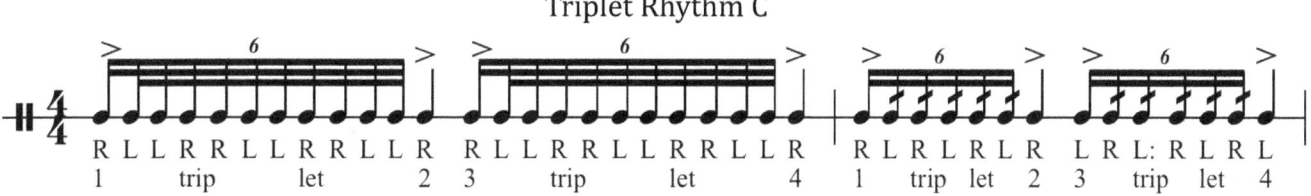

## Triplet Rhythm D

## Evenly Spaced Triplets

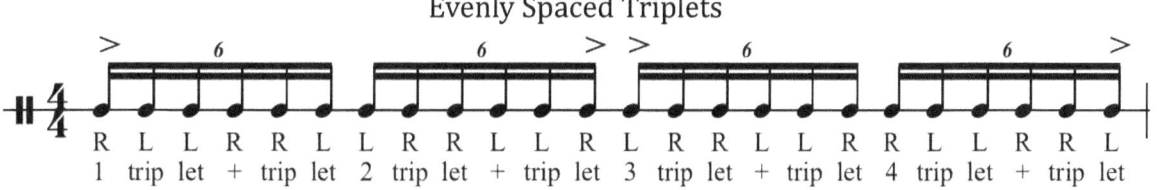

# 14. 13 Stroke Roll

**PAS:** *#13*
**NARD:** *#18*
**Other Names:** *Ra de 13, Redoble de Negra con Puntillo, 13er Gebunden Wechelseitig*
**Alternation:** *yes*
**Origin:** *unknown*

The 13 Stroke Roll is a variant of the Double Stroke Open Roll (5) containing exactly 13 notes. It appears on both the NARD and PAS rudiment sheets. It was first printed in America, by Bruce and Emmett in 1862, though was certainly in use, earlier. It can be played in duple or triple meter, in a variety of note values. This roll is directly related to the rudiment Single Stroke 7 (4), in that it merely doubles the first six notes.

PAS Notation

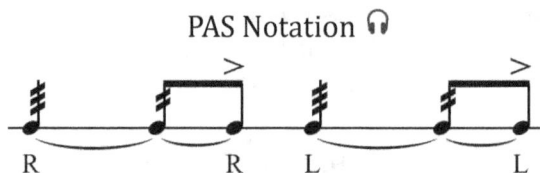

PAS Notation Interpreted

NARD Notation

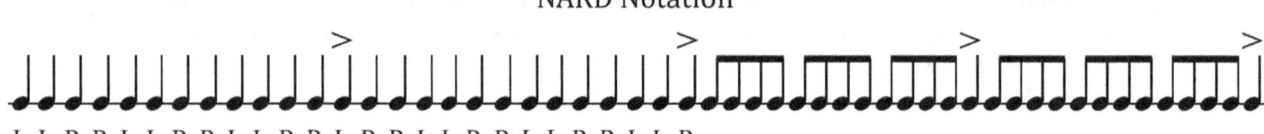

16th Rhythm to the downbeat

Triplet Rhythm Fast

Triplet Rhythm Slow

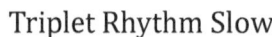

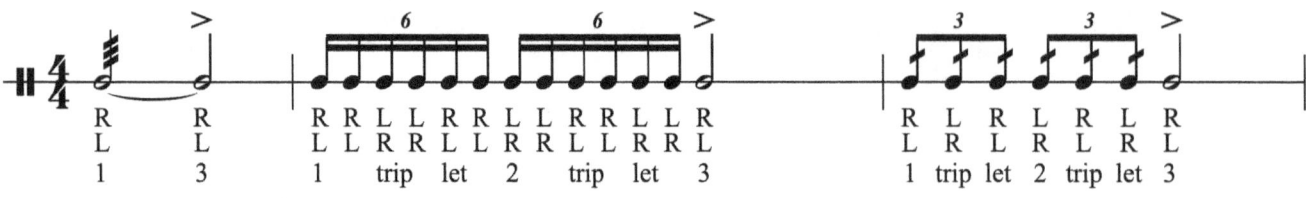

## 6/8 Rhythm Fast

## 6/8 Rhythm Slow

## Combination Exercise

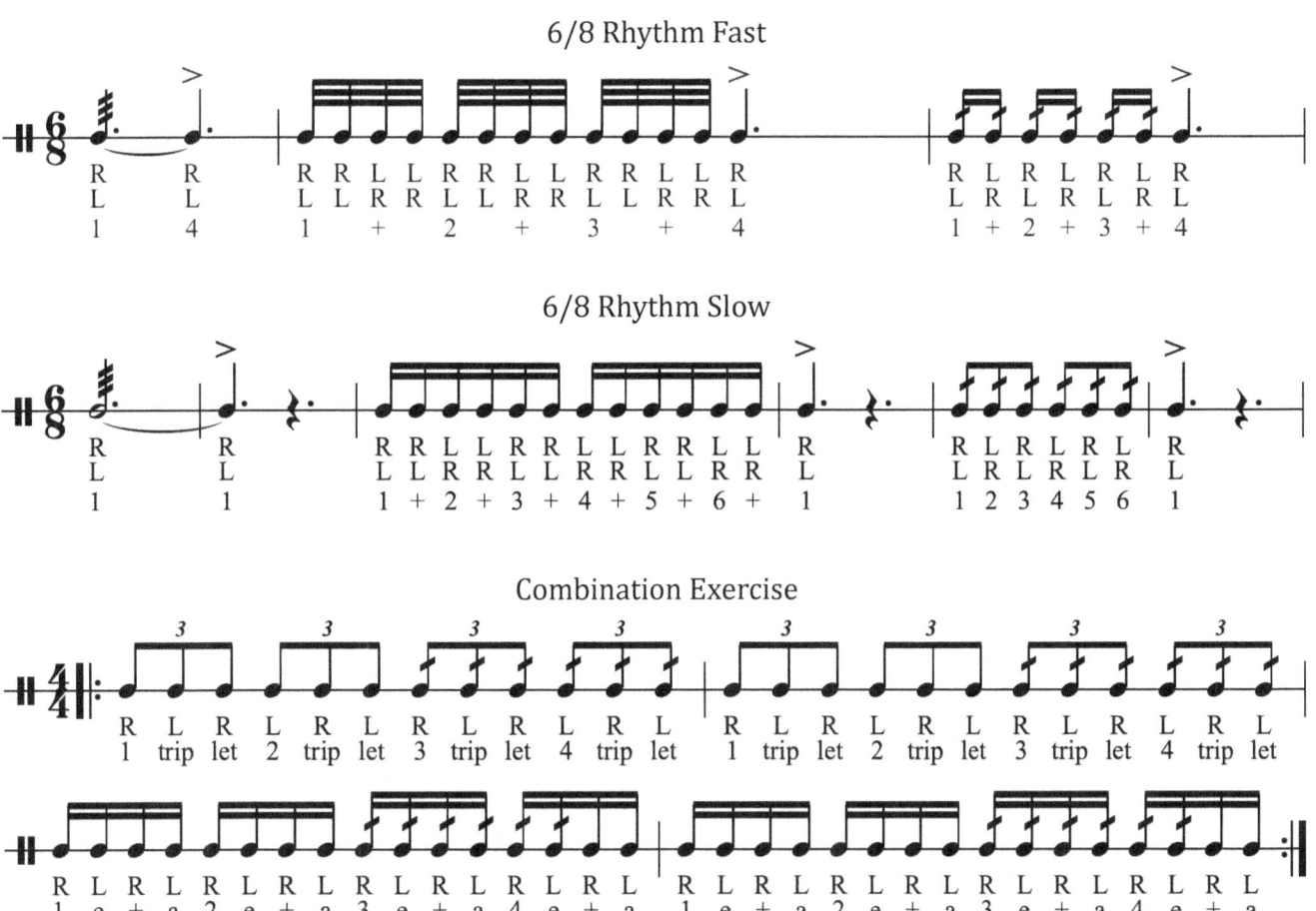

# 15. 15 Stroke Roll

**PAS:** *#14*
**NARD:** *#19*
**Other Names:** *Ra de 15, 15er Ruf*
**Alternation:** *no*
**Origin:** *unknown, possibly France*

The 15 Stroke Roll is a variant of the Double Stroke Open Roll (5), containing exactly 15 notes, and it appears on both the NARD and PAS rudiment sheets. It was used in American manuals by at least 1810, and has been a staple American rudiment, ever since. It can be played in duple or triple meter, and is often seen in 2/4 as a dotted quarter note, with a timing that is oddly, open to interpretation. The 2/4 version of the roll will be explained further on the following page.

### PAS Notation 🎧

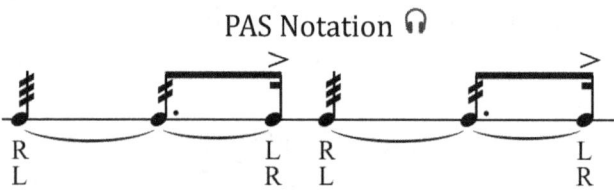

### PAS Notation Interpreted

### NARD Notation

### 16th Rhythm to the downbeat

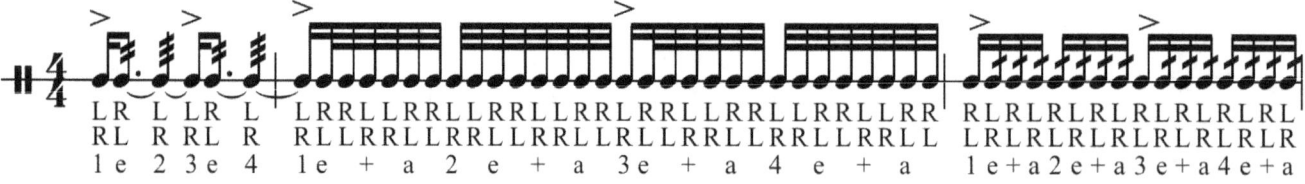

### 6/8 Rhythm

The 15 Stroke Roll in 2/4 has a few possible interpretations, for the same notation. The "most correct" interpretation is notated here, but it is not the only way to play this figure. "Most correct" is in quotations, because not all rudimental drummers agree on what is correct. Very often the roll will be notated as a dotted quarter note, as in the first measure of the following example. Here, the roll is shown as a group of fourteen $32^{nd}$ notes, played over three 8ths. This is polyrhythmic, as the notes do not evenly fit into 8ths or quarters, at this speed. The notes fit evenly across the space of three 8ths, or one dotted quarter. This is awkward, at best, though roughly corresponds to the interpretation of the Army Old Guard Drum Corps, and many other ancient drumming experts.

2/4 Polyrhythmic Interpretation

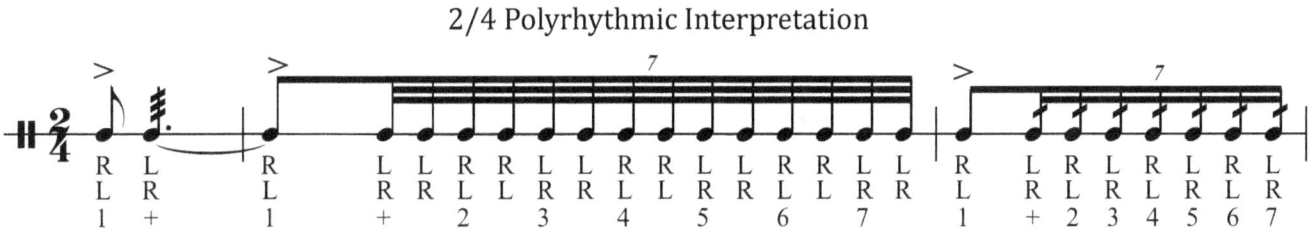

Marching (or tapping your foot) on straight quarter notes will result in only the last note matching up precisely with a step. Even subdividing into 8ths is unhelpful. Below, the X note heads indicate the placement of standard straight $8^{th}$ notes. It is clear that the seven notes of the roll's skeleton do not line up with the downbeat 2 or the upbeat of 2, even though the roll starts precisely on the upbeat of 1, and ends on 1 of the following measure. The upper set of counts corresponds to the notes being played, and the lower set of counts corresponds to the referential X note heads.

2/4 Polyrhythmic Interpretation (with 8ths for reference)

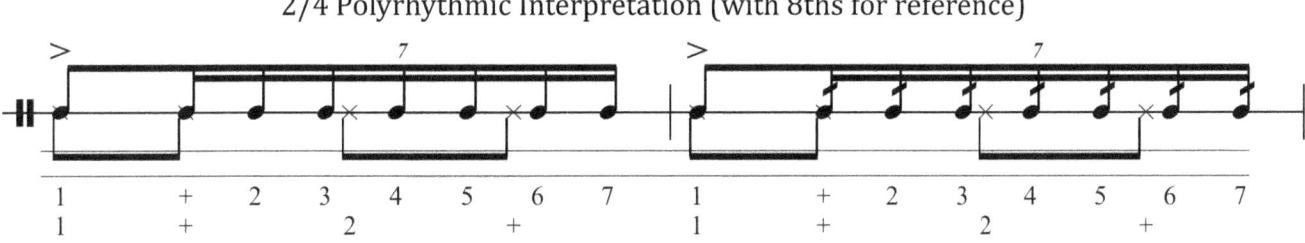

As mentioned earlier, there are other interpretations of this roll. One possible alternative is to start the roll earlier than notated, as in the previous "16th Rhythm to the Downbeat" example. Another alternative is to end the roll later than the downbeat, instead landing on the second 16th note in the measure. Both of these alternatives fundamentally disregard the notation in favor of a longer duration for the roll. One further alternative is to change the speed of the roll in the middle, so that some of the notes are played as doubled 16ths, and others as doubled $16^{th}$ triplets. This final interpretation has the roll accelerate in the middle, so it is not an even 15 strokes. None of these choices, including the notated polyrhythmic septuplet, is attractive. However, the 15 Stroke Roll notated with a dotted $8^{th}$ is fairly common in older rudimental repertoire, and it must be played, one way or another.

# 16. 17 Stroke Roll

**PAS:** *#15*
**NARD:** *n/a*
**Other Names:** *Roffel van Drie Tellen, 3 Pace Roll, Længre Hvirvel, 17er Ruf, Redoble Largo, Redoble de Blanca*
**Alternation:** *yes*
**Origin:** *unknown, ancient*

The 17 Stroke Roll is a variant of the Double Stroke Open Roll (5) containing exactly 17 notes. While a roll lasting for the duration of a half note has essentially always existed in percussion, Americans did not label the roll as a rudiment, or explicitly specify that half note rolls should be played with 17 notes until the early 20th century (possibly, as late as the 1930s). It is an old concept, with a relatively recent upgrade to the status of an official rudiment. Most often, the 17 Stroke Roll is played in a duple meter with standard 16th notes doubled, but it can also appear as a nonuplet or group of nine. In this application, two 17 Stroke Rolls can fit in a single measure of 4/4, which is much like the quintuplet interpretation of the 9 Stroke Roll (10), but twice as long.

Rolls longer than 17 strokes can be played, and have been written in rudimental repertoire. A whole note roll is usually interpreted as 33 strokes, for example, when played in a 16th note skeletal base. The same whole note played in an 8th note triplet skeleton will be 25 strokes. These longer rolls are rarely (possibly never) included in American rudiment lists, perhaps because it is assumed that a player who can play every roll up to 17 strokes will have an inherent understanding of the patterns governing double stroke rolls, and will be able to extrapolate how the longer rolls must be played to fit into music. This book will also stop at 17 under this same assumption.

PAS Notation

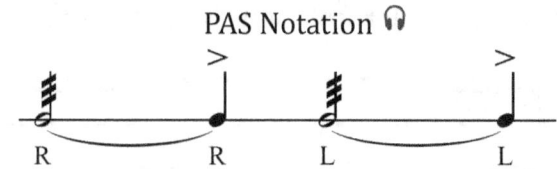

PAS Notation Interpreted

Chicken and a Roll

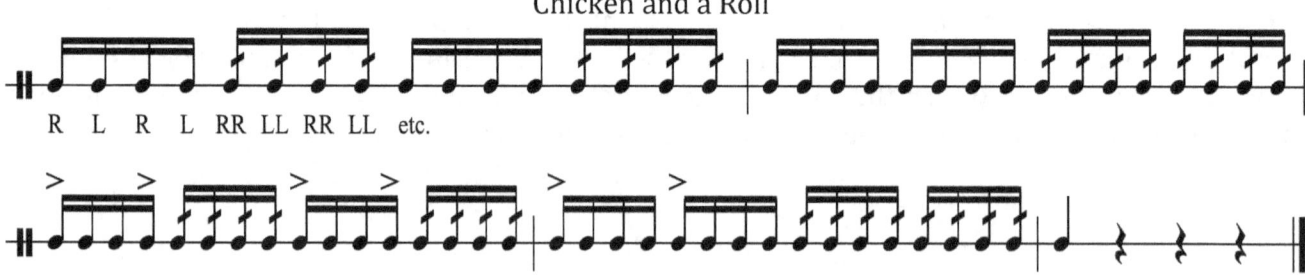

## Nonuplet Rhythm

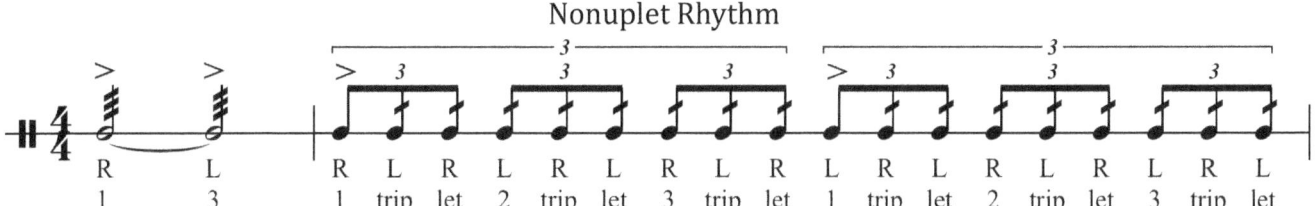

The above interpretation requires a skeleton of 9 notes to a beat. This is a difficult concept, though it can be understood as a quarter note triplet (3 quarters over 2 beats), where each quarter is further split into three (written as 8th triplets), then most of those resulting nested triplet notes are played as a double stroke (or two 16th triplet notes with the same hand). This interpretation is unusual, though it is possible, and may be encountered (rarely), in older repertoire. Similarly, some repertoire may indicate a 19 Stroke Roll written on a half note, the same way the 17 Stroke Roll is written in the PAS notation. A nonuplet interpretation with 18 strokes in doubles, plus a single stroke on the following downbeat is the only way to fit 19 strokes into that space. The phrasing below, with the nested triplets applies to this roll, as well.

## Nonuplet Skill Buildup

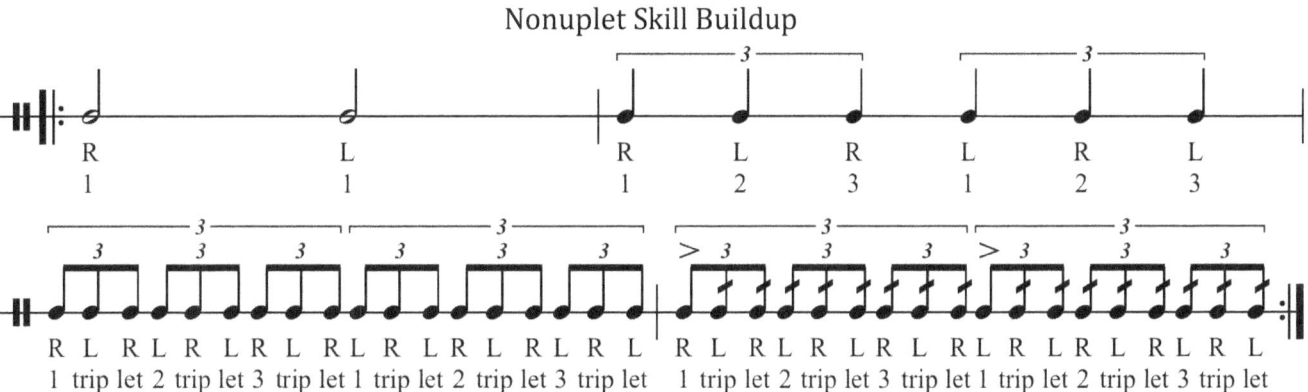

# 17. Multiple Bounce Roll

**PAS:** *#4*
**NARD:** *n/a*
**Other Names:** *Buzz Roll, Concert Roll, Orchestral Roll, Symphonic Roll, Classical Roll, Press Roll, Crush Roll, Scratch Roll, Redoble de Zumbido, Rullo, Redoble, Repiqueo*
**Alternation:** *yes*
**Origin:** *classical*

The Multiple Bounce Roll has only been considered a rudiment in the USA, since the 1960s. Before that, it was regarded as a classical technique, but something to be avoided by rudimental players. In other rudimental traditions, such as Scottish pipe band, Mexican banda de guerra, Galician pipe band, the Carnevale di Ivrea in Italy, and only relatively recently, in British Corps of Drums, the Multiple Bounce Roll is used as the primary rudimental roll. It is a common occurrence in American rudimental playing of the last several decades.

Multiple Bounce Rolls can be played in several ways. The underlying base rhythm of the roll can change, depending on the tempo. At a high tempo, a slower denomination for the underlying rhythm makes more sense. At a slow tempo, more notes of a faster denomination are needed to fill the space with a good roll. Practicing the roll with different numbers of strokes per beat is helpful. Try to connect the multiple bounce or buzzed strokes together into a smooth, seamless roll, regardless of the number of strokes per beat. Some veteran concert or orchestral players go to the extreme of actually playing strokes completely out of time from the music, because they have a particular rolling speed that works for the ideal sound. They use this speed, whether or not it corresponds to the music around them. To do so, they must be able to count accurately with the music, and move their hands at a separate and unrelated speed. It is not an easy thing to do, so starting with exact metric subdivisions, as below, is a necessity for less experienced players.

PAS Multiple Bounce Roll 🎧

Alternative Notation Styles

Possible Base Denominations

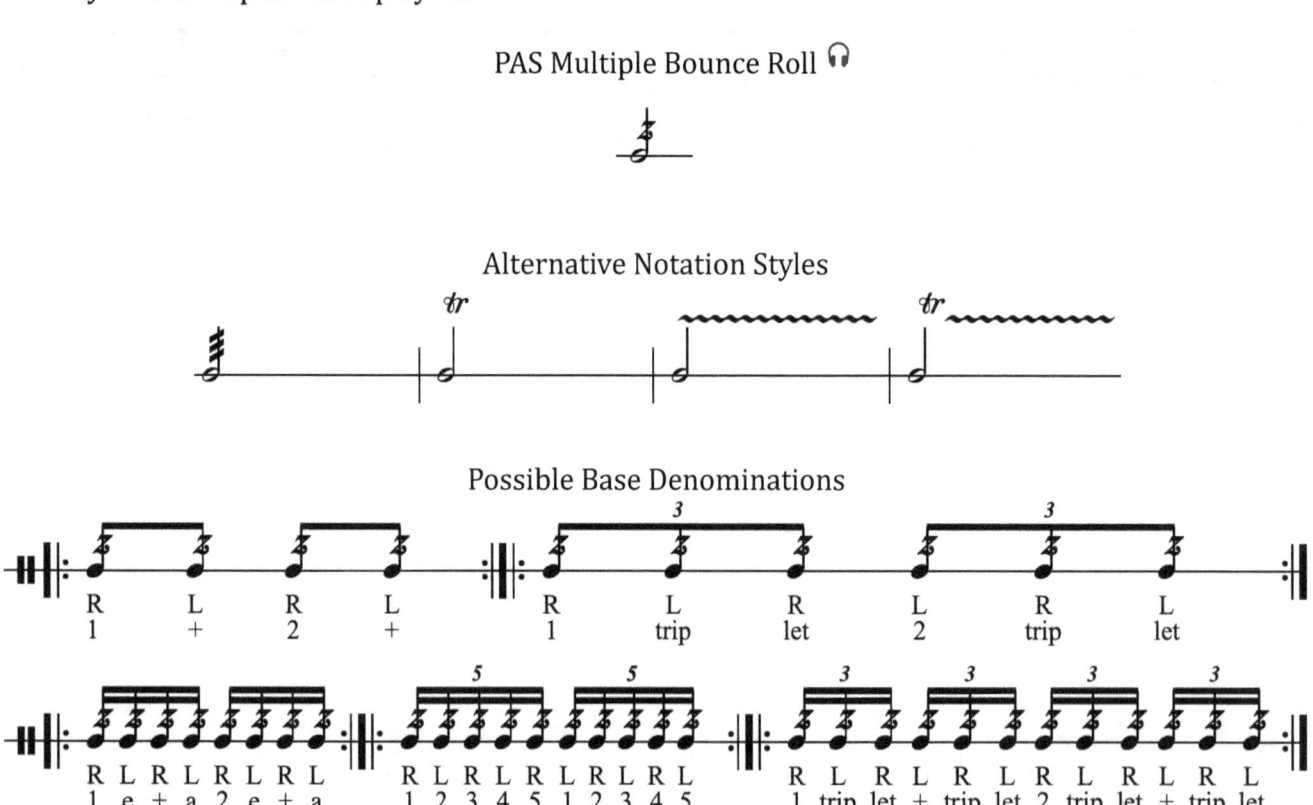

Multiple Bounce Rolls can also be played with a different number of bounces per hand, depending on the situation. The drum tuning, the sticks, the room, the tempo of the piece, and the dynamic marking for the roll, all contribute to the selection of a number of bounces per hand. This is often intuitive for an experienced player, but it is worth trying out different numbers for practice. The fewest number of bounces that is acceptable is three, because two would be a definite Double Stroke Open Roll (5), and one would be a Single Stroke Roll (1). Neither of those can be substituted for a Multiple Bounce Roll. The following measures have rolls with three to seven bounces per hand. Play at a tempo where all of the bounces for each hand can be executed in a single wrist motion, using rebound from the drum. DO NOT play each note individually from the wrist or fingers, as that will not translate into a connected and smooth sounding roll.

IMPORTANT: ALL bounces must come from a SINGLE movement of the wrist, and the rebound of the drum head – they are NOT really independent notes, but part of a singular buzz stroke.

When playing at low volumes (pianissimo or piano), five or six bounces can be useful. These bounces should be easy to produce, with a low stick height and slower hand motions, near the edge of the drum head. In contrast, at high volumes (forte or fortissimo), fewer bounces will suffice. It will be hard to produce more than three or four bounces when using the faster hand motions and high stick heights in the center of the drum that are demanded by loud playing.

Although it is difficult to notate, or even demonstrate in real time, it is not necessary to always roll with every bounce perfectly aligned to exact metric divisions. It is actually beneficial, in some cases, to have the last bounce of one hand slightly overlapped by the first bounce from the next hand. In other words, instead of a perfectly even spacing between the third note of a triple stroke and the first note of the following triple stroke (according to a perfect triplet grid), the last note and first note may be compressed closer together – more like a Flam (32) than two separate notes. This will mitigate the inherent decrease in sound over the duration of each buzzed stroke. Each successive bounce of a multiple bounce stroke is smaller and has less energy. Starting the new, louder bounces closer in time than is perfectly accurate can make the roll sound smoother and more even, as well as more connected – effectively covering up the diminished volume at the end of each stroke. Easier said than done, but when you have eventually achieved the perfect Multiple Bounce Roll, you may notice that you are naturally overlapping the strokes, intuitively.

Suggested Drum Kit Application

# 18. Crushed Ruff

**PAS:** *n/a*
**NARD:** *n/a*
**Other Names:** *Press Roll, Crush Roll, Crush Stroke, Crushed Buzz, Short Buzz, Dry Crush, Zut*
**Alternation:** *no*
**Origin:** *classical, jazz*

The Crushed Ruff has many names, and some of these terms are used as synonyms for the Multiple Bounce Roll (17), which can be confusing. Some of the names are used by percussionists colloquially, but have not often been printed in methods or articles. Crushed Ruff has been selected as the main term here, because it is very commonly used in percussion literature, and is not easily confused for a standard Multiple Bounce Roll. It does add to the confusion over the term Ruff (24), but its short burst of sound is consistent with the Ruff concept.

Unlike most other rudiments, the Crushed Ruff can be played more than one way. It has been listed as a rudiment in the past, as well as a jazz drum set technique and a classical snare technique. The US Army, Buddy Rich, Ed Freytag, and James Campbell all refer to the technique as a rudiment, among others. Its widespread use in many types of music, makes it worthy of inclusion here – despite it not being featured on the standard rudiment sheets.

The Crushed Ruff can be played with a single buzzed stroke, with two simultaneous buzzed strokes, or two nearly simultaneous buzzed strokes, like a buzzed Flam. The wide variation in names might suggest that perhaps, there are multiple rudiments here. Unfortunately, the several names and the three main techniques do not correlate well enough to make that definitively true. In a survey of over 100 years of percussion literature, Crushed Ruff and Crush Roll normally refer to a two-handed execution, but Press Roll, Crush Stroke, and several other terms have been used to refer to both one-handed and two-handed techniques, with no general consensus from experts. The intended sound is roughly the same for all names and techniques – a short, unconnected buzz, or a quick burst of sound. Here, we will prioritize the two-handed Crushed Ruff, because it is the most common name and technique combination in published literature. Feel free to work on a single-hand variant with the same basic sound.

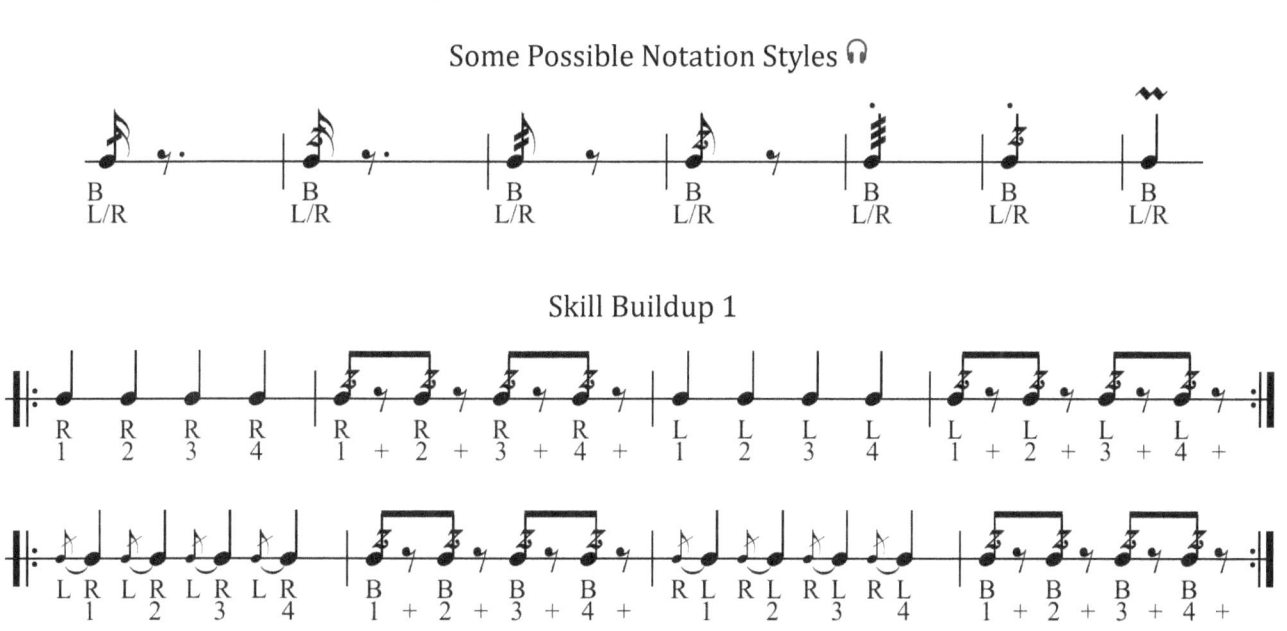

Some Possible Notation Styles 🎧

Skill Buildup 1

In this next exercise, keep every buzz separated. Do not let them connect. Go slowly and get a good sound from each Crushed Ruff.

## Skill Buildup 2

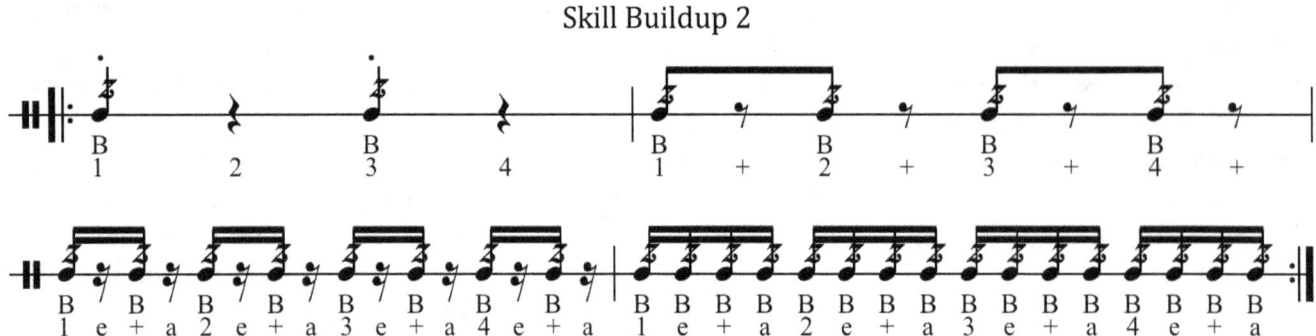

This exercise mimics the sticking patterns of the Flam Tap (36) and Flam Accent (35), but with the Crushed Ruff.

## Common Sticking Exercise

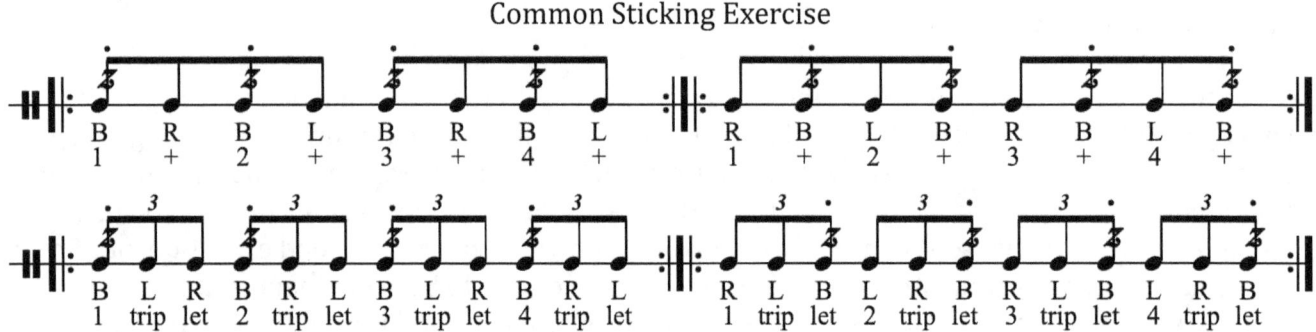

# 19. Triple Stroke Roll

**PAS:** *#5*
**NARD:** *n/a*
**Other Names:** *n/a*
**Alternation:** *yes*
**Origin:** *unknown*

The Triple Stroke Roll is distinct from the Multiple Bounce Roll (17) when played slowly enough to count the strokes, but Multiple Bounce Rolls can sometimes be played similarly, with three notes per hand. A Multiple Bounce Roll made of groups of three notes will still be a smooth and sustained sound, while a Triple Stroke Roll is always audibly, and obviously, made up of alternating groups of three notes. The line where one rudiment becomes the other is not exact. The drum, the room, the sticks, and the player, all influence the clarity of the bounces, and therefore, will affect the speed at which one roll might seem to transform into the other, to the listener. The Multiple Bounce Roll can be played with other numbers of bounces on each hand, but the Triple Stroke Roll, obviously cannot.

This roll has only been in common rudimental use in the United States from the 1960s, or later. It was mentioned by Sam Ulano in 1959, and was pretty rare before that, possibly appearing in unpublished drum corps repertoire. A 1941 issue of *The School Musician* states, "actually the production of such a roll isn't possible." Clearly, it is possible (being an official PAS rudiment), but it wasn't taken seriously as a rudimental concept before the latter half of the 20th century.

Learning to play the Triple Stroke Roll at a variety of speeds, or open-close-open, is difficult. Many factors contribute to the success or failure of an individual drummer's Triple Stroke Roll. These factors make it so that producing the roll, even after it is learned, can never be taken for granted. Technique considerations: desired stroke speed, stroke angle, grip type (traditional/matched, number of fingers in fulcrum, thumb position, fulcrum position on fingers), grip angle, grip height, type of stick, type of drum/pad/surface, drumhead tension, body proximity to playing surface, relative motion of wrist/elbow/shoulder, dynamic level, etc. These considerations are also true for any rudiment, but rolls in particular are difficult. The Triple Stroke Roll is often regarded as more difficult than the Multiple Bounce Roll, or Double Stroke Roll (5). Thus, it is the roll that is affected the most, either positively or negatively, from changes to any of the above factors.

Other rudiments containing a triple stroke: Flam Accent (35), Flam Tap (36), Flam Paradiddle-diddle (40), Pataflafla (41), Inverted Flam Tap (43), Cheese (45), Eggbeaters (49), and Shirley Murphy (50). Some of these are explicit in the primary sticking, and others are hidden within combinations of grace notes and primary notes.

PAS Notation 🎧

R R R L L L R R R L L L

Counted and Alternative Phrase

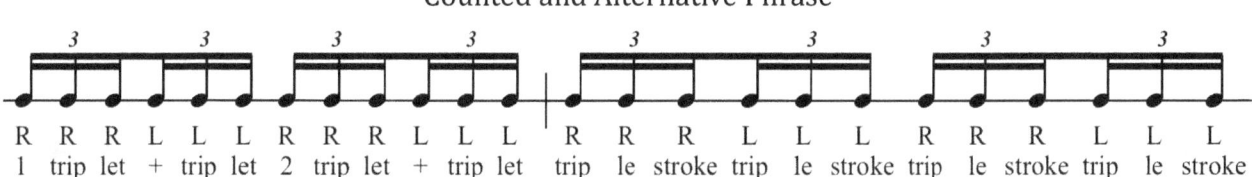

R R R L L L R R R L L L   R R R L L L R R R L L L
1 trip let + trip let 2 trip let + trip let   trip le stroke trip le stroke trip le stroke trip le stroke

## Single Hand Skill Buildup Exercise 1

## Single Hand Skill Buildup Exercise 2

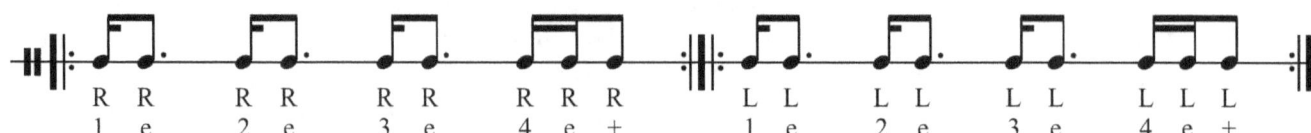

## Single Hand Skill Buildup Exercise 3

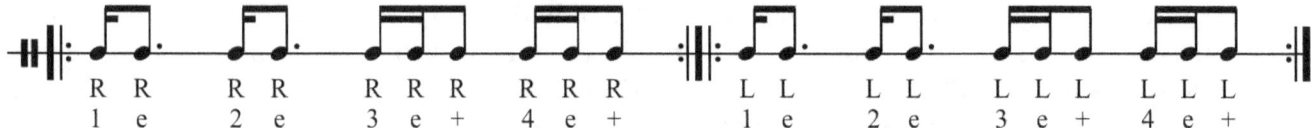

## Single Hand Skill Buildup Exercise 4

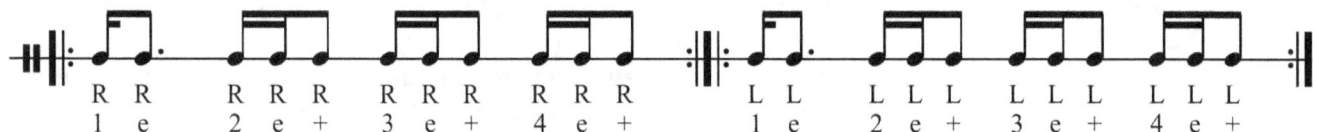

## Single Hand Skill Buildup Exercise 5

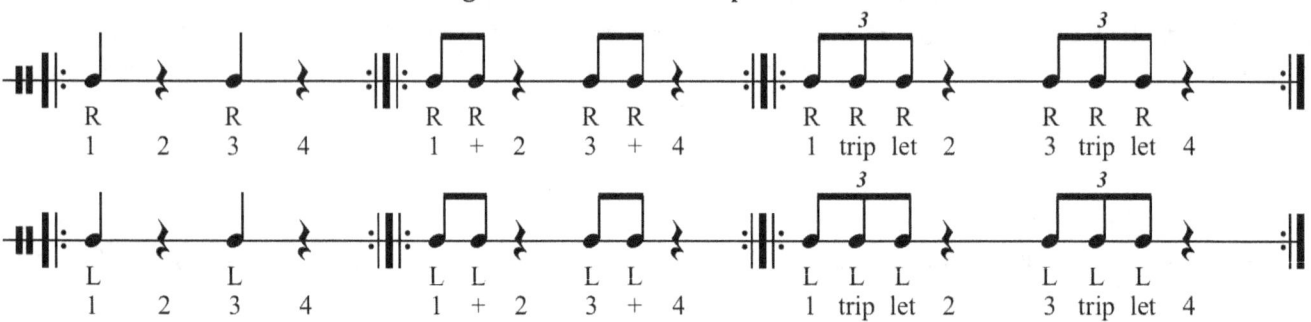

Exercises 6 and 7 contain measures containing quadruple strokes, which provide a hand workout by overshooting the triple stroke requirement.

## Single Hand Skill Buildup Exercise 6

Single Hand Skill Buildup Exercise 7

Single Hand Skill Buildup Exercise 8

Single Hand Skill Buildup Exercise 9

Two Hand Skill Buildup Exercise 1

Two Hand Skill Buildup Exercise 2

## Two Hand Skill Buildup Exercise 3

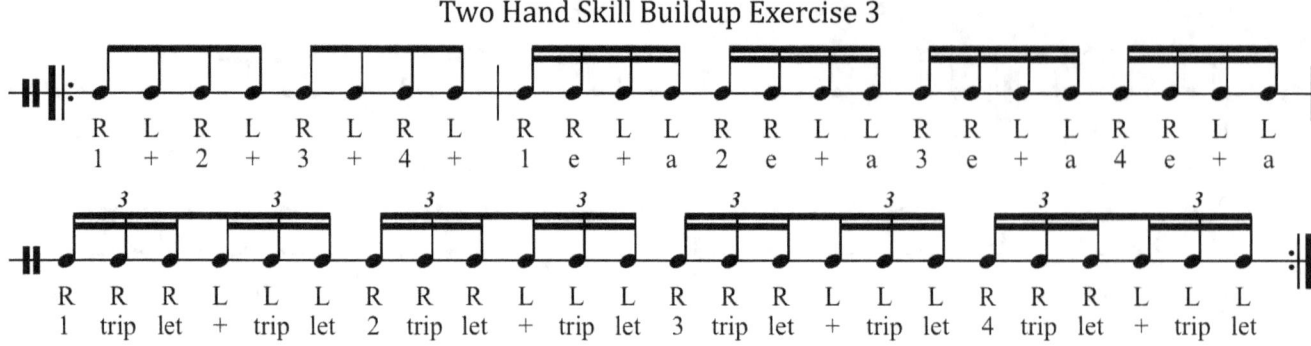

R L R L R L R L | R R L L R R L L R R L L R R L L
1 + 2 + 3 + 4 + | 1 e + a 2 e + a 3 e + a 4 e + a

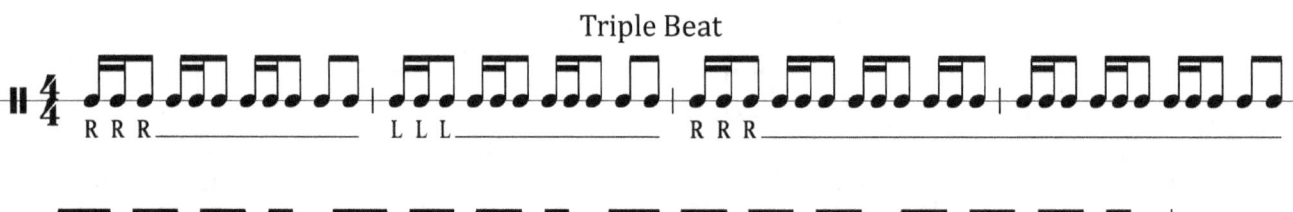

R R R L L L R R R L L L R R R L L L R R R L L L
1 trip let + trip let 2 trip let + trip let 3 trip let + trip let 4 trip let + trip let

## Triple Beat

R R R _____ L L L _____ R R R _____

L L L _____ R R R _____ L L L _____ R

## Suggested Drum Kit Application

R R R R R R R R R R R R
1 + a 2 + a 3 + a 4 + a

# 20. Single Paradiddle

**PAS:** *#16*
**NARD:** *#21*
**Other Names:** *Paradidle, Padadiddle, Stroke Paradiddle*
**Alternation:** *yes*
**Origin:** *England*

The Single Paradiddle is a combination of two single strokes and one double stroke, for a total of four notes. It usually begins with an accent, and is effectively a means of switching which hand falls on the downbeat. At some points in history, the Single Paradiddle we know today would have been referred to as the Stroke Paradiddle, while the standard Paradiddle actually featured two successive accents on the single strokes.

The name Paradiddle is derived from the ancient practice of using syllables to indicate sticking. In England, the words Pou and Tou were sometimes used, while in France, Pa and Ta served the same purpose. In this same vein, the first part of Paradiddle can be seen as the separate syllables Pa and Ra, indicating strokes on opposite hands. Diddle is a percussion term for a double stroke. When Pa, Ra, and Diddle are combined into Paradiddle, the name specifies the sticking of two singles and a double, RLRR or LRLL. Historical spellings include Padadiddle and Paradidle, but the logic holds true for those variations, as well.

The Paradiddle first appears in American playing in the late 18th century, including in a handwritten 1797 manuscript by Isaac Day, and has been in constant use ever since. Some scholars attribute the pattern to the British, and others to the Americans. The first written Paradiddles may occur in a British manual dated vaguely between 1770 and 1790, specifically mentioned as a timpani technique, but there is still some scholarly debate on the issue.

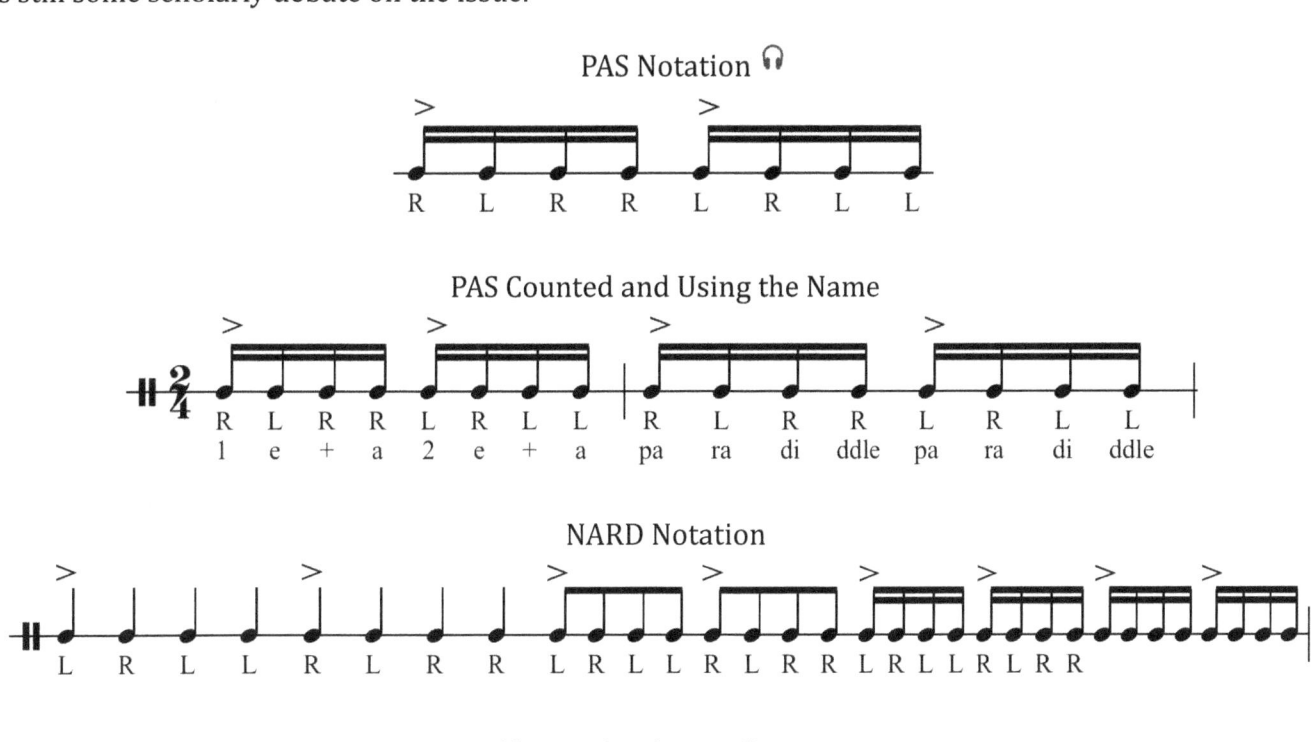

PAS Notation

PAS Counted and Using the Name

NARD Notation

Alternative Accent Pattern

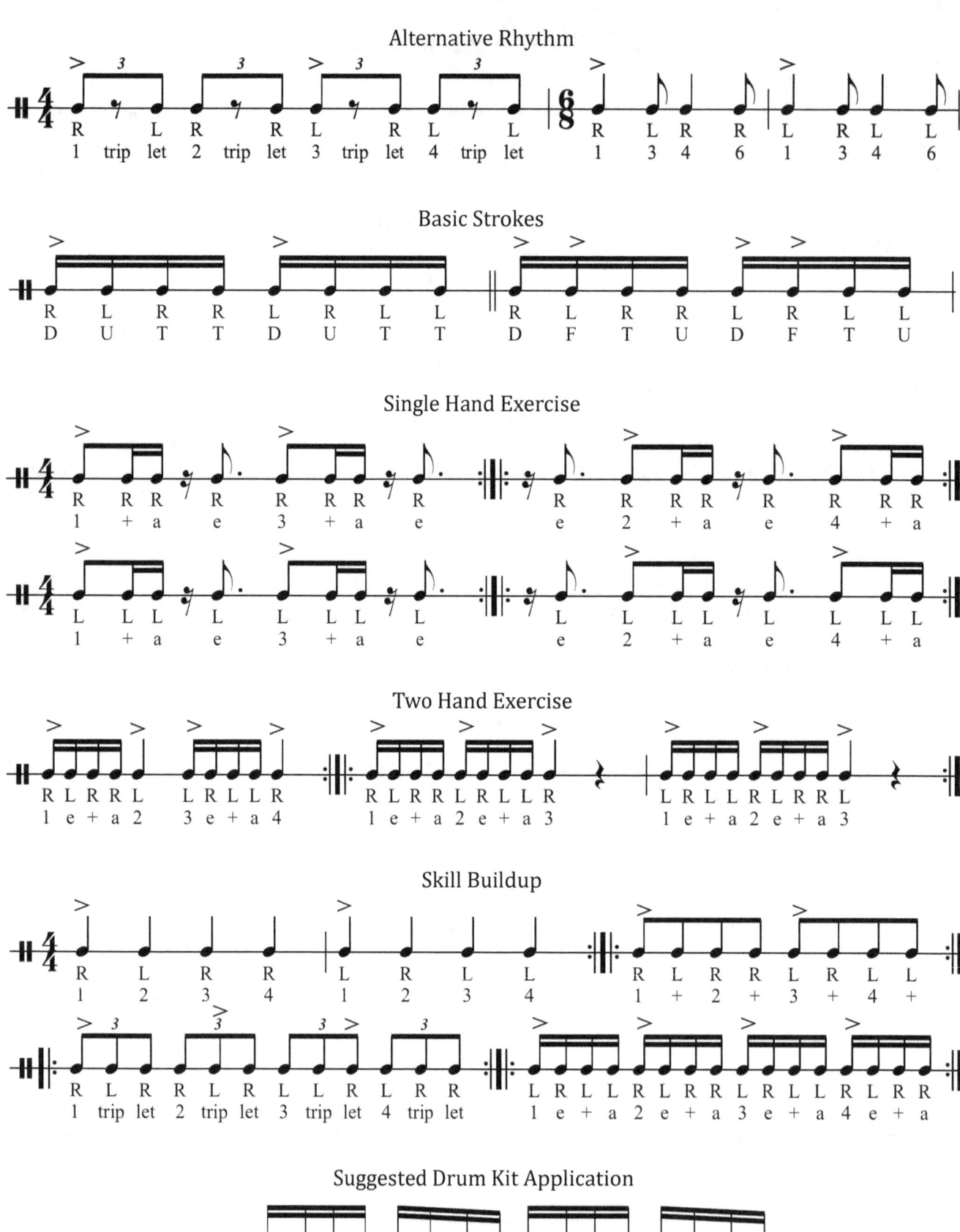

## Alternative Rhythm

## Basic Strokes

## Single Hand Exercise

## Two Hand Exercise

## Skill Buildup

## Suggested Drum Kit Application

Many rudiments can appear in inversions, where the downbeat falls on a different part of the rudiment than the way it is commonly listed on rudiment sheets. Paradiddles may be the most often cited example of this idea, with four inversions possible, by starting the rudiment on the downbeat from any of the four notes. This does not change the fundamental order in which the sticking appears, only which point in the sticking is viewed as the beginning of the pattern. This will be notated below, but RLRR LRLL is considered the standard sticking, and the other three inversions include: LRRL RLLR, RRLR LLRL, and RLRL LRLR. Though these other stickings do not look like Paradiddles to the untrained eye, the classic sticking pattern has not actually been reordered, but simply shifted over, in time. Another way of thinking about this concept is to use the name instead of the R and L sticking. ParadiddleParadiddle would be the standard sticking and the three other inversions would include: RadiddlepaRadiddlepa, DiddleparaDiddlepara, and DdleparadiDdleparadi. In each case, the spelling "paradiddle" can be found intact within the letters, meaning the actual order of the sticking has not changed. There are several competing sets of terms for these inversions. A good set of names has been included above, with some reasonable alternatives in parentheses below. This is not a comprehensive list of the possible naming conventions, some of which are confusing, or completely contradictory to the names here.

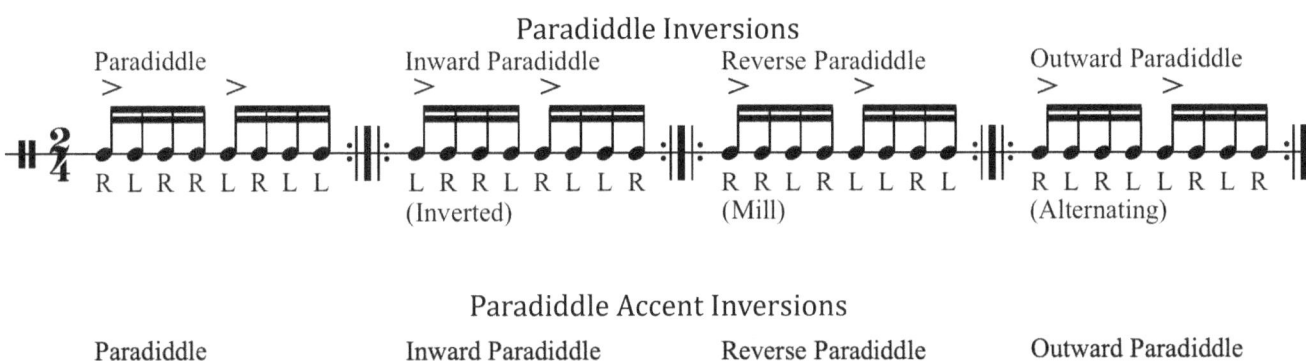

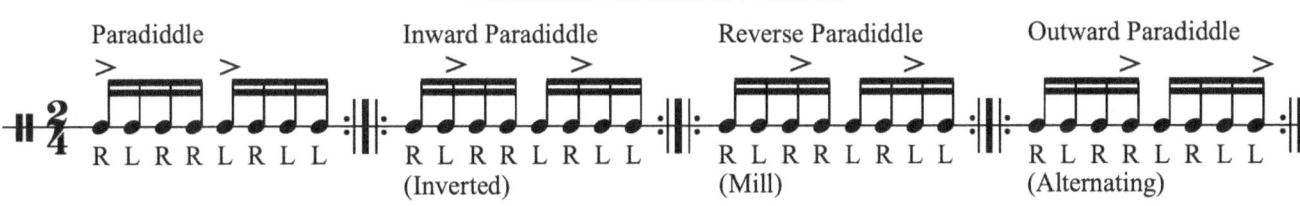

# 21. Double Paradiddle

**PAS:** *#17*
**NARD:** *#11*
**Other Names:** *n/a*
**Alternation:** *yes*
**Origin:** *USA*

The Double Paradiddle is a combination of four single strokes and one double stroke, for a total of six notes. It essentially just adds two single strokes to the beginning of the standard Single Paradiddle (20). While it is not actually double the length, the word Double in the name is useful in that it adds two syllables to the beginning of the Paradiddle, which correspond to the number of extra notes. The Double Paradiddle first appears in Ashworth's 1812 manual, and has been common in the USA, ever since. It is likely to be of American origin, though could also possibly be derived from the British. It is most commonly found in triplets or 6/8 time, but can also be played in a duple feel.

## PAS Notation

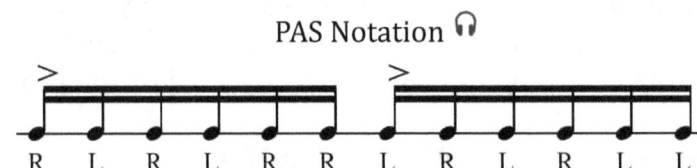

## PAS Counted and Using the Name

## NARD Notation

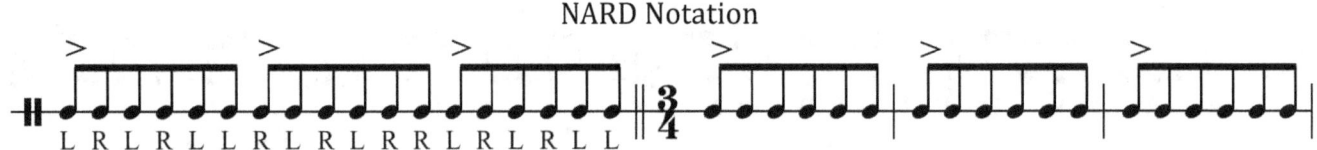

## Alternative Accent Pattern

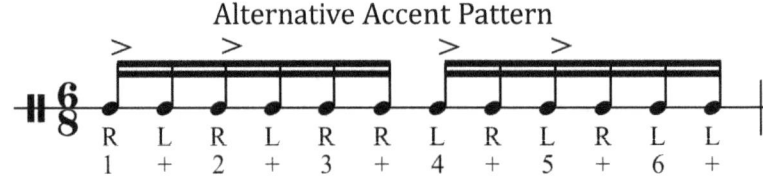

## Basic Strokes

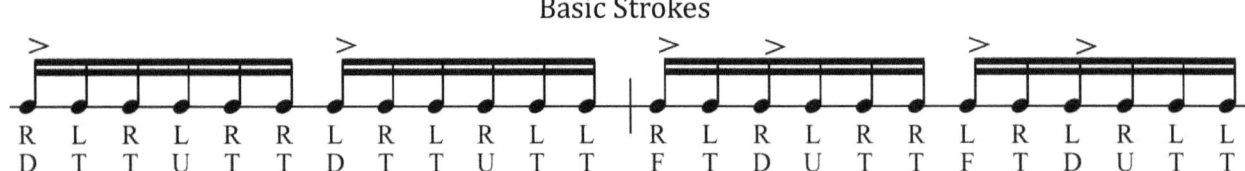

## Single Hand Exercise

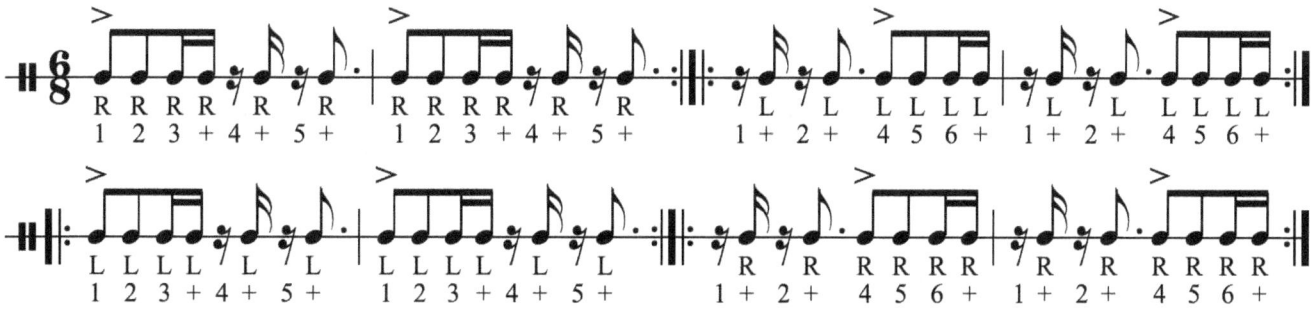

## Skill Buildup

## Suggested Drum Kit Application

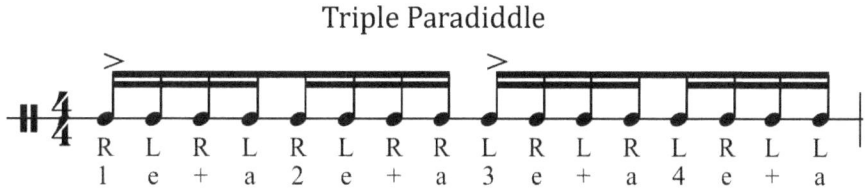

The PAS 40 includes a Triple Paradiddle, which further adds another pair of single strokes to the front end of the Double Paradiddle, for a total of 8 notes. It is not featured on the NARD sheets, and wasn't named or included in rudiment lists until the late 1930s. It will not be featured independently in this book, because it is arguably not traditional (can easily be interpreted as four single strokes, followed by a Single Paradiddle), and its exclusion as a separate rudiment, leaves more room for other topics. It is not inherently necessary to think about or practice it as its own rudiment, and is regarded by some as somewhat superfluous (if the Single Stroke Roll, Single Paradiddle, and Double Paradiddle are sufficiently well developed) – just like the Double Stroke Rolls longer than the 17 Stroke, it can be extrapolated easily.

## Triple Paradiddle

# 22. Single Paradiddle-diddle

**PAS:** *#19*
**NARD:** *n/a*
**Other Names:** *n/a*
**Alternation:** *no*
**Origin:** *USA*

The Single Paradiddle-diddle is a combination of two single strokes and two double strokes, for a total of six notes. The fact that it is specified to be "single" is somewhat misleading, because there is no Double Paradiddle-diddle, or other larger iteration commonly taught or listed on standard rudiment sheets.

While the Flam Paradiddle-diddle (40) is a fairly old, traditional American rudiment, the Single Paradiddle-diddle is a relatively new variation. It first appears in print, possibly as late the 1960s, and is thus a PAS rudiment (but not a NARD selection). It is quite similar to the 6 Stroke Roll (7), in that it contains two double strokes and two single strokes, which is precisely the number and type of strokes in the 6 Stroke Roll. Depending on where in the 6 Stroke Roll or the Paradiddle-diddle a player starts, and what rhythm for the roll they use, these two rudiments can sound almost identical or quite different.

### PAS Notation 🎧

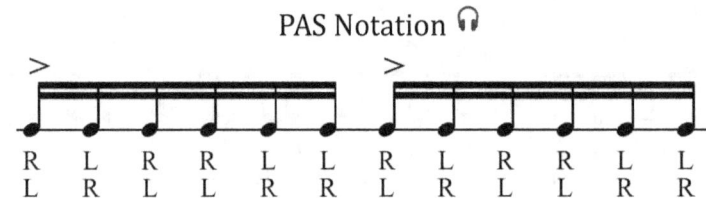

### PAS Counted and Using the Name

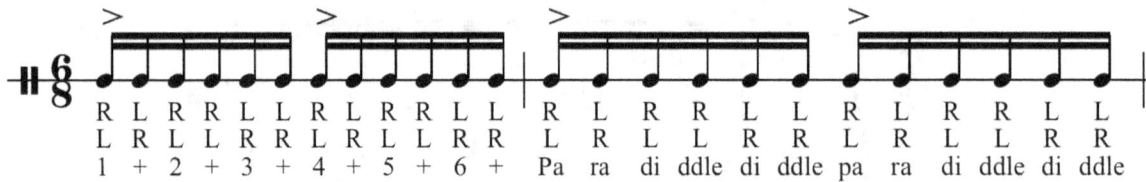

### Basic Strokes

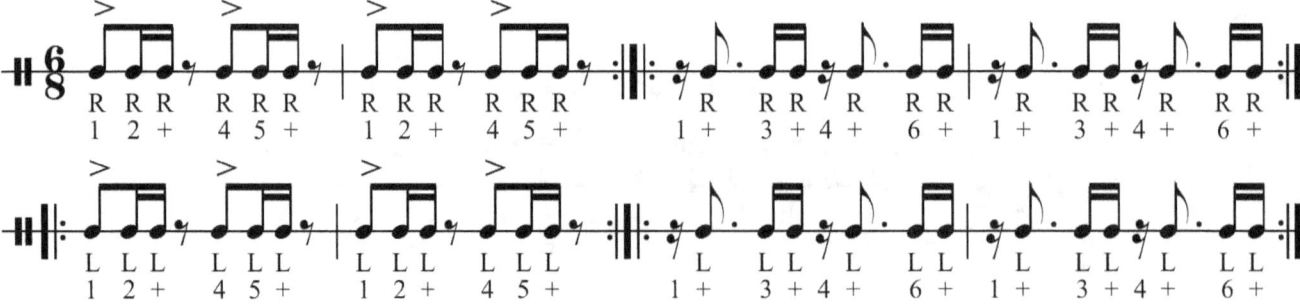

### Single Hand Exercise

## Two Hand Exercise

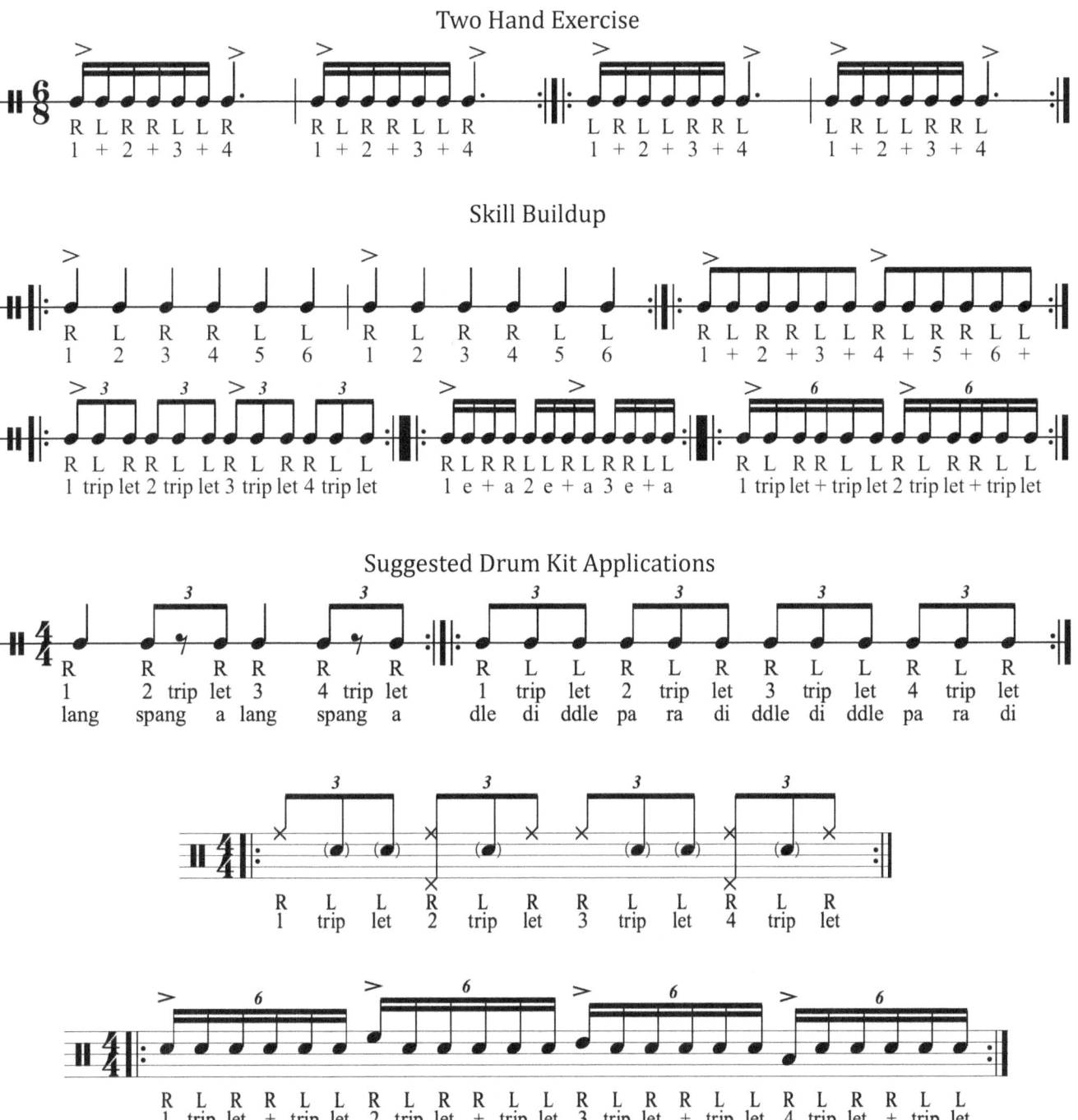

## Skill Buildup

## Suggested Drum Kit Applications

# 23. Drag

**PAS:** *#31*
**NARD:** *n/a*
**Other Names:** *Half Drag, Dragge, Dragg, Half Dragge, Open Drag, 3 Stroke Roll, 3er Ruff, Halbe Ruff, Ra, Ra de 3, Rau, Rau de 3, Ran de 3*
**Alternation:** *yes*
**Origin:** *unknown, possibly Switzerland*

The Drag can be notated a couple of ways – with grace notes, or with a tremolo slash. A classic Drag consists of two grace notes (played on the same hand, as a double stroke) preceding a single primary note (played with the opposite hand). All notes are equally spaced. A right-handed Drag would be played with a left hand double stroke and a right hand single stroke. The timing of the grace notes is subject to interpretation, and can vary from 16th notes up to 64th notes, depending on where they are found and how they are used. It is common in the modern era, however, to notate the exact timing required for a Drag, without the use of any grace notes. A tremolo slash is used on the stem of a note of half the speed of the intended double stroke. For example, if the Drag should be played as 32nd notes, a 16th note will be notated with a tremolo slash, followed by a note of any value without a tremolo slash, corresponding to the primary note in the classic grace note notation style. With this notation, the player executes the Drag exactly at the note values indicated, and it is not subject to interpretation.

Drags are extremely ancient, with their exact origin unknown. Most rudimental styles employ them, and Drags are technically the shortest possible Double Stroke Roll – a 3 Stroke Roll. Some styles of drumming label them as such, while others insist that they are separate from the various numbered rolls that they resemble. They appear in American drum manuals in the 18th century, and are first named by Ben Clark, in around 1797-1800. Clark calls them 3 Stroke Rolls. The name Dragg or Dragge is used in earlier English sources, and Americans reverted to this naming convention, later. They are sometimes called Half Drags to differentiate from the Single Drag and Full Drag, which we would now call variations on the Single Drag Tap (26). They are also, unfortunately, referred to as Ruffs (or conflated with Ruffs), in many places.

Drags are extremely similar to Ruffs (#24 in this book, shown in the next section), to the point where many drummers consider them interchangeable. They are not. There is plenty of historical precedent to show that Ruffs and Drags are different rudiments and many historical drum manuals list both as independent skills. Drags are played open, with all three notes, clearly audible. Ruffs are played closed, where the grace notes are so close together, that they often cannot be counted. Ruffs can be played so closed, that a buzz stroke is used, instead of a distinct pair of notes. Drags must always contain exactly three notes. They cannot be buzzed, and should not be played so closed that they blur together. Drags played slowly have more space between the notes, proportional to the tempo, while Ruffs sound the same (closed) at any tempo. When notated with grace notes, there is often no visual difference between a Drag and a Ruff. Context is the only way to determine which rudiment to use, and sometimes, a guess must be made. In modern rudimental tremolo slash notation, Drags are obvious, and cannot be confused for Ruffs. In concert or orchestral music, Ruffs are almost always required, instead of Drags.

PAS Notation 🎧

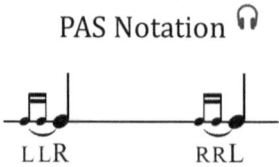

LLR          RRL

## PAS with several possible interpretations

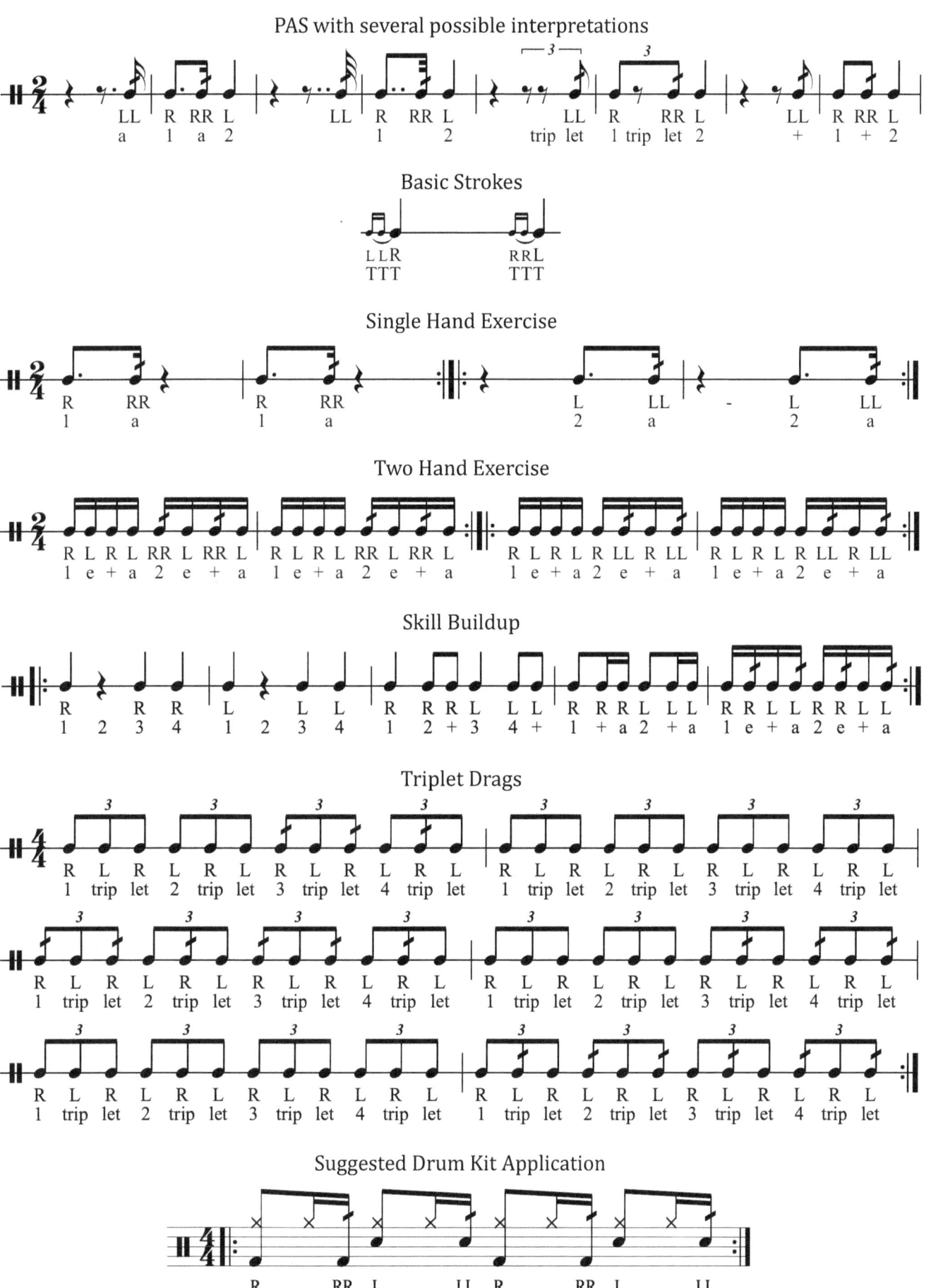

## Basic Strokes

## Single Hand Exercise

## Two Hand Exercise

## Skill Buildup

## Triplet Drags

## Suggested Drum Kit Application

# 24. The Ruff

**PAS:** *n/a*
**NARD:** *#8*
**Other Names:** *Ruffe, Ruf, Rough, Roofe, Closed Drag, Close Drag, Tra, Ra*
**Alternation:** *yes*
**Origin:** *unknown, possibly England or France*

The Ruff consists of two grace notes on the same hand, followed by a single primary note on the opposite hand – A Double, and a Single. On the surface, this appears to be so incredibly similar to the definition of a Drag (23) as to be the same rudiment. In reality, the Ruff is more like a Flam (32) than a Drag, in that the grace notes do not change proportionally, with the speed of the primary notes around them. The Ruff is generally always played closed, with the grace notes as close to the primary note, as is reasonably possible. A very slow or very fast tempo should not affect the execution, and each Ruff should sound the same. Although the grace notes appear to show exactly two notes, and a very closed double stroke is the technically correct way to play a Ruff, in practice, a short buzz can be used in some contexts, for the same basic effect. It then becomes more of a "Multiple Bounce Flam" than anything like a Drag. This is not always acceptable, however, and two very closed grace notes should be practiced.

The name "Ruff" gets used far too often! "Ruffs" of one sort or another can be single stroked, double stroked, or buzzed, and none of these are the same as the Drag. Ruff, or a different spelling of the same sound, has been used in English, since the 1600s. In some cases, the name refers to single stroked rudiments, such as the 3 Stroke Ruff (or Tap Ruff)(2) and the 4 Stroke Ruff (3). In 1861, Keach, Burditt, and Cassidy used the name Ruff to refer to a clearly double stroked rudiment that was "like the Flam". They appear to be referring to the same Ruff discussed on this page. In the same year, Elias Howe listed a double stroked rudiment named Ruff, and a separate double stroked rudiment named Half Drag. Howe's Ruff is also compared to the Flam, while the Half Drag is not. These are also completely separate rudiments from the Multiple Bounce rudiment, herein called the Crushed Ruff (18), which is found primarily in jazz and classical music, but has been referred to as a rudiment, under various names, since the early 20th century.

Some famous or important American authors to list the Double Stroked Ruff and the Double Stroked Drag as different rudiments in the same book include: George Bruce (Barrett), John Philip Sousa, Sanford Moeller, Vincent Mott, and the US War Department. Between 1861 and the formation of NARD in 1933, listing both rudiments was common, and this list is far from complete. Between NARD's formation and the 1980s (when the PAS 40 were published), most books simply listed the Ruff (with a couple of exceptions), because that is the only one of the two rudiment names that NARD officially recognized in their 26 rudiments. Drag was used in conjunction with other patterns, such as Drag Paradiddles, but not the straight Drag rudiment.

The PAS 40 uses only the name Drag, and there are no Ruffs of any type on the sheet. The Drag is clearly intended to fill the same role as The Ruff from the NARD 26, because the Drag on the PAS sheet has an asterisk next to it, denoting its supposed inclusion on the NARD 26. Some modern drummers are campaigning for the use of the word Ruff only in context of the single strokes, but history just isn't on their side. Rest assured, these are all definitely different rudiments, and should not be casually interchanged, despite the confusing names and notation.

In British books, it became standard in the 19th century to list a Close Drag, or Closed Drag, and an Open Drag. This naming convention avoided a lot of the confusion that the name Ruff caused in the USA. The British then reserved the name Ruff for the 4 Stroke Ruff. Pipe bands have two types of Drags, Scottish and Open – both with two written grace notes. Scottish Drags are played with a single dead stroke grace note, or very short buzzed grace note, in place of the two written grace notes. Open Drags are played like an American Drag. France also has open and closed versions of a two-grace-note rudiment. This means that there are at least four rudimental traditions that separate open and closed two-grace-note figures like the Ruff and Drag: Britain, France, pipe band, and USA. Despite the arguing and confusion, the separation of the two rudiments is not unusual, and these are all separate from the single stroked Ruffs.

The notation for the Ruff is identical to the older style of Drag notation, with the same two grace notes. Context and logic must be applied when selecting the appropriate spacing. Sometimes it is unclear, and the performer must make a judgment call. In a classical context, closed Ruffs are always preferred to the more open Drags. In rudimental playing, the age of the piece being played, the composer, and the framework of rudiments around the grace notes can sometimes help identify whether a Ruff is appropriate.

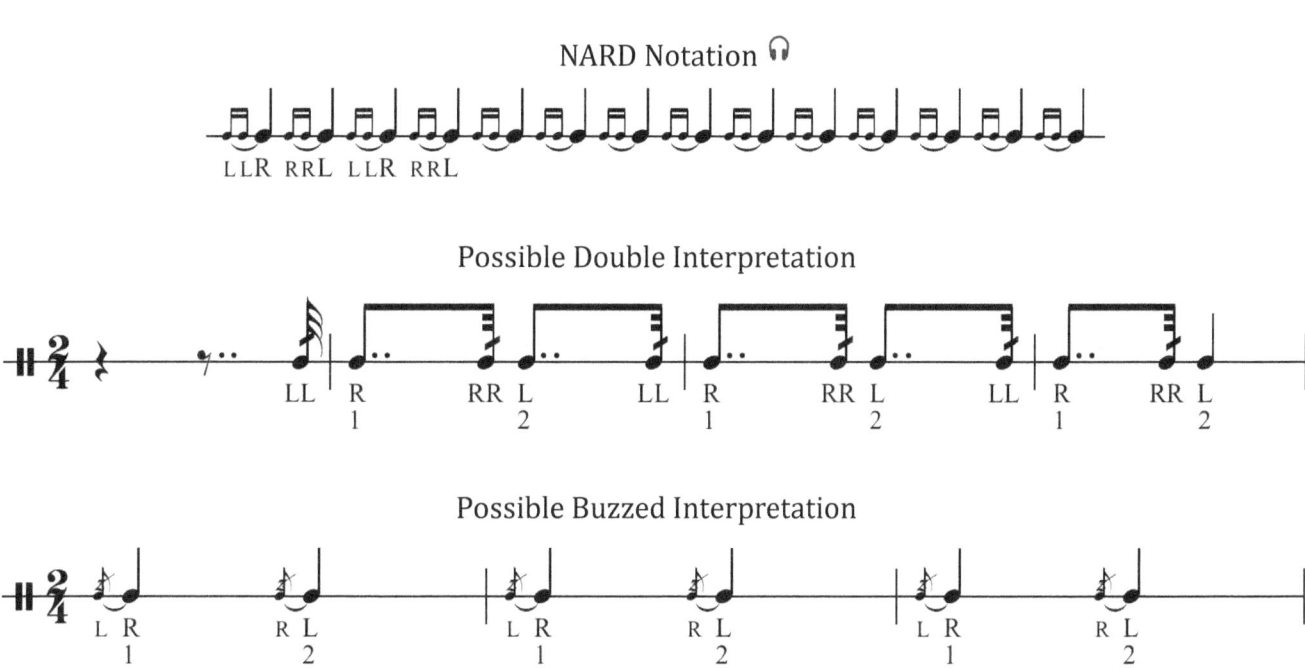

# 25. Lesson 25

**PAS:** *#34*
**NARD:** *#25*
**Other Names:** *Compound Stroke, Ratatap, Ratamott, The Preparative, Quick Scotch, Three and a Two, Accent #3, Quick Three and Two Beats*
**Alternation:** *no*
**Origin:** *possibly England or USA*

The Lesson 25 begins with two grace notes on the same hand, followed by three alternating primary notes (usually written as two 16th notes, and an 8th note). In other words, it is a Drag (23) followed immediately by two single strokes.

The Lesson 25 is derived from a couple of British and American duty signals, "The Preparative" and "The Quick Scotch", in which the rhythm is featured. The first American instance of it being named as a rudiment is from 1818, when Hazeltine calls it "a stroke a three and a two." His rudiment contains an extra note, when compared to the modern understanding, but the spirit is the same. Several different names were offered for the pattern, but none stuck. The current name, Lesson 25, makes little sense without lots of background information. It is currently #34 on the PAS sheet, which confounds almost all new drummers.

The name Lesson 25 originated with Gardner Strube, in 1869, when he published a list of 25 "Lessons." Each lesson had a name, e.g. "Lesson, No. 1. The Long Roll." The 25th lesson was left without a name. Strube mentions the "Quick Scotch", but that is clearly not its name. It is unclear whether Strube did not know the name, did not like any of the previously used names, or whether the publisher made a mistake. Many drummers subsequently referred it to as the 25th Rudiment, or Lesson 25, as a substitute for a name. W.F. Ludwig and V.L. Mott have proposed other names, such as Ratatap or Ratamott, respectively, but none have had lasting success. On the NARD sheet, it retains its number 25, so the name makes some sense. The PAS 40 ignored that number and placed it with other similar patterns, not in the 25th position. This book has been organized such that it is the 25th rudiment, to prevent confusion – despite the number itself being completely arbitrary. Certainly by accident, the name contains the correct number of syllables for the notes in the rudiment, and can be used to help remember the pattern.

PAS Notation 🎧

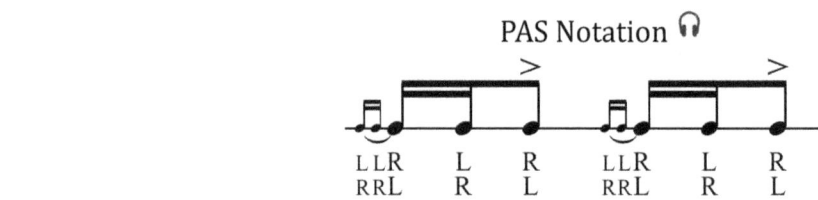

PAS Counted and Using the Name

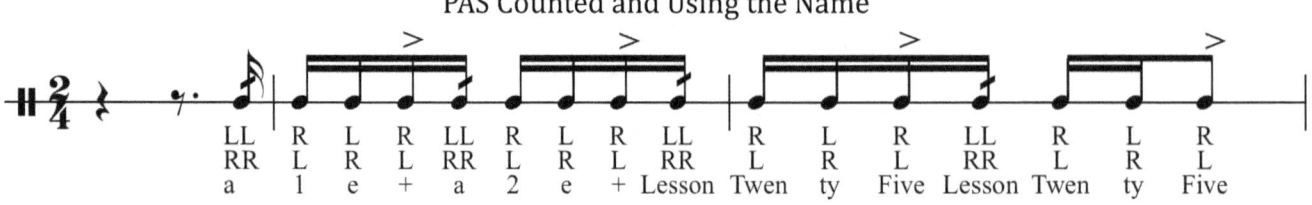

NARD Notation

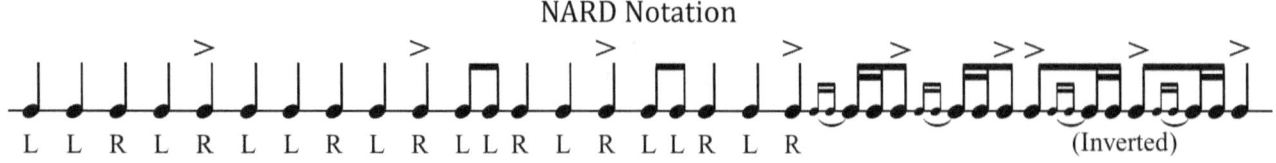

## Basic Strokes

## Single Hand Exercise

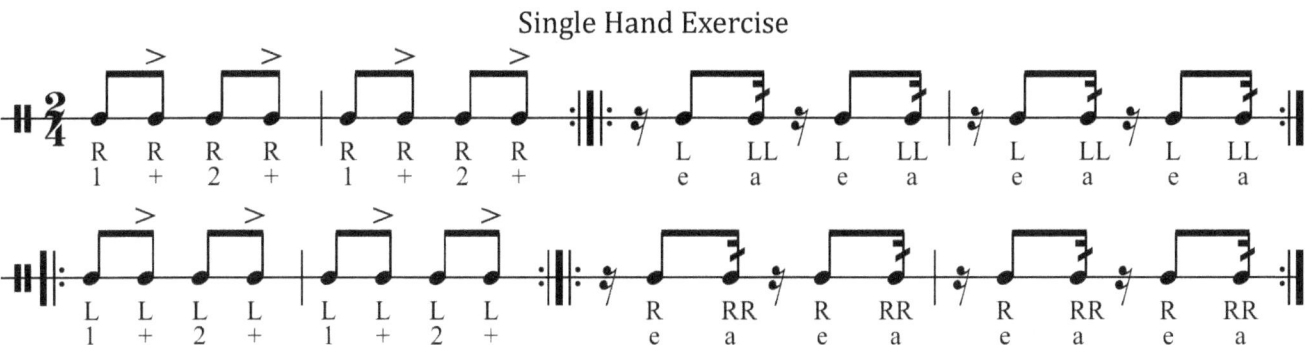

## Two Hand Exercise

## Skill Buildup

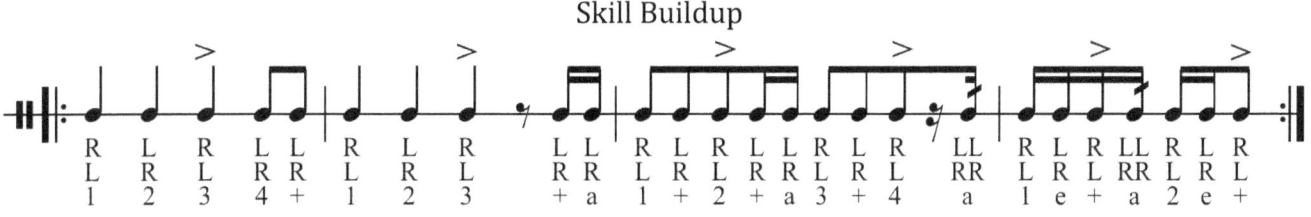

## Suggested Drum Kit Application

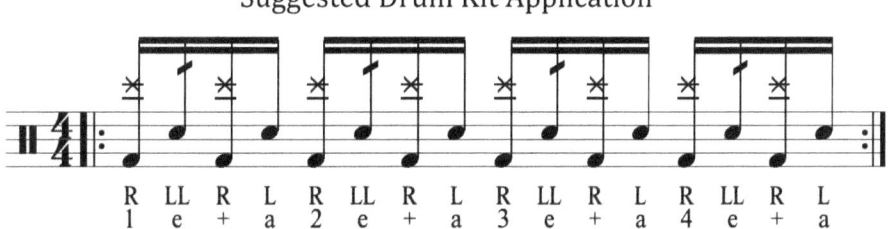

# 26. Single Drag Tap

**PAS:** *#32*
**NARD:** *#9*
**Other Names:** *Single Drag, Single Drag and Stroke, Drag and Stroke, Ruf, Coup du Rigodon, Halv Appel, Halbe Ruf*
**Alternation:** *yes*
**Origin:** *unknown, likely Switzerland or France*

The Single Drag Tap consists of two grace notes on the same hand, preceding a primary note on the opposite hand – a Drag (23) followed by a stroke with the hand that played the grace notes (often accented). Put another way, it is a double stroke, followed by two single strokes. A commonly used inversion starts with the Tap, and then follows with the Drag (single-double-single). The PAS sheet shows the Single Drag Tap starting only from the grace notes, but the NARD list shows both versions, from the grace notes and from the Tap.

The Single Drag Tap most likely originated in Switzerland or France, and made its print debut as a named rudiment in the USA around 1797-1800 (probably directly taken from the British). It has historically been called simply, the Single Drag. The word "Tap" was added to the name in the 1980s (probably as a clarification). The rudiment names Drag, Single Drag, and Full Drag, all sound confusingly synonymous at face value – but, Single Drag Tap instantly conveys that there is another note beyond the Drag. It is an unfortunate name, because the note that is referred to as the named "Tap" is actually accented in many interpretations. Since taps are a different type of stroke from accents, this doesn't fully make sense. Some past manuals used the name Drag and Stroke, instead of Drag Tap, which is in the same spirit, but does not conflict as much with the possible presence of an accent.

Although it has a special name, the Single Drag Tap is actually a 4 Stroke Roll, in the same manner that the Drag is a 3 Stroke Roll. It follows the convention of all of the even-numbered rolls, such as the 6 Stroke Roll or the 10 Stroke Roll, having two single strokes, and the remainder of the notes played in double strokes. It is the shortest possible even-numbered Double Stroke Roll (5).

PAS Notation

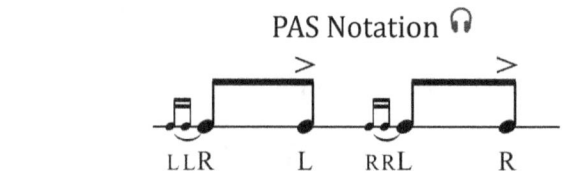

PAS Counted and Using the Name

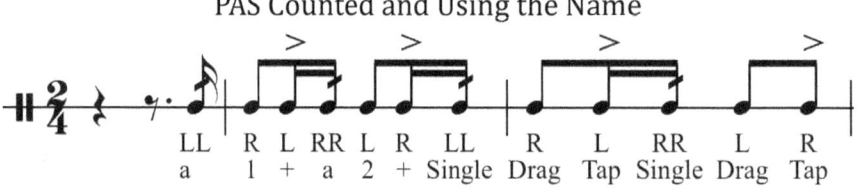

NARD Notation

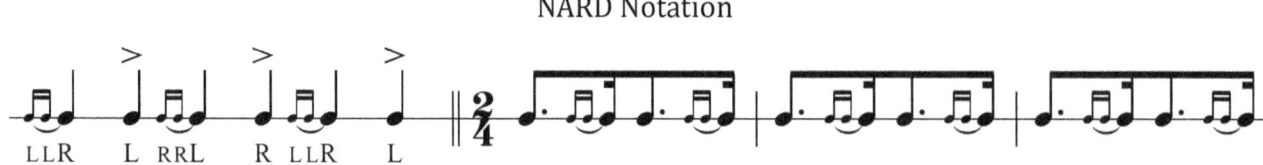

## Basic Strokes

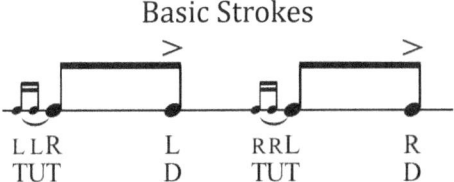

## Alternative Notation

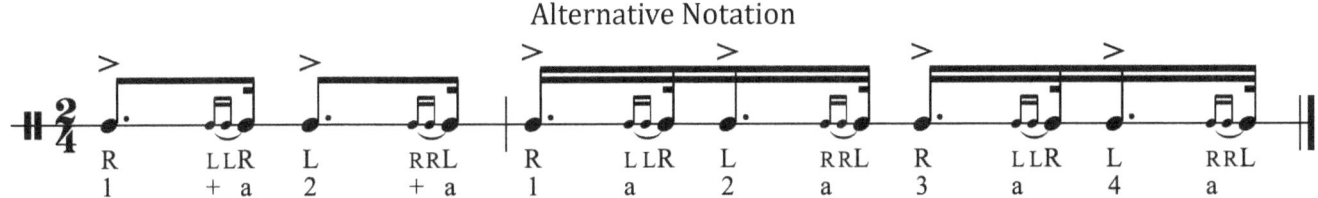

The alternative notation above may be interpreted as Alternative Rhythm 1 (below), despite not matching the actual notation at all. It is also as common, or possibly even more common, in rudimental repertoire than the PAS rhythm. Several exercises below will use this rhythm, instead of the PAS version.

## Alternative Rhythm 1

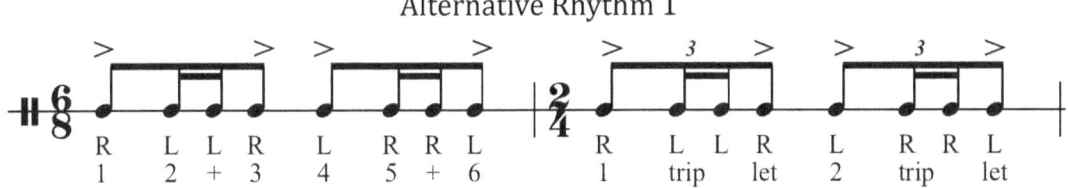

## Alternative Rhythm 2

## Alternative Rhythm 2 Interpreted

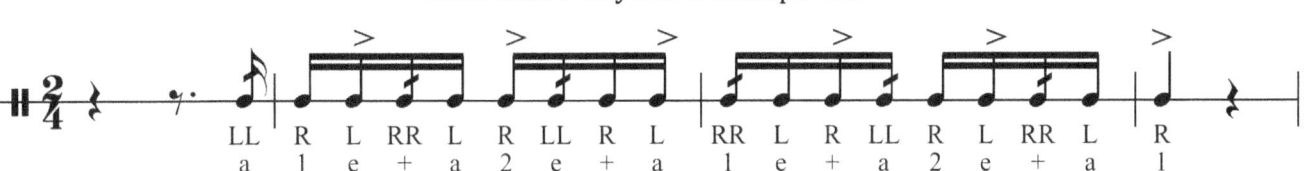

## Single Hand Exercise

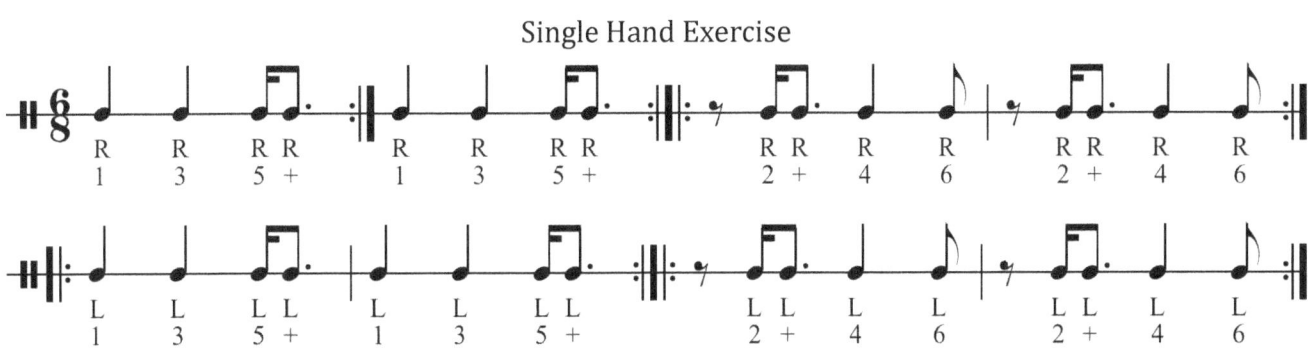

## Two Hand Exercise

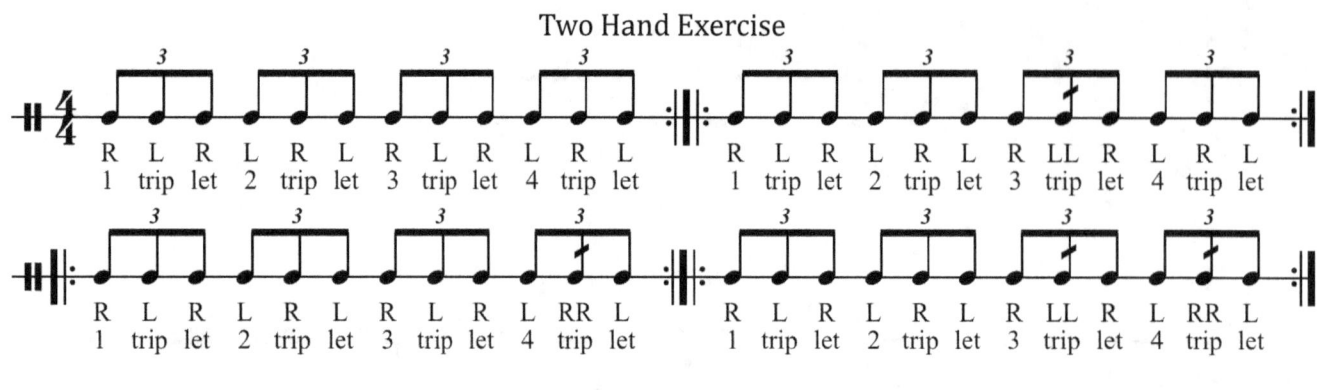

## Skill Buildup

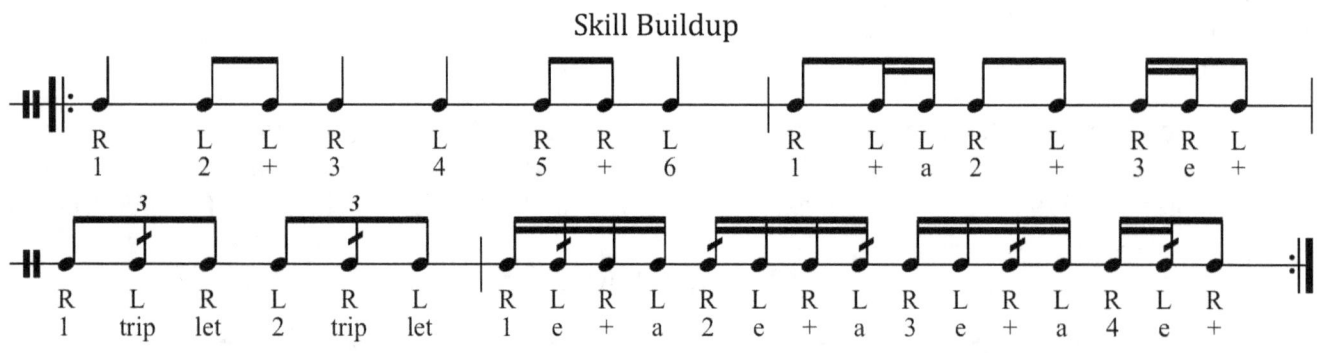

# 27. Double Drag Tap

**PAS:** *#33*
**NARD:** *#10*
**Other Names:** *Double Drag,*
*Double Drag and Stroke, Dragg,*
*Double Dragg, Coup de la Diane,*
*Doppelter Tagwachtstreich*
**Alternation:** *yes*
**Origin:** *unknown, likely*
*Switzerland or France*

The Double Drag Tap consists of two Drags played on the same side followed by a single stroke, for a total of seven notes (double-single-double-single-single). For example, two lefts, followed by a right, then another two lefts, followed by a right, then a further left. It essentially adds one more Drag to the beginning of a Single Drag Tap (26), doubling the number of Drags played, hence the name.

The name Double Drag Tap is somewhat misleading because, like the Single Drag Tap, the "Tap" portion is often accented, making it NOT the Basic Stroke called Tap. In older publications, it is sometimes referred to as the "Double Drag and Stroke", which makes more sense. More commonly, it was called the Double Drag, and the "Tap" or "Stroke" was implied, but not stated.

The notation for the Double Drag Tap can take several rhythmic forms. In the USA, it is commonly seen in straight 8th notes (as on the PAS sheet), or dotted 8ths and 16ths (as shown on the NARD sheet). In Europe, especially France and Switzerland, it is sometimes played as a quintuplet, often paired with the quintuplet version of the 9 Stroke Roll (10), but seems to have lost this timing when brought into British, and later, American playing. In Europe, it was historically used in the Reveille sequence, but in British and American drumming, it was found in the Dinner Call.

### PAS Notation

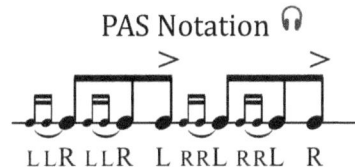

### PAS Counted and Using the Name

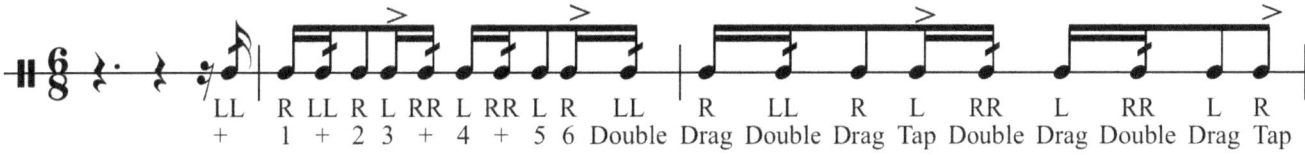

### NARD Notation

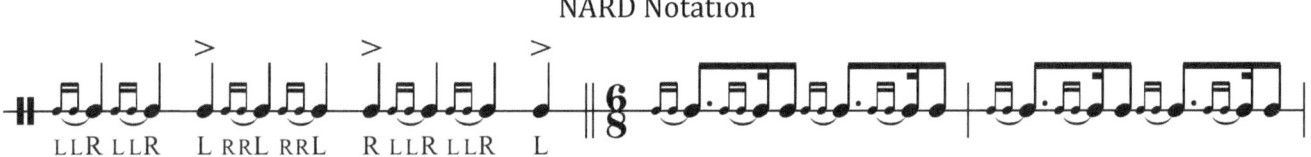

### Basic Strokes

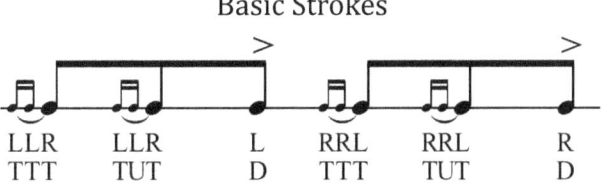

**Alternative Rhythm 1a** – This is the 6/8 rhythm shown on the NARD sheet interpreted very open

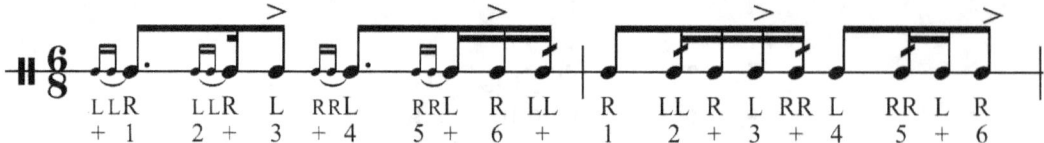

**Alternative Rhythm 1b** – This is the same NARD rhythm as 1a but interpreted more closed, or with a "scherzo" style

**Alternative Rhythm 2** – European Interpretation

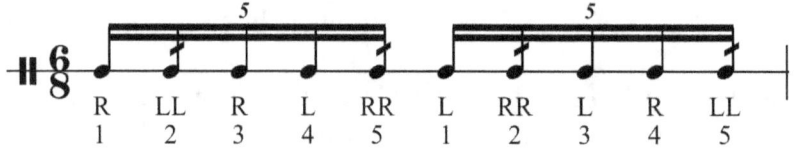

### Single Hand Exercise

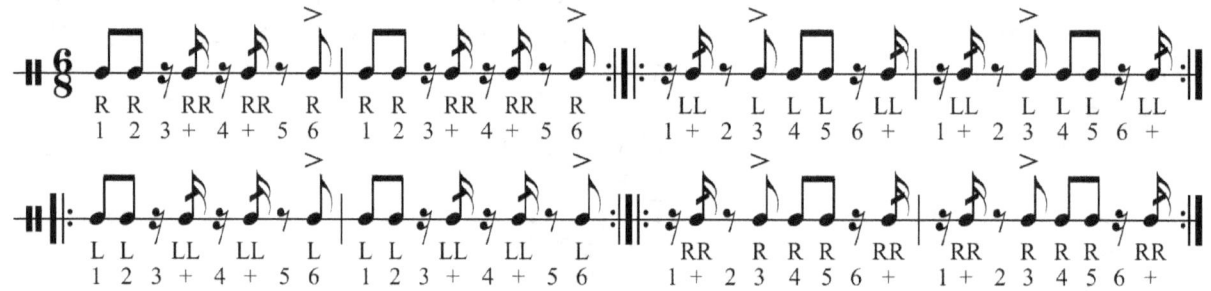

### Two Hand Exercise

### Skill Buildup

# 28. Drag Paradiddle No. 1

**PAS:** *#36*
**NARD:** *#22*
**Other Names:** *Stroke and Drag Paradidle, Stroke and Drag Paradiddle, Paradiddle Drag Beat, Drag Paradiddle #1*
**Alternation:** *yes*
**Origin:** *England*

The Drag Paradiddle No. 1 consists of a single stroke followed by a double stroke on grace notes, and then a Single Paradiddle (20). For a right-handed Drag Paradiddle No. 1, it is a right accent, two left taps, then a Paradiddle (right-left-right-right). The double stroke of the Drag (23), is typically played faster than the surrounding notes, such that the rudiment fits nicely in a triplet, or three beats of 6/8 time. It can also be thought of as a Double Paradiddle (21), in which the second note is played as a double stroke.

Samuel Potter may have been the first to name the rudiment in 1815, as the Stroke and Drag Paradiddle, but it entered the American rudimental vocabulary in 1862, when H.C. Hart called it the Paradiddle Drag Beat. It found its modern name in 1869, with Gardner Strube, who also seems to have invented, or first published the Drag Paradiddle No. 2, necessitating the numbering of both versions, to avoid confusion.

There are several various other rudiments called Drag Paradiddle, so this can be an area of confusion. Moeller listed five separate versions, for example. In many cases, rudiments called Drag Paradiddle without specifying a number, or using the word "Stroke" in the name, begin with the double stroke of the Drag, and not with an initial single stroke. Although extremely similar in name and execution, these other rudiments beginning with a double stroke are separate rudiments and not part of the standard No. 1 and No. 2 naming convention. The numbered Drag Paradiddles both begin with a single stroke.

PAS Notation

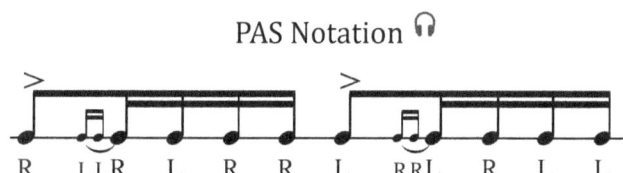

PAS Notation Interpreted

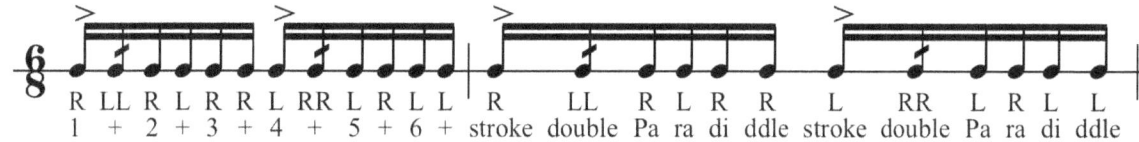

NARD Notation

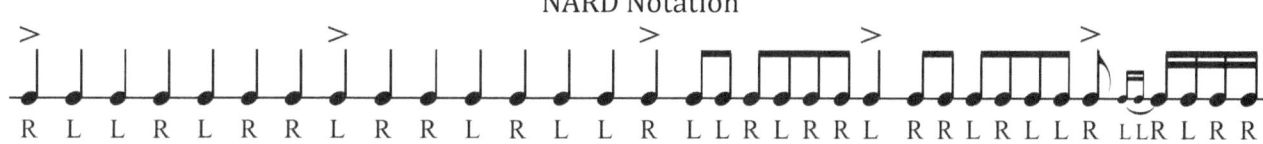

Basic Strokes

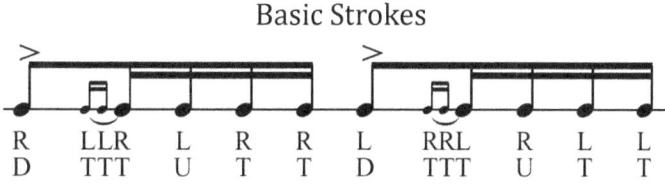

## Single Hand Exercise

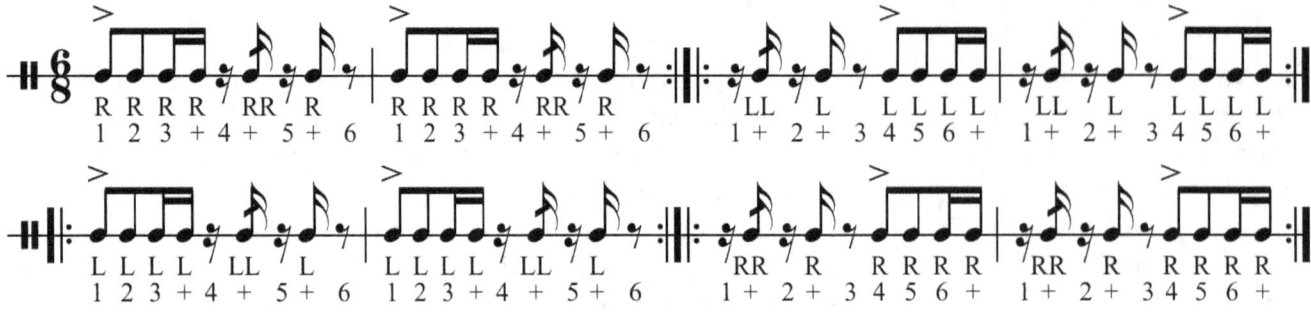

## Two Hand Exercise

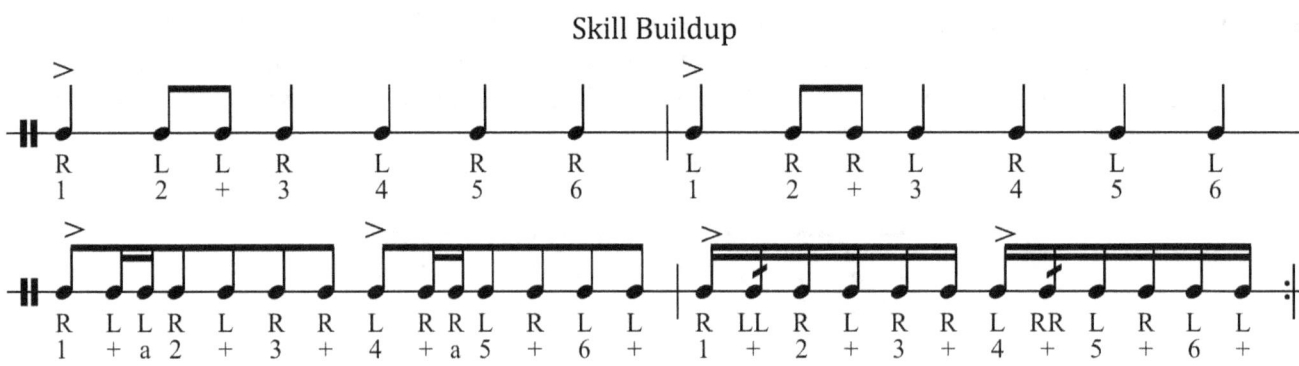

## Skill Buildup

# 29. Drag Paradiddle No. 2

**PAS:** *#37*
**NARD:** *#23*
**Other Names:** *Drag Paradiddle #2, Stroke and Double Drag Paradiddle*
**Alternation:** *yes*

The Drag Paradiddle No. 2 consists of a single stroke followed by a double stroke on grace notes, then another single stroke, and then another set of grace notes played as a double stroke, and then a Single Paradiddle (20). For a right-handed Drag Paradiddle No. 2, it is a right accent, two left taps, right tap, two more left taps, then a Paradiddle (right-left-right-right). The double stroke of the Drag (23) is typically played faster than the surrounding notes such that the rudiment fits nicely in a measure of 2/4 time. It can also be thought of as a Triple Paradiddle, in which the second and fourth notes are played as a double stroke.

Gardner Strube first published an American Drag Paradiddle No. 2 in 1869. There were a couple of possible antecedents that were similar in both the USA and Britain, but nothing with exactly the same pattern. When the No. 2 was published, the No. 1 received its number for the first time, since there were now two of them. There are other rudiments with a similar pattern that are usually referred to as Drag Paradiddles, but they are not officially numbered, and they often begin with a Drag instead of a single stroke. There are very few, or perhaps no, Drag Paradiddle variations outside of the UK and USA. Including those patterns that also contain Flams, there are around seven unique Drag-Paradiddle-like rudiments, all found in the British, American, or pipe band (Scottish) traditions.

PAS Notation

PAS Notation Interpreted

PAS Notation Interpreted musical notation

NARD Notation

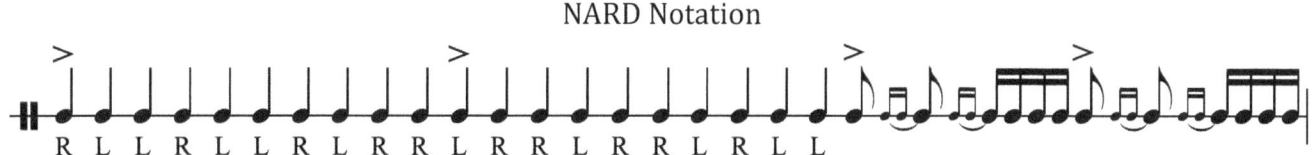

## Basic Strokes

## Single Hand Exercise

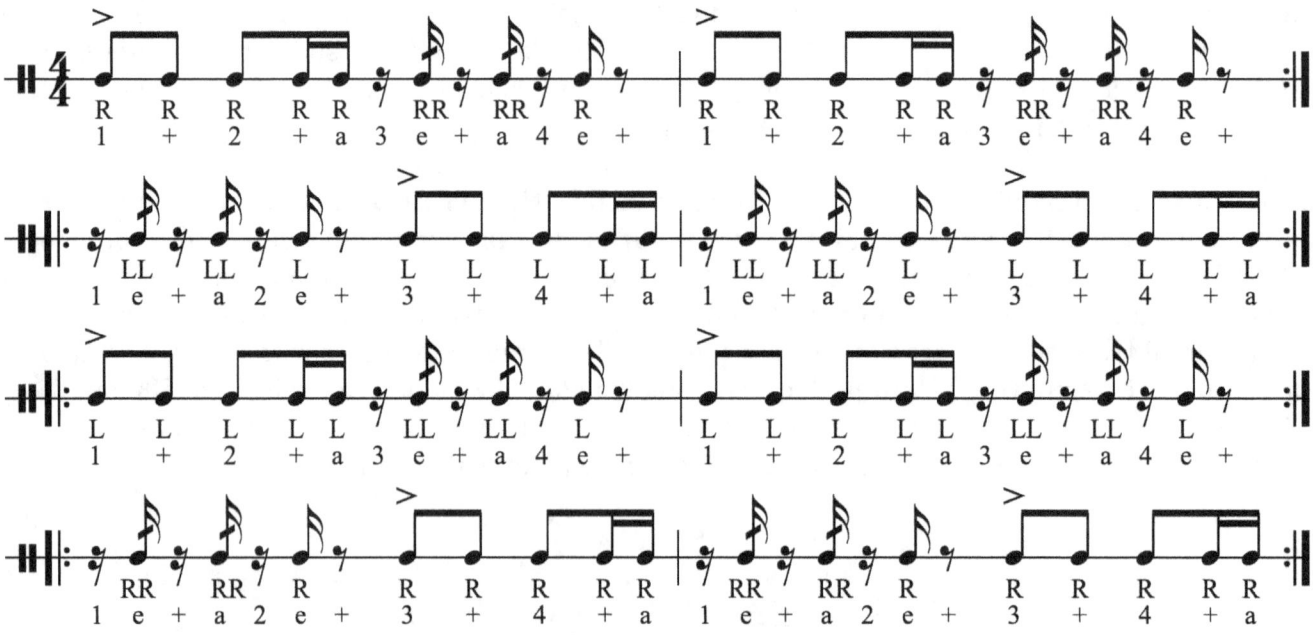

## Two Hand Exercise

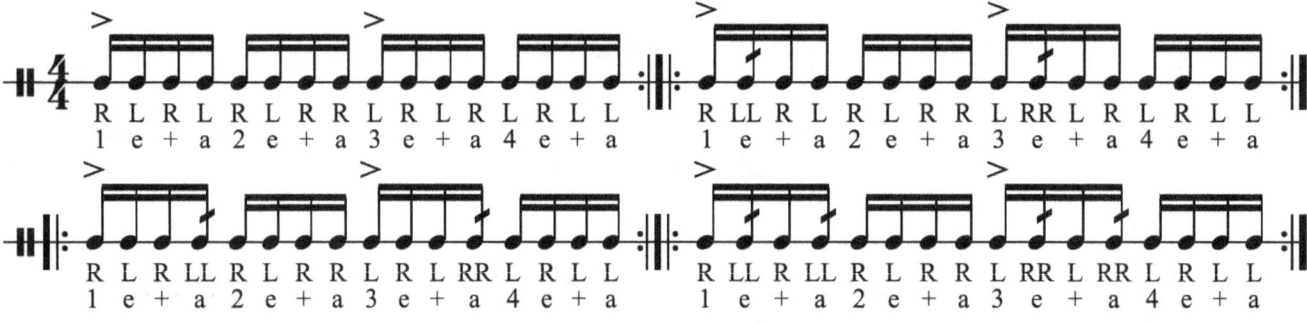

## Skill Buildup

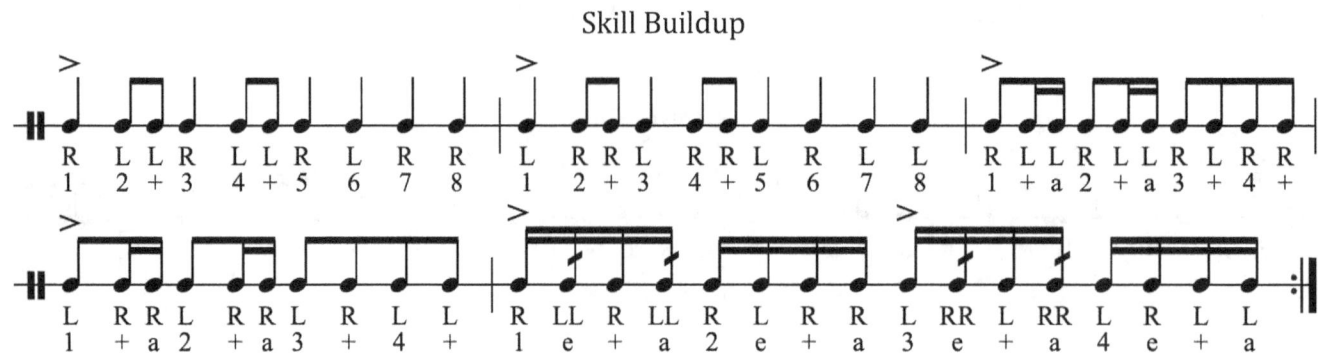

As previously mentioned, other Drag Paradiddle variations exist. Here are a few examples of others that are not PAS or NARD standards, most of them beginning with a double, instead of a single stroke, and thus necessitating a closed, or Ruff-like interpretation.

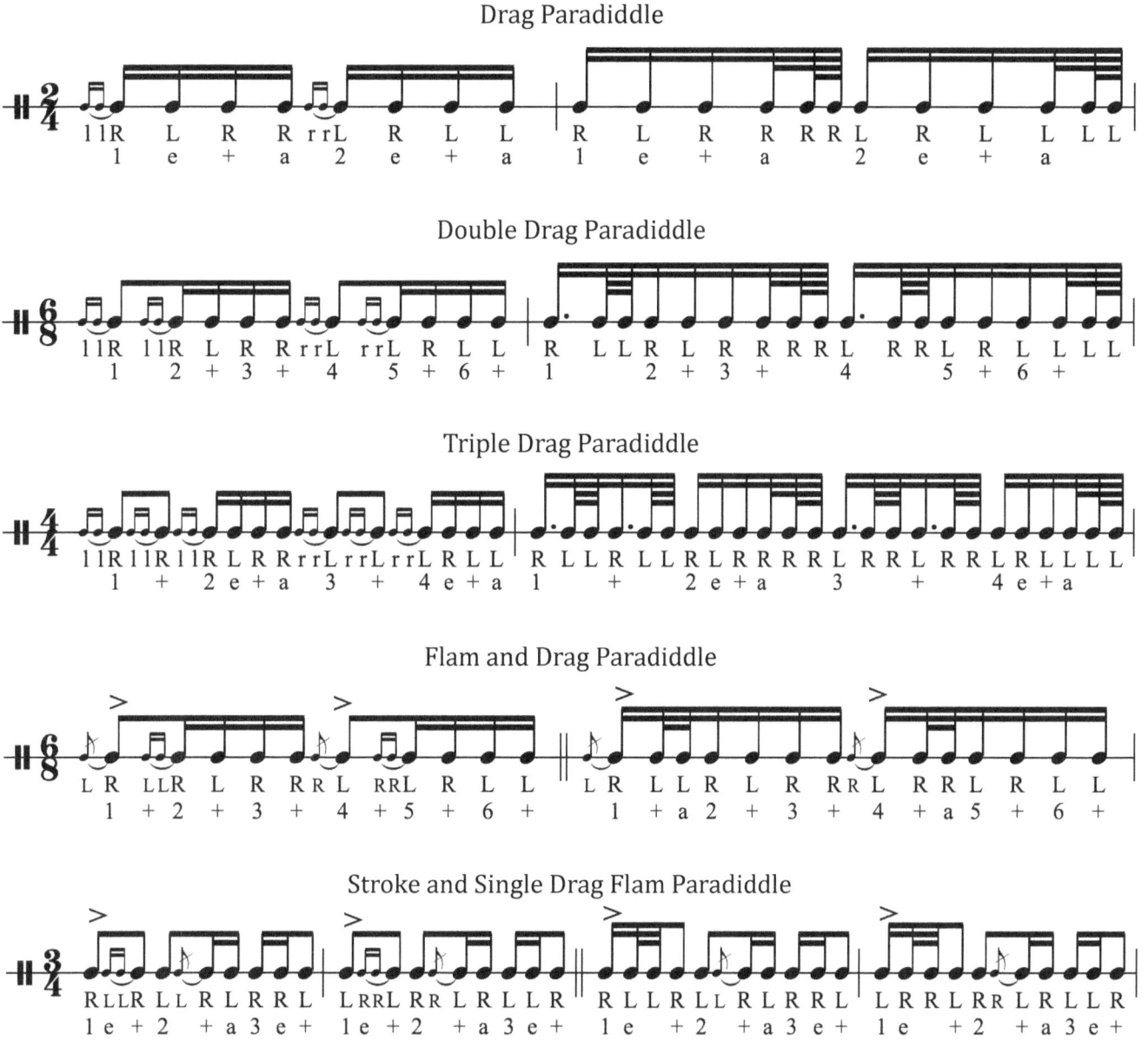

(Stroke, Single Drag Tap, Flam Paradiddle, Tap)

# 30. Single Ratamacue

**PAS:** *#38*
**NARD:** *#12*
**Other Names:** *Single Rotamacue, Quick 3 Roll and 3 Quick Single Blows, Zitterstreich*
**Alternation:** *yes*
**Origin:** *USA*

The Single Ratamacue consists of a pair of grace notes played as a double stroke followed by four alternating single strokes (the last of which, is accented). A right-handed Single Ratamacue is played with two lefts, then right, left, right, left. In other terms, it is a double stroke, preceding a Single Stroke Four (3).

Ashworth was the first to publish a Ratamacue of any kind in 1812, when he listed both the Single and the Double Ratamacue. Today, the first syllable is usually pronounced rat, as in the rodent. In the past, there is evidence that it may have been pronounced rot, to decompose. In 1817, for example, it was spelled Rotamacue, with an O at the beginning. American English, in the early 1800s, was probably spoken a bit more like British English. Thus, the rot sound might be correct under either spelling. It would certainly make the spelling more phonetically consistent to say "rah-tah-mah-kyew" (with every A making roughly the same sound) than "rat-ah-muh-kyew", as we do today.

## PAS Notation 🎧

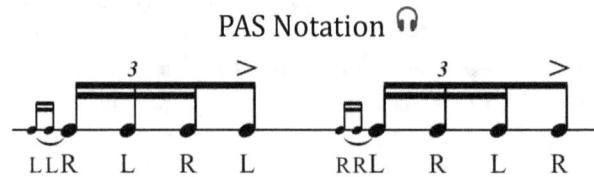

## PAS Notation Interpreted and Using the Name

## NARD Notation

## Basic Strokes

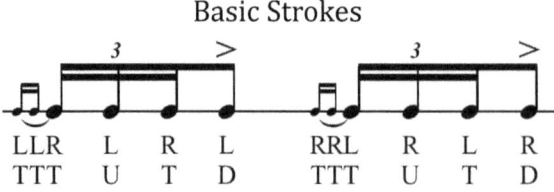

Rhythmically, the Single Ratamacue is usually played with the grace notes faster than the single strokes, much like other Drag rudiments, but this is not always the case. The spacing of the grace notes is inherently variable, with some players opting for a closed "Ruffamacue", and others playing an open "Dragamacue." The widest possible interpretation, makes all the notes the same length (including the grace notes). In this case, where all the notes are played evenly, it becomes almost an inversion of a Double Paradiddle (21), starting on the Diddle. In a very broad sense, the ancient interpretation seems to be more closed. In the 20th century, it became popular to play the "inversion of a Double Paradiddle," but today, most players land in between these extremes.

### Alternative Rhythms

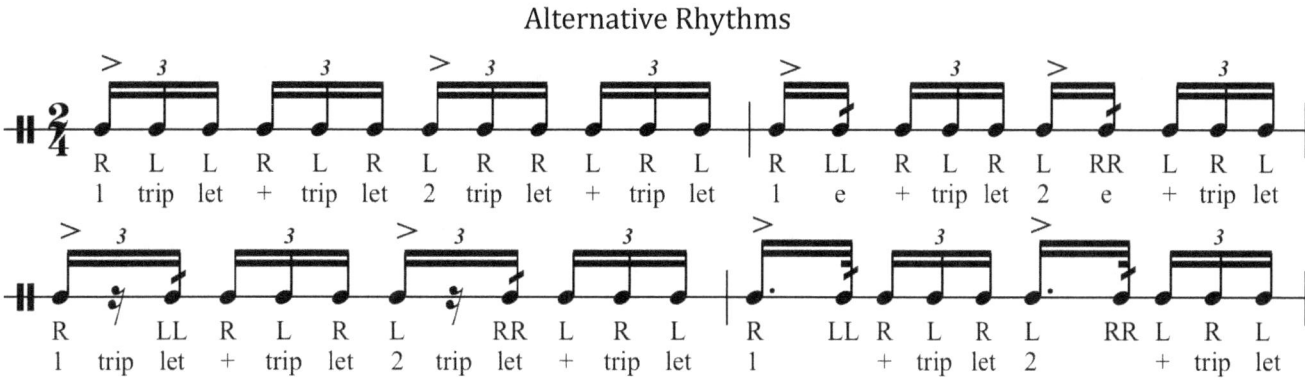

The following exercises all use the most open interpretation for the grace notes, but feel free to insert a more closed execution, as desired.

### Single Hand Exercise

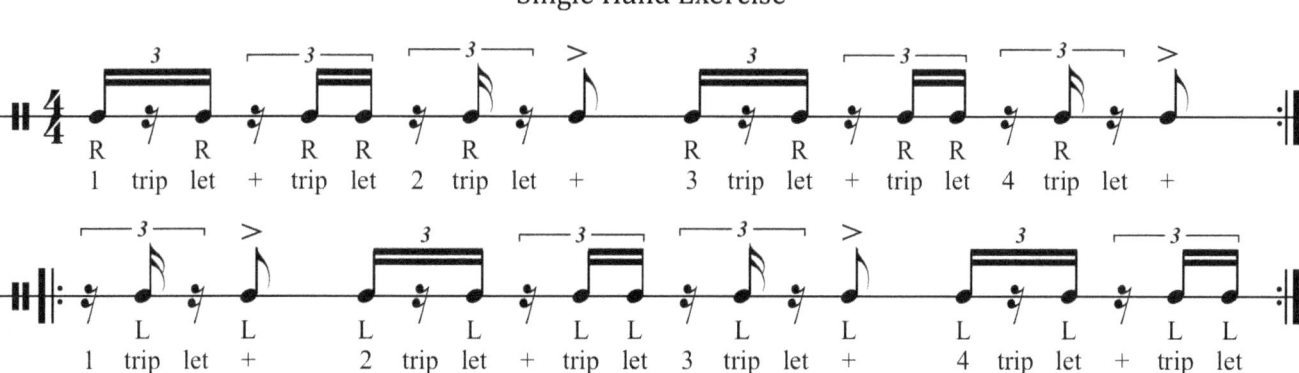

## Two Hand Exercise

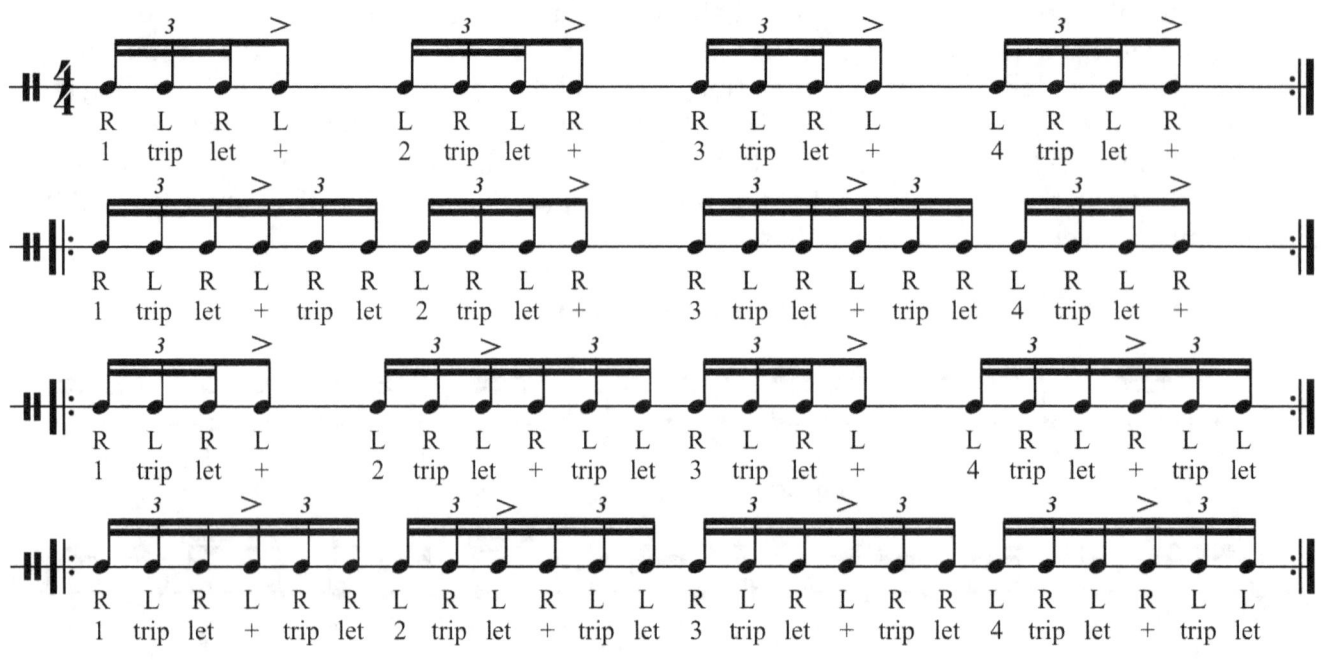

## Skill Buildup

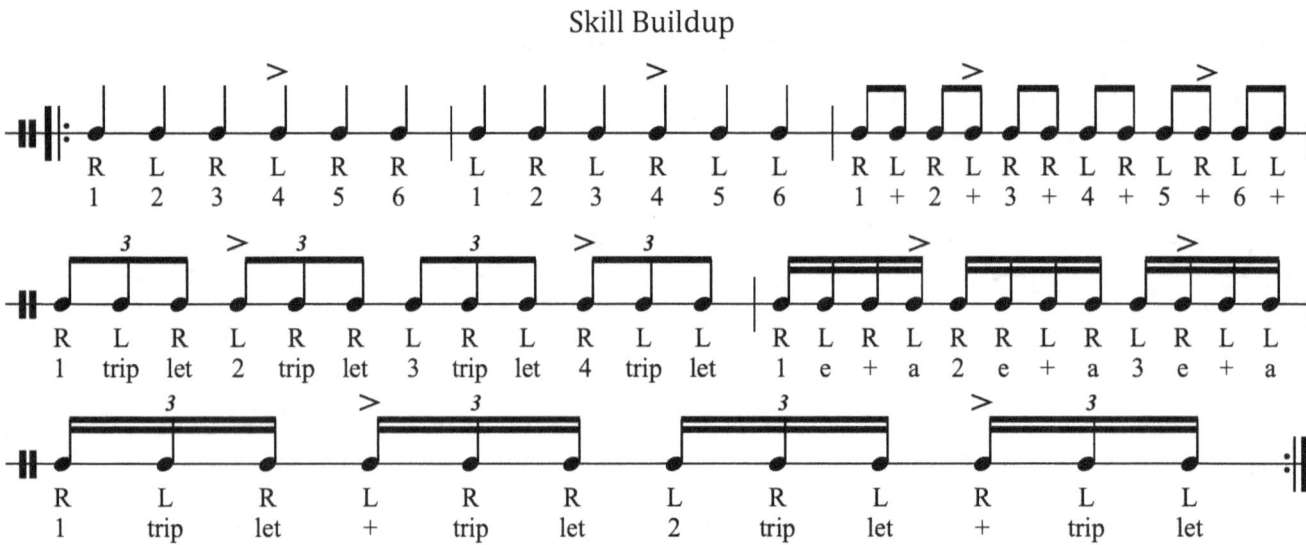

# 31. Double Ratamacue

**PAS:** *#39*
**NARD:** *#26*
**Other Names:** *Double Rotamacue*
**Alternation:** *yes*
**Origin:** *USA*

The Double Ratamacue consists of a pair of grace notes played as a double stroke followed by a single stroke, making a Drag (23), then another pair of double stroked grace notes, preceding four alternating single strokes (the last of which, is accented). A right-handed Double Ratamacue is played with two lefts, then a right, two further lefts and a right, and then left, right, left. In other terms, it is a Drag, and then a Single Ratamacue (30).

Ashworth published both the Single and the Double Ratamacue, in 1812. As with the Single Ratamacue, Rumrille and Holton published the alternative spelling Rotamacue, in 1817. This spelling, and the fact that Ashworth was British-born, and may have had different standard vowel sounds than modern English, leads to the conclusion that the pronunciation might have always been more like the O, than the A. The Double Ratamacue fits nicely into 6/8 or other triple meters, rather than the 2/4 or duple meters that feature the Single Ratamacue – because of the extra Drag at the beginning, which gives it a third 8th note worth of time.

PAS Notation

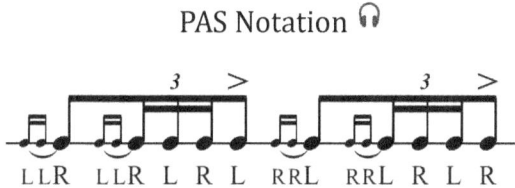

PAS Notation Interpreted and Using the Name

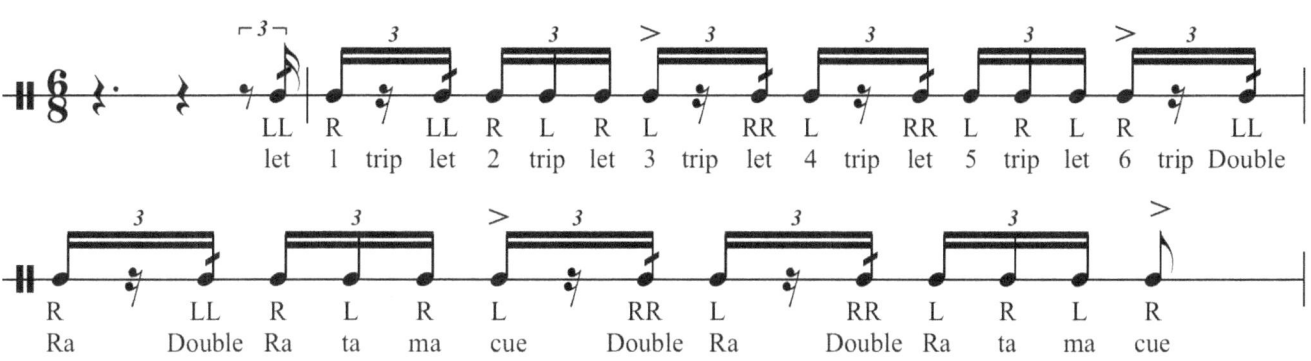

NARD Notation

## Basic Strokes

Like the Single Ratamacue (30), the Double Ratamacue is usually played with the grace notes faster than the single strokes, much like other Drag (23) rudiments, but this is not always the case. The spacing of the grace notes is inherently variable, with some players opting for a closed "Ruffamacue" and others playing an open "Dragamacue." The widest possible interpretation makes all the notes the same length, including the grace notes.

## Alternative Rhythms

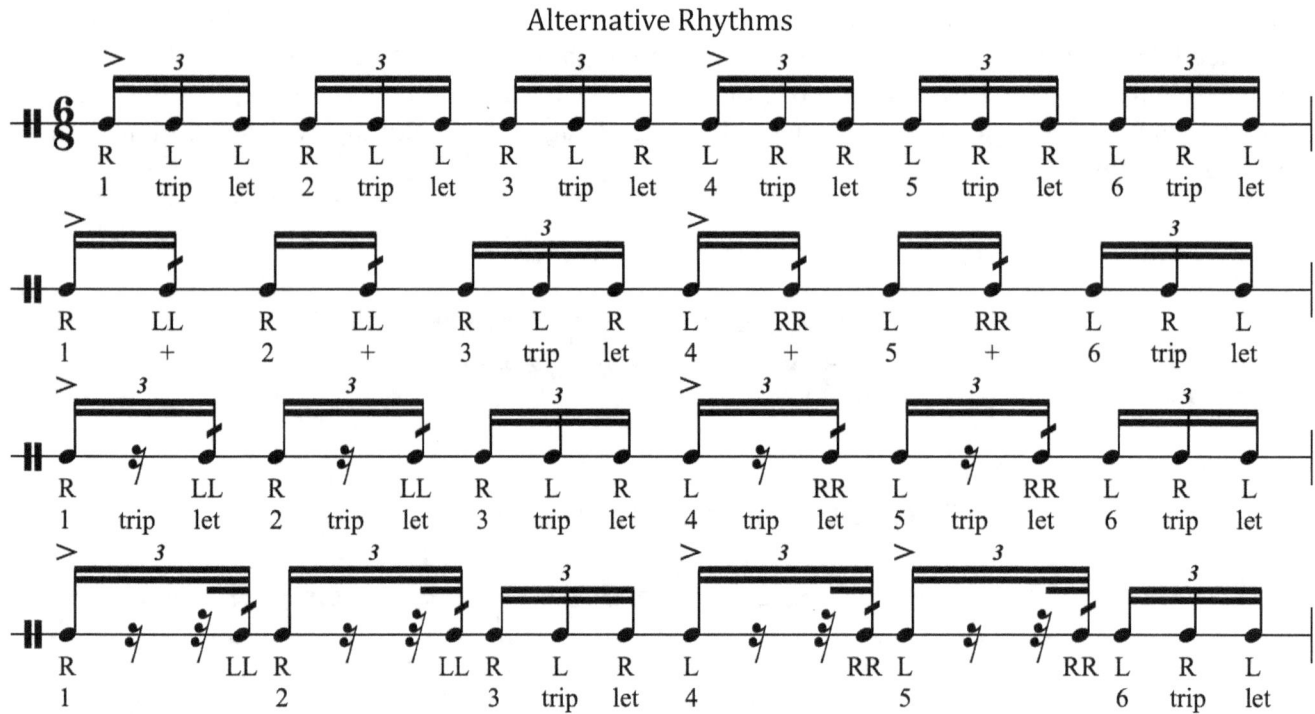

The following exercises all use the most open interpretation for the grace notes, but feel free to insert a more closed execution, as desired.

## Single Hand Exercise

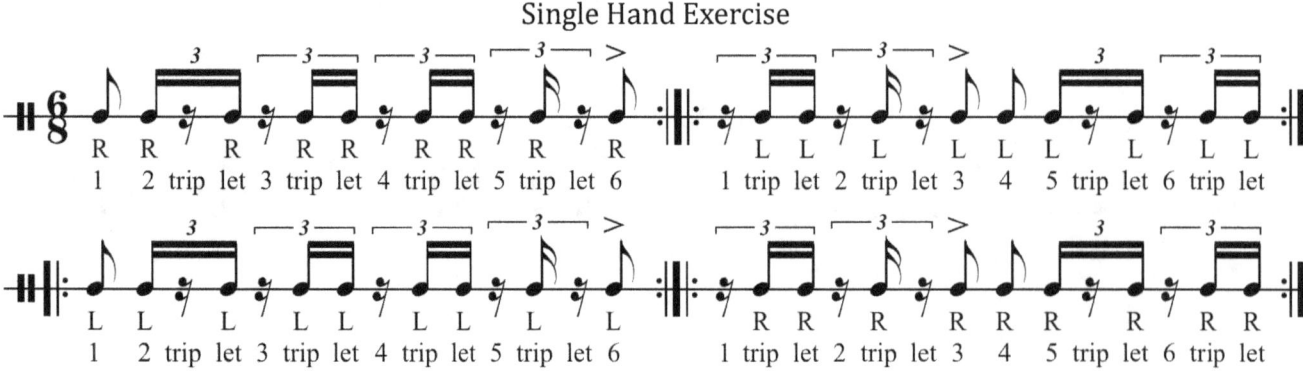

## Two Hand Exercise

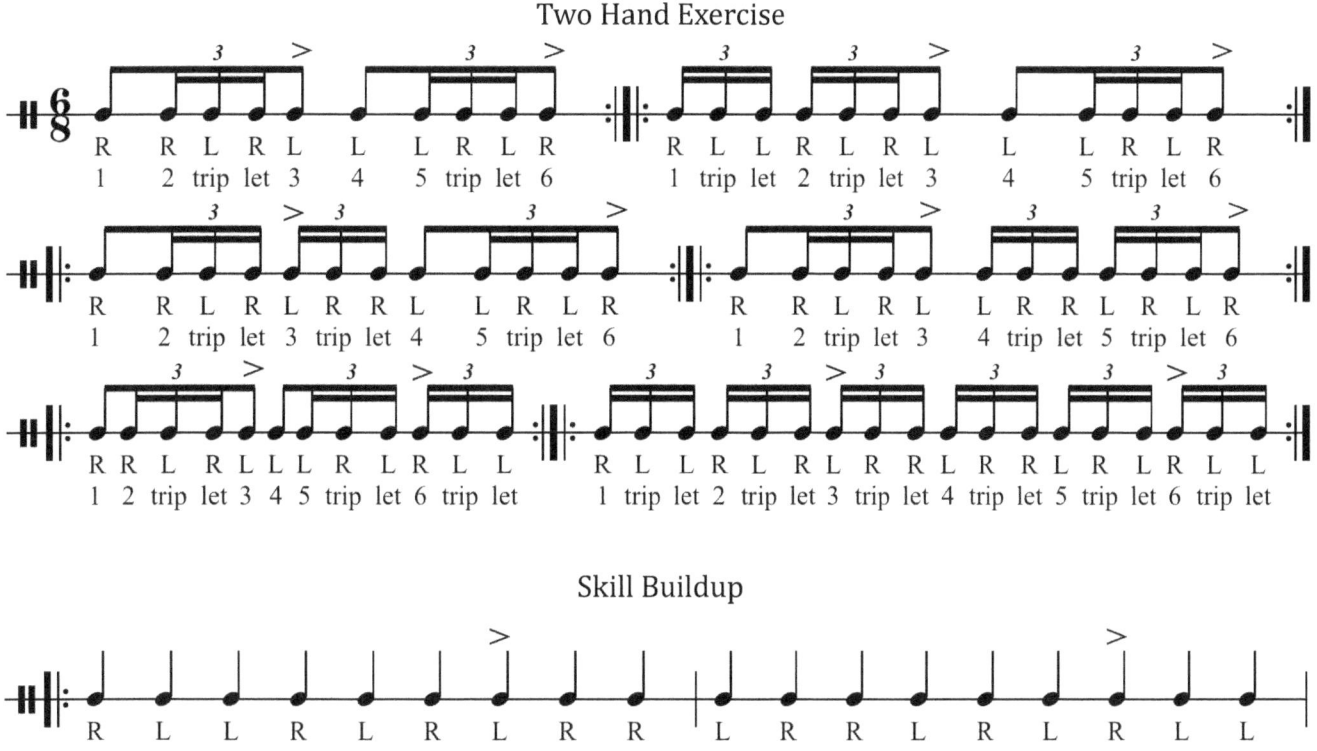

## Skill Buildup

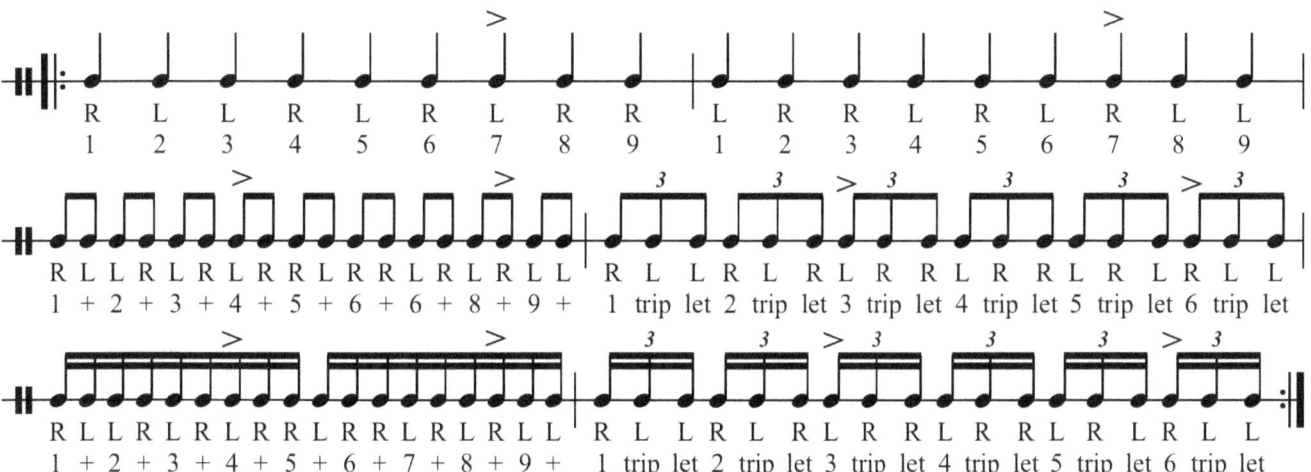

There is also a Triple Ratamacue, NARD #13 and PAS #40, which has been a part of American drumming since 1862 (sometime called the Treble Ratamacue). It will not be given its own section in this book, because of the extreme similarity to the Single and Double Ratamacues. It has no distinct skills or features, but is notated below, for reference.

### Triple Ratamacue PAS Notation

# 32. Flam

**PAS:** *#20*
**NARD:** *#4*
**Other Names:** *Pla, Tla, Fla, Fli, Plon, Plan, Plau, Plao, Schleppschlag, Schleppstreich, Schleifschlag, Vlamslag, Slip, Coup Double, Schlepper, Doppelschlag, Einfache Vorschlag, Mordiente de Una Nota, Släpslag, Kort Forslag*
**Alternation:** *yes*
**Origin:** *unknown, ancient*

The Flam consists of two notes executed nearly simultaneously – a grace note, played with one hand, and a primary note, played with the other hand. The intended effect is two separate sounds in very close temporal proximity. It is *not* one single sound with both hands (a Double Stop (33)), *nor* is it two sounds far enough apart to be counted independently (a Charge Stroke (34)).

The Flam has been present in American drumming for as long as there has been American drumming. It appears in the text of Baron de Steuben's 1779 infantry manual and is notated in other 18th century American publications. In Europe, it is assumed to have existed since the inception of rudimental drumming, and is one of the most common rudiments. The name Flam is English, but it is very similar to the name for the same pattern in most other languages.

The Flam can only be executed correctly by applying two of the Basic Strokes, the Up Stroke and the Down Stroke. Failure to use the appropriate strokes is a near guarantee that the result will not be a passable Flam. The grace note of the Flam is inherently an Up Stroke – starting low and ending high. The primary note that follows the grace note is inherently a Down Stroke – starting high and ending low. Both strokes are played together *at the same time*. This is key. Of course, the definition of a Flam is that the notes do not sound simultaneous. Both strokes start at the same time, yet the notes sound at two separate times, only because the sticks start at different heights – high for the Down Stroke, and low for the Up Stroke. The stick that is closer to the drum will produce sound first, followed by the stick that is farther from the drum. The difference in the starting stick heights, is the only factor in how open or closed the Flam sounds. There is no need to worry about timing between the hands, only about the height difference between the starting points of the strokes.

To restate the previous paragraph more simply: use two different stick heights, but start the strokes at the same time.

The proper pedagogical line is to say that the grace note of the Flam falls ahead of the beat, and that the primary note falls precisely on the beat. To say otherwise is heresy. This is fine for Flams in the open, and is the platonic ideal, but this does not always happen in context, unfortunately. When playing a more complicated Flam rudiment, like the Flam Paradiddle (38) or Flam Accent (35), for examples, it is unlikely that the grace note will actually happen ahead of the beat – and this is ok. There really is no way to keep the grace note ahead of the beat in all situations, especially if it is part of a set of 3 or 4 successive notes on the same hand. The best answer is to use your ears. If it sounds on time, in the context of whatever rudiment is being played, then there is no issue. If the Flam sounds late – it is.

In modern American terms, a Flam is labeled by the hand that plays the primary note. A Flam played LR is a Right Flam, because the right hand plays the primary note. Conversely, RL is a Left Flam, because the primary note is played by the left hand. The preceding grace notes are ignored for identification purposes. In other cultures, and even in ancient American manuals, this convention is sometimes reversed.

One further technical note: there is no horizontal component to the Flam. The sticks should never travel sideways, forward, or backward during the execution of a Flam. It is tempting for inexperienced drummers to engage in unnecessary horizontal motion when playing several successive Flams with alternating stickings – but this should be avoided in all cases.

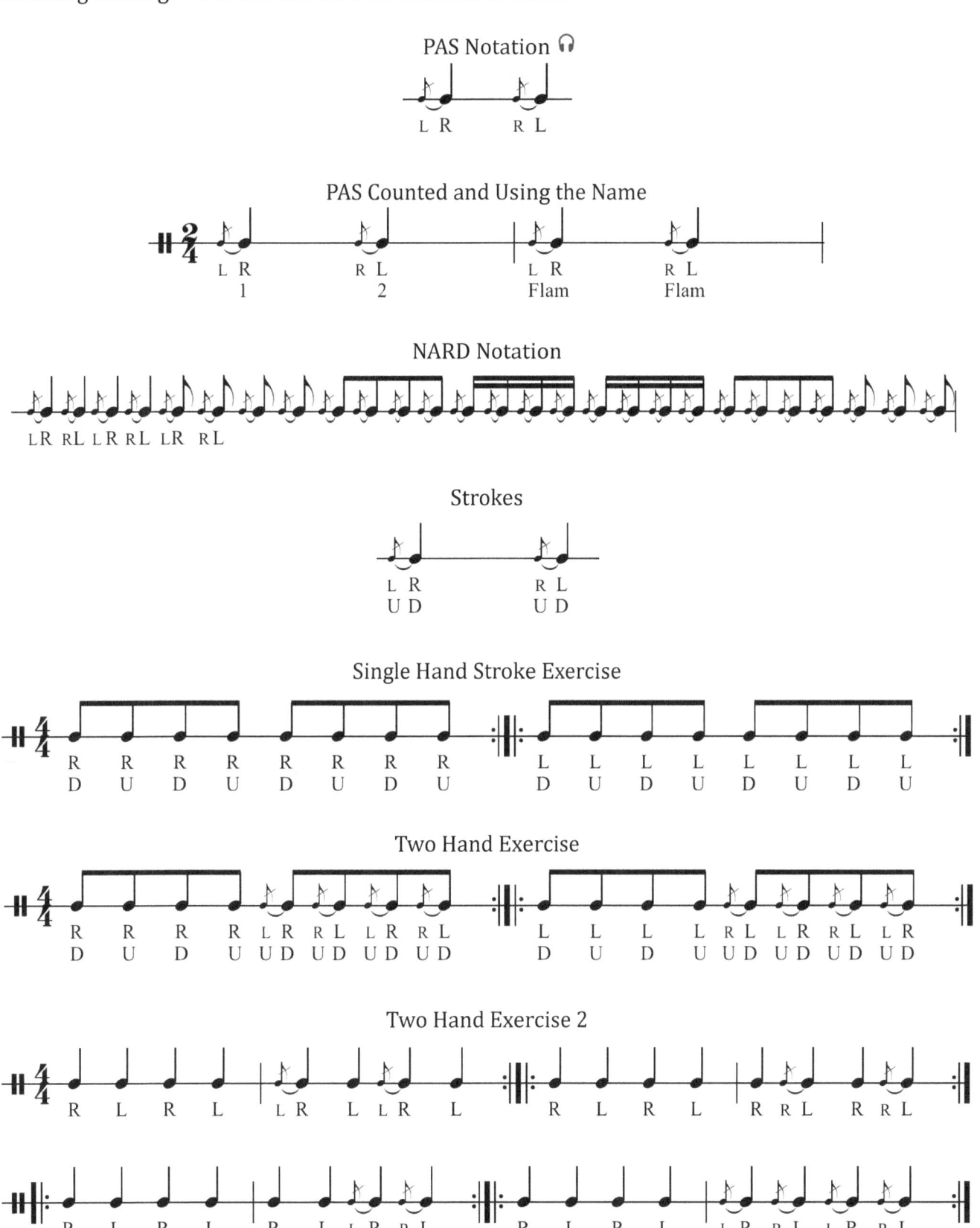

## Two Hand Exercise 3

L R L R L R L R R L R L R L R L   L R L R R L R L L R L R R L R L

## Skill Buildup

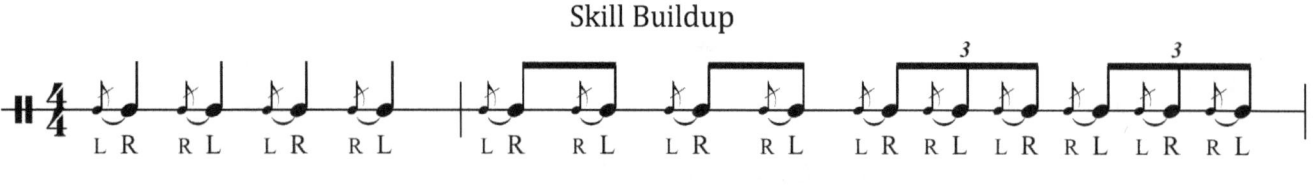

L R R L L R R L   L R R L L R R L   L R R L L R R L L R R L

L R R L L R R L L R R L L R R L L R R L L R R L L R R L L R R L

## Suggested Drum Kit Application

L R    L R    L R    L R
1  +  2  +  3  +  4  +

# 33. Double Stop

**PAS:** *n/a*
**NARD:** *n/a*
**Other Names:** *Double, Unison, Unison Hands, Both, Flats, Pop Flam, Popped Flam, Double Vertical, French Flam, Dead Stroke, Harmonic Flam, Double Whammy, Double Piston Stroke, Doppelter Schlag, Trau, Rücker, Zusammenschlag, Dubbele Slagen, Doppelschlag*
**Alternation:** *n/a*
**Origin:** *unknown, ancient*

The Double Stop is an essential part of percussion, though it has rarely (or never) been featured on an American snare drum rudiment sheet. Double Stops are two strokes that strike the drum simultaneously, to produce a single sound from both hands. They differ from Flams, in that the Flam (32) is two slightly offset sounds that are very nearly played together (but are not, actually), while the Double Stop is purely at exactly the same time.

As a snare drum technique, there is little evidence for their use in the USA before the modern DCI era. As a general percussion technique, they are an essential part of drum kit, multi-tenors, timpani, keyboards, and other multi-percussion setups, where two different instruments or notes, have to be struck together. Outside of the USA, there is good evidence for Double Stop snare drum rudiments dating back to at least the late 18th century, and possibly much earlier (though evidence is thin before this time). Bavarian drummers were using them, and writing them down, by 1781. Denmark-Norway, Austria, The Netherlands, and Prussia all have records of similar rudiments from the 19th or 20th centuries.

In the USA, over the last 30 or 40 years, the Double Stop has gained a surprisingly large catalog of unofficial names, for being rarely recognized as a rudiment. Some of these names pertain more to keyboard percussion technique, such as the Double Piston Stroke. Others are wrong, or are extremely misleading – for example, French Flam is completely nonsensical, because French drummers play normal Flams, called Fla – and there is no difference from an American Flam. Dead Stroke is also confusing, because that term is usually used to denote a stroke with no rebound, not a two-handed note. Others refer to the resulting sound. Playing both hands at once does induce a different set of overtones from a single stroke, or a Flam, which is why it is sometimes called Popped or Harmonic. It isn't usually any louder than playing a single note, but it is used for its differing timbre on the snare – to the extent that it is used on snare, at all.

The "official" English language term, Double Stop, is actually a string instrument term for pressing two strings down to the fret board, at the same time – thus, doubly stopping them. This term was borrowed by classical percussionists for keyboard percussion instruments, playing simultaneous intervals with two mallets, and then further borrowed by drummers, for playing both hands together. The sticking indication for a Double Stop on snare is usually the letter B (for both), as opposed to right or left, individually. On other percussion instruments, such as drum kit, it will be obvious that a Double Stop must occur when two notes happen on different surfaces, or notes, on the same beat.

One helpful tip on playing Double Stops accurately, is to start by placing both stick tips on the head together, then raise them together, and execute both strokes together. Since they started from exactly the same point, there is a greater chance that they will sound together at the end of the motion. This is impractical in a real playing context, and should be abandoned as soon as the strokes are landing simultaneously with consistency.

## Notation Styles

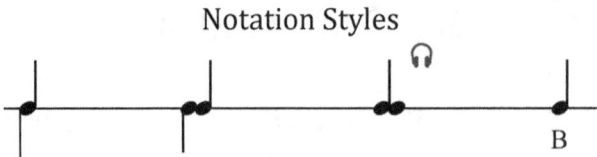

## Quarter Exercise

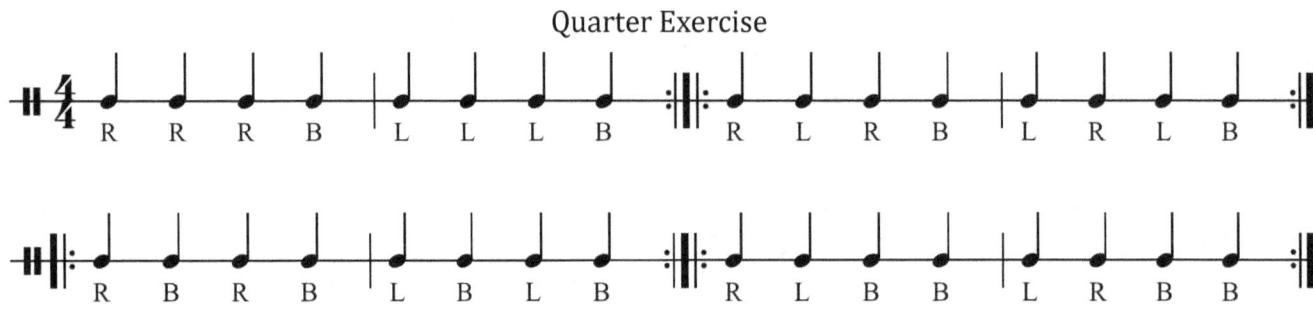

## Exercises with Common Sticking Patterns

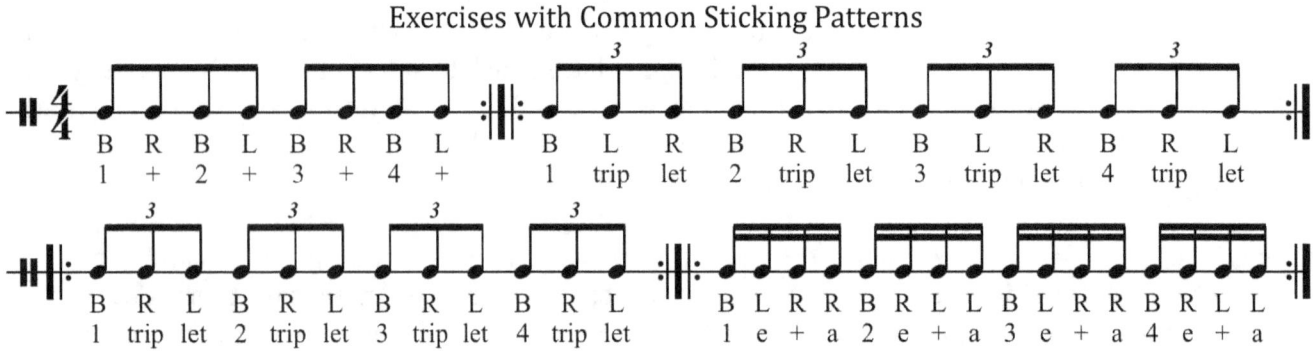

## Skill Buildup

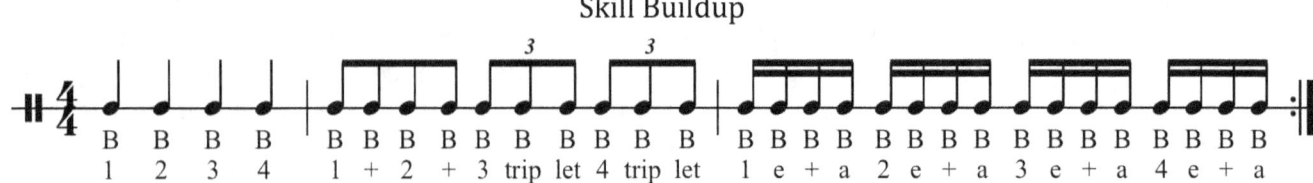

## Suggested Drum Kit Application

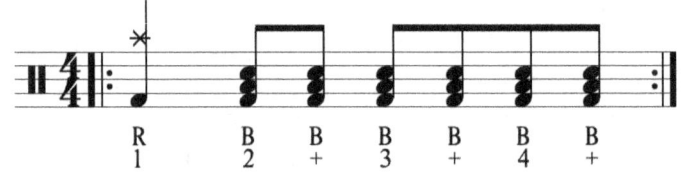

# 34. Charge Stroke (or Open Flam)

**PAS:** *n/a*
**NARD:** *n/a*
**Other Names:** *Coup de Charge, Sturmschlag, Dedans, Doppelter Streich, Doppelstreich, Trau, Tarau, Talá, Tra, Tau, Tran, Lange Voorslag, Dubbele Slag*
**Alternation:** *no*
**Origin:** *unknown, ancient*

The Charge Stroke is a concept that is fairly unknown in the modern USA, although it can be described, more or less, as an Open Flam (or a set of two notes, struck very close together, by opposing hands). These notes are often accented, and always played more open than a standard Flam (32) – enough so, that a difference can clearly be heard between a Charge Stroke and a Flam. Though not currently known as an American rudiment, the Charge Stroke (or something like it) is actually one of the most common rudiments in the rest of the rudimental world. It seems that Americans are among the few types of rudimental drummers who have never really embraced the Charge Stroke, at least not as a lasting standard.

Several American rudimental drum books of the late 19th and early 20th century, including one by famed composer and Marine Corps bandleader, John Philip Sousa, in 1886, listed both an Open Flam and a Close or Closed Flam. None explained the difference particularly well (since American drumming repertoire does not generally use Open Flams, it may well be that some authors did not know what they actually were), nor did the Open Flam catch on, as a standard American rudiment. It disappeared from essentially all American books after World War II. The Open Flam concept seems to have been imported from Britain, where it was commonly seen in rudimental manuals from the Samuel Potter's 1817 military method through the civilian drum corps oriented methods of the 1930s. Today, American drumming does have a rudiment called the Malf (a reverse spelling of Flam), which places the primary note before the grace note. This is something like a Charge Stroke, but is often played right on the beat, with the grace note falling afterward, completely reversing the idea of the Flam, as well as the name. Though the Malf is not a exactly a Charge Stroke, it is fairly consistent with the Swedish Nedslag, or Træf, which dates from at least the 1820s, possibly earlier, and is still used today.

The normal execution for a Charge Stroke is to place one note ahead of the beat, by either one 32nd note, or possibly even one 16th note, and accent either the first note, or both notes. The two hand motions start at slightly different times, unlike the simultaneous beginning of a Flam, so it is actually two separate strokes. The French style of Charge Stroke places an accent on only the first of the two notes. The Swiss style of Charge Stroke places an accent on both notes. Other rudimental systems fall into one of these two categories, with a slight worldwide preference overall for having both strokes accented in the Swiss style. The British Open Flam, which some Americans tried to import (without lasting success), is usually explained like the Swiss style of Charge Stroke – both notes are accented. This is the style that will be notated below because it is the "most American" of the Charge Strokes.

Notation Styles (these are only some of the possibilities) 🎧

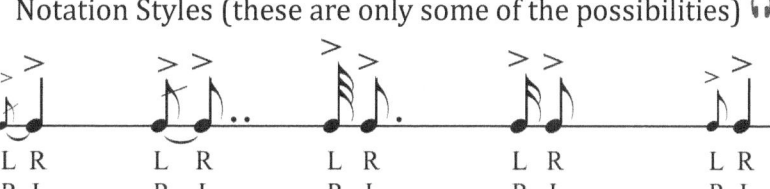

## Exercise as 16th Notes

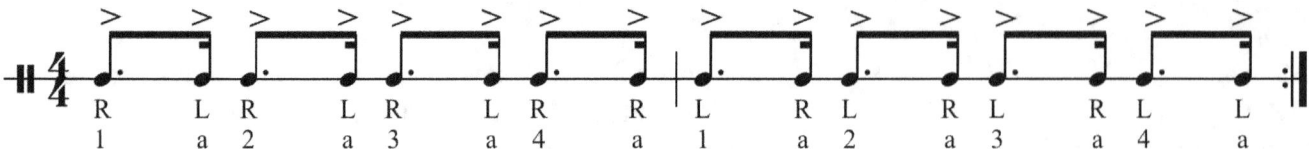

## Exercises as 32nd Notes

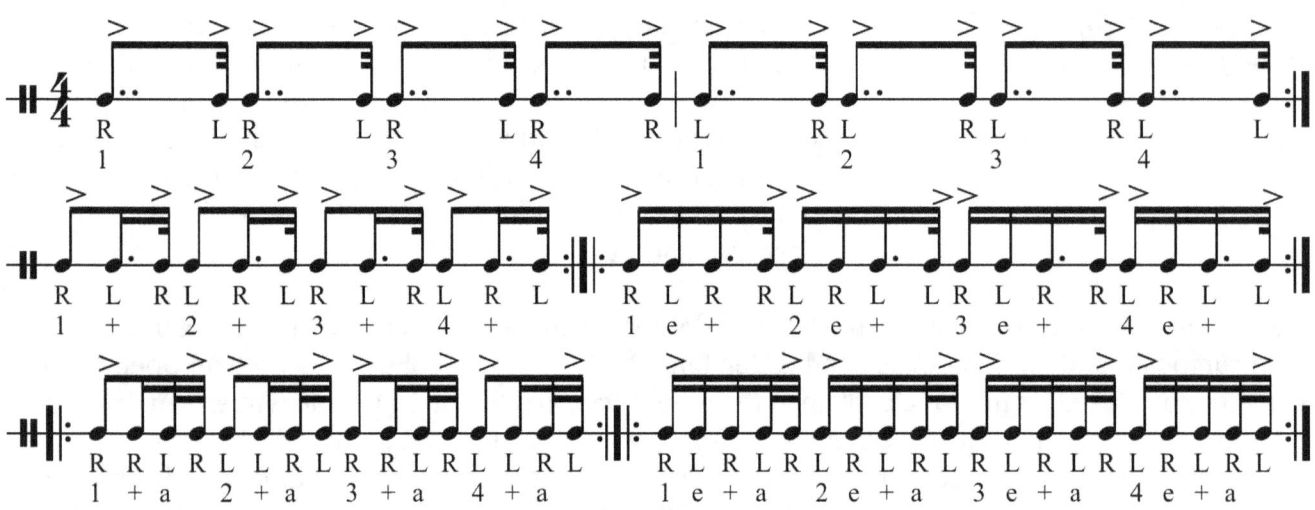

## Exercises with Grace Notes (same rhythms as above)

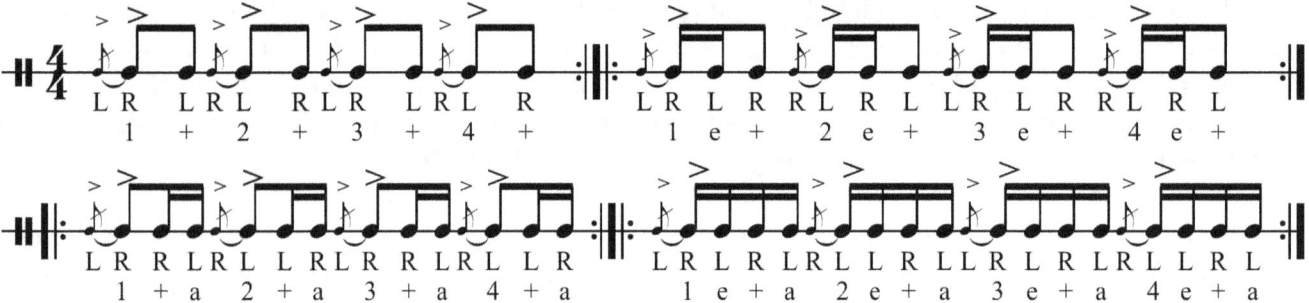

## Suggested Drum Kit Application

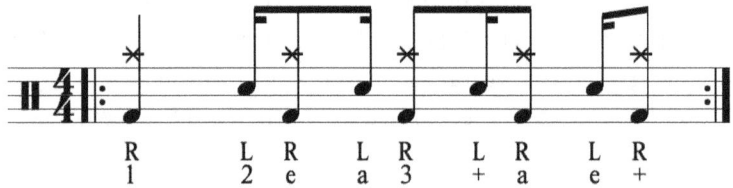

# 35. Flam Accent

**PAS:** *#21*
**NARD:** *#5*
**Other Names:** *Flam-and-a-Two, The Full Flam and Two Half Blows, Flam and Two Strokes, Flam Accent No. 1, Flam-A-Tap, Patafla, Flapata, Flipata, Tresillos de Corchéas con Mordentes*
**Alternation:** *yes*
**Origin:** *unknown*

The Flam Accent consists of an accented Flam (32) followed by two single strokes – one with the low hand of the Flam, and another with the high hand of the Flam. The primary notes are simply alternating single strokes, and the grace note is placed on the first note of each group of three. While the Flam is normally accented, the name is useful because the three syllables of "Flam-Ac-cent" fit nicely to the primary notes of the rudiment. The original American term was Flam-and-a-Two, dating to 1810, which makes a lot of sense, but cannot be spoken along with the notes.

Although the primary notes are alternating single strokes, when the grace note is factored in, each hand actually plays a single stroke, followed by a triple stroke. The second note of the triple is where the Flam falls, making the rudiment considerably more difficult to play quickly than it looks at first glance.

### PAS Notation

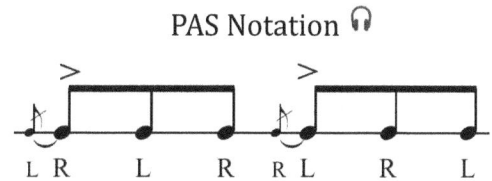

### PAS Counted and Using the Name

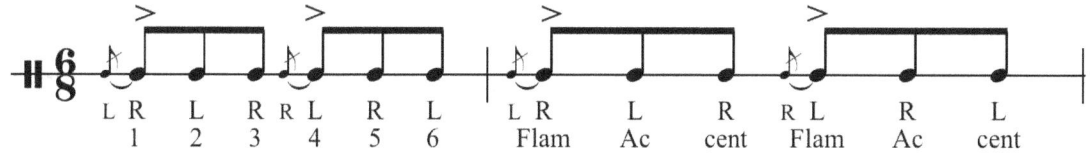

### NARD Notation

### Basic Strokes

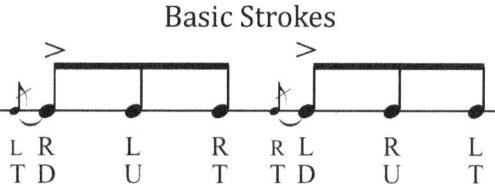

## Single Hand Exercise

## Two Hand Exercise 1

## Two Hand Exercise 2

## Skill Buildup

# 36. Flam Tap (or Flam Accent No. 2)

**PAS:** *#22*
**NARD:** *#20*
**Other Names:** *Stroke and Flam, Faint and Flam, Flam Pou, Stroke Flam, Full Blow and Flam, Flam-a-Poo, Flam and Faint, Flam and Stroke, Flamma, Flapa, Flipa, Batard*
**Alternation:** *yes*
**Origin:** *unknown, possibly England*

The Flam Tap consists of a Flam (32) and a single stroke (the Tap) played with same hand that plays the primary note of the Flam. It can also be viewed as an open double stroke, with a single grace note – or, simply described as a Flam, plus another stroke, with the high hand of that Flam. For example, a right hand Flam (with a left grace note, and a right primary note), followed by a right hand tap. Another way of thinking about several Flam Taps in a row, is as a series of triple strokes that are oddly overlapped at the Flams. The Flam Tap first appeared in American drumming in the early 19th century, with the first instance possibly being from about 1804, where it was called the Flamma.

The Flam Tap has been combined here in this section with the Flam Accent No. 2, because they both share the same sticking. The Flam Accent No. 2 also consists of a Flam and a Tap, with the hand that plays the primary note of that Flam. The difference is only in the rhythm. The primary notes of a series of Flam Taps are usually played with an even set of notes of the same value (a consistent stream of 16th notes), for example. The Flam Accent No. 2 is played as a shuffle, an uneven spacing with the Flam lasting twice the value of the Tap. This can be notated in 6/8 or as triplets with the same feel. George Bruce (George Barrett) named the Flam Accent No. 2 in 1862, and it was seemingly invented by removing the second primary note from the Flam Accent No. 1 (the normal Flam Accent (35)), leaving only the first and third primary notes, and the grace note. Although the Flam Accent No. 2 does not appear on the NARD or PAS rudiment lists, it has been taught continuously, up through the present day in American books. Most books that mention it over the past 160+ years, refer to it as a unique rudiment, and use the name Flam Accent No. 2 – but, a small number use the name Flam Tap in 6/8, or the similar Flam Taps in 6, and acknowledge its closer relationship to the Flam Tap. It has been included here, and not with the Flam Accent No. 1, because the normal method of separating one rudiment from another is by the sticking. Many rudiments have rhythmic variations or accent variations, but the sticking is the primary feature. The Flam Accent No. 2 is just a rhythmic variation for the exact sticking of the Flam Tap, despite its common name referring to the Flam Accent.

PAS Notation 🎧

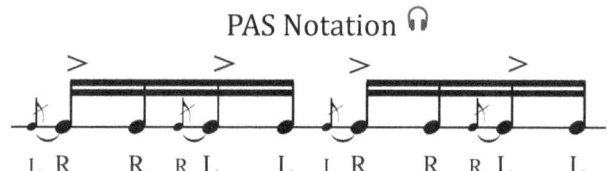

PAS Counted and Using the Name

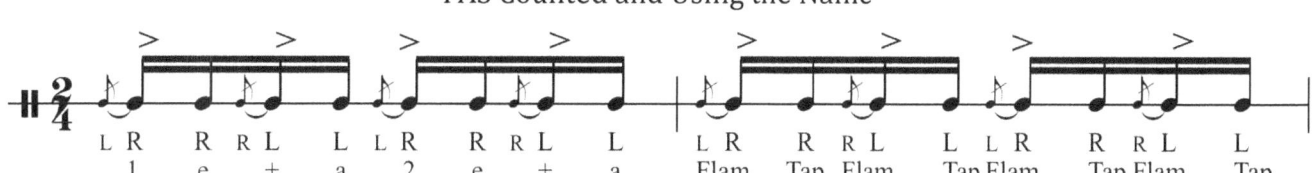

## NARD Notation

L R RR L L L RR R L L    RR  L L    RR  L L

## Basic Strokes

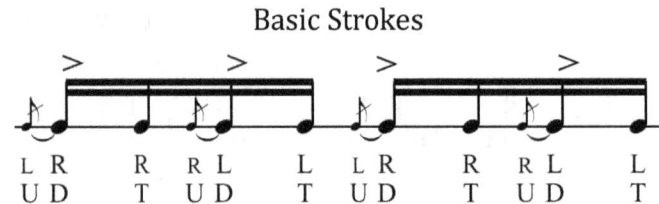

L R  R RL  L  L R  R RL  L
U D  T  U D  T  U D  T  U D  T

In some of the older naming conventions, the Tap (stroke, faint, blow) is mentioned before the Flam (32), which may lead some to believe that these names refer to the Inverted Flam Tap (43). This is not the case, however, because the order in which the Flam Tap is played can be reversed without being inverted. This is tricky to understand, at first. The only difference between a Flam Tap and an Inverted Flam Tap is which hand plays the Tap, not in which order the Tap is played. As stated above, the hand that plays the primary note of the Flam is used for the Tap in a standard Flam Tap, while the hand that plays the grace note is used for the Tap in an Inverted Flam Tap. It is not simply a reversal of the order of the notes, but a complete change in the sticking. To put it another way, Flam Taps can start on the upbeat, instead of the downbeat, and will still be Flam Taps, if the standard Flam Tap sticking is preserved.

## Reversed Flam Tap

L  L R  R RL  L  L R  R RL
1  e  +  a  2  e  +  a

(this is like an Inverted Invert, but without changing the accent position, the Inverted Invert can be seen in *Encyclopedia Rudimentia*)

## Single Hand Exercise

R R R   R R R    R R R   R R R        R   R R R   R R  R   R R R   R R

L L L   L L L    L L L   L L L        L   L L L   L L  L   L L L   L L

## 2 Hand Exercise

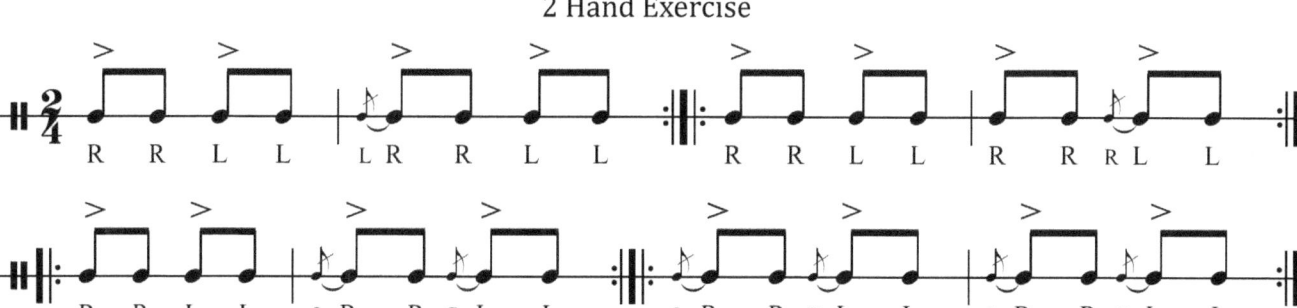

## Skill Buildup

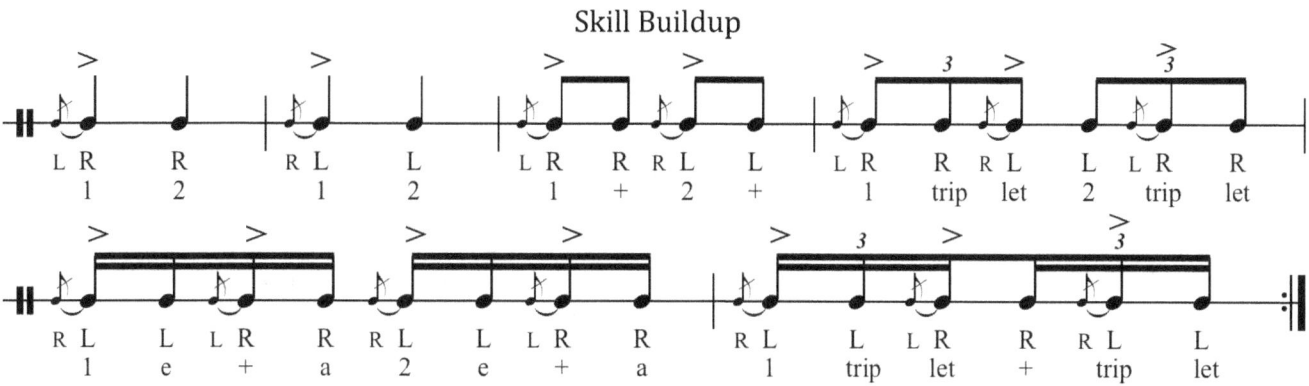

## Flam Accent No. 2 Rhythm

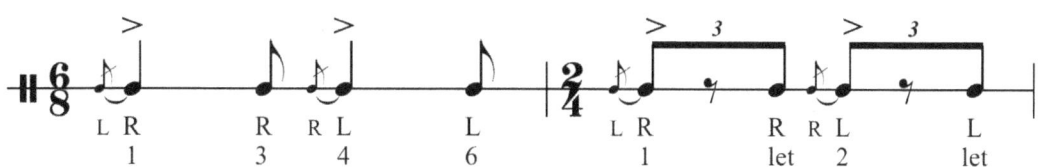

## The Reversed Exercise

# 37. Flamacue

**PAS:** *#23*
**NARD:** *#7*
**Other Names:** *Flamamacue*
**Alternation:** *no*
**Origin:** *USA*

The standard Flamacue is a series of five primary notes, with a grace note preceding the first and last. It begins with a Flam (32) followed by a series of three single strokes, the first of which is accented, and then one additional Flam. All of the primary notes alternate, which causes both Flams to be played from the same hand. In some cases, the Flamacue can be repeated in succession, so that it is only four notes long, instead of five. In this application, the final Flam is left off and the first four notes are repeated, often ending with fifth note (the Flam), on the final iteration. It is odd that the Flamacue can be both four and five notes long in different situations – but both are common applications, and many drummers refer to both versions as the same Flamacue.

The original name for the Flamacue as a rudiment was Flamamacue, as named by George Bruce (George Barrett) and Dan Emmett in 1862, with an added "ma" syllable in the middle. The standard rudimental presentation has five primary notes, and the modern name only has three syllables. The additional syllable in the original name is closer, but is still insufficient to match the sound of the rudiment. Flamamacue-flam or Flamacue-a-flam would be more useful names for learning the pattern. The name was shortened to Flamacue within seven years of its apparent invention and has remained the same, ever since. The original name does match the four syllables in the alternate four-note pattern when the rudiment is repeated in close succession (though this may be accidental).

It has been erroneously printed that the Flamacue is "the only American rudiment." This is completely false. Several other rudiments were invented in the USA, and there is no evidence that the Flamacue is special in this regard. It is unclear where this incorrect information originally came from, but American drummers are likely responsible for most (or all) of the Paradiddle variations and all of the Ratamacues – just to name rudiments that were invented before the Flamacue. Many more have been invented in America since the Flamacue. The Flamacue is interesting for another reason – it is the only "traditional" rudiment to feature its sole accent in the middle. (The Open Double and Single Flam Drag Beat was a short-lived rudiment, also from 1862, but published by H.C. Hart, that features the same length, rhythm, and emphasis, albeit with an internal Flam, instead of an accent.) Many rudiments have accents on the first or last note, and some have no accent at all.

PAS Notation

PAS Counted and Using the Name

## NARD Notation

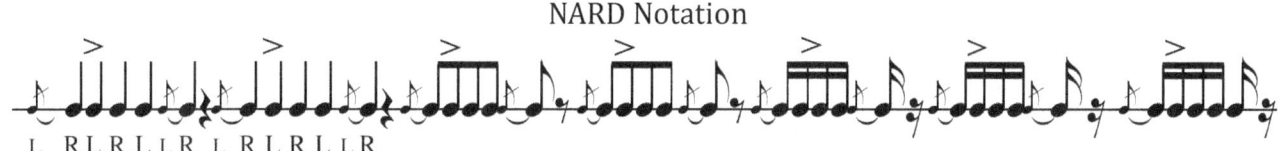

L R L R L L R L R L R L L R

## Alternative – Multiple in Succession

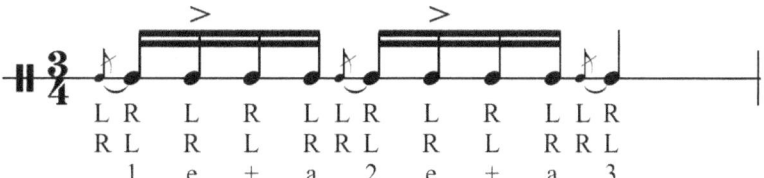

## Alternative Rhythm – 6/8 or triplets

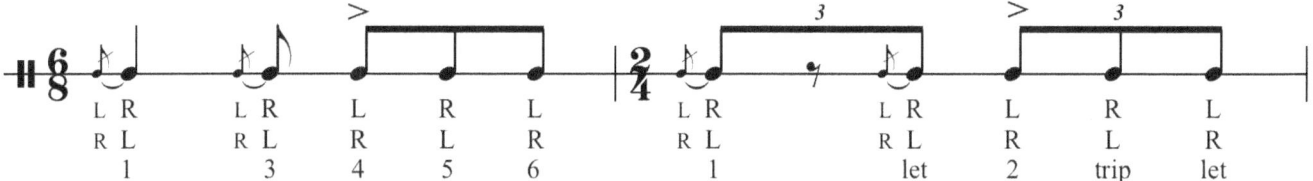

## Basic Strokes

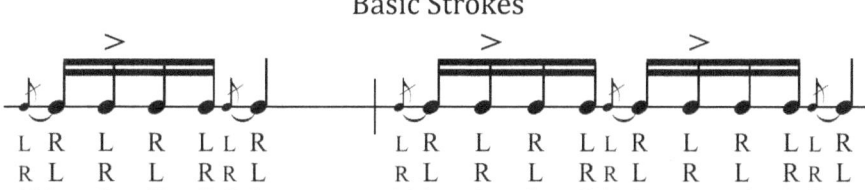

## Single Hand Exercise

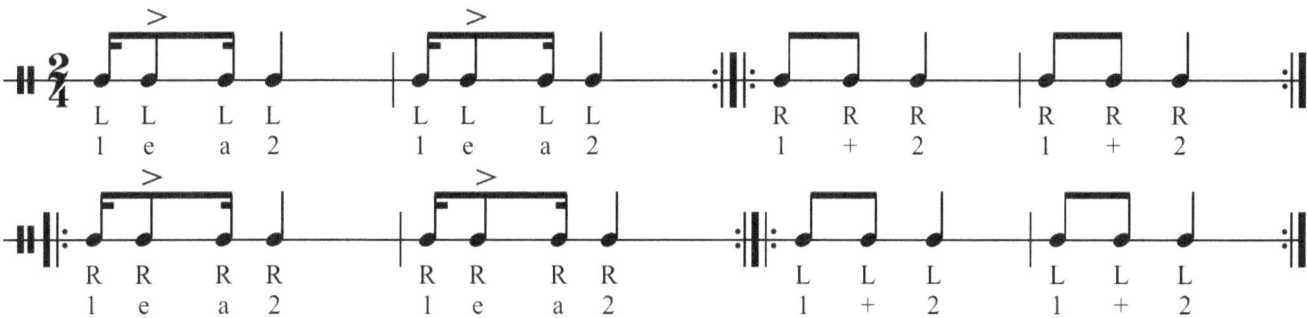

## 2 Hand Exercise

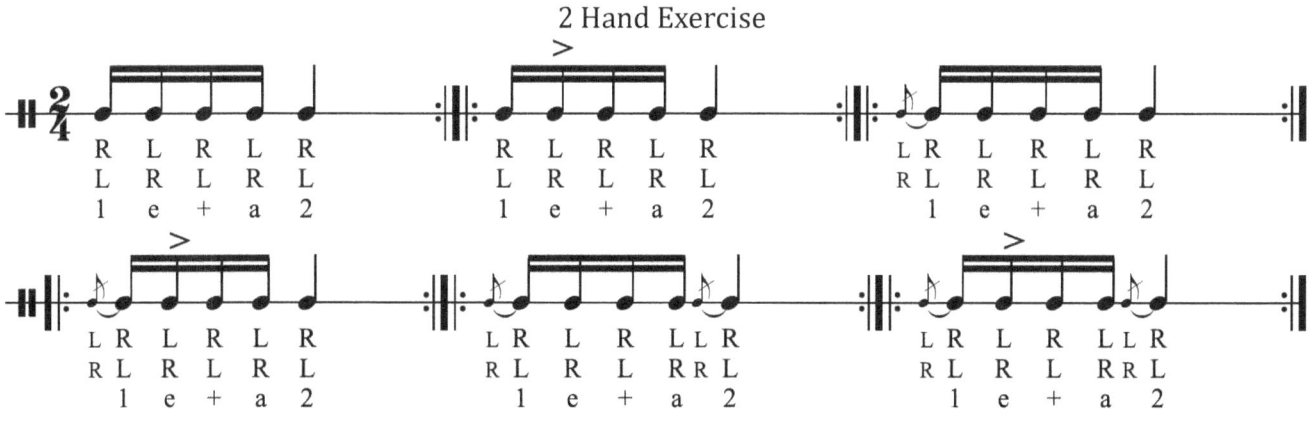

## Skill Buildup

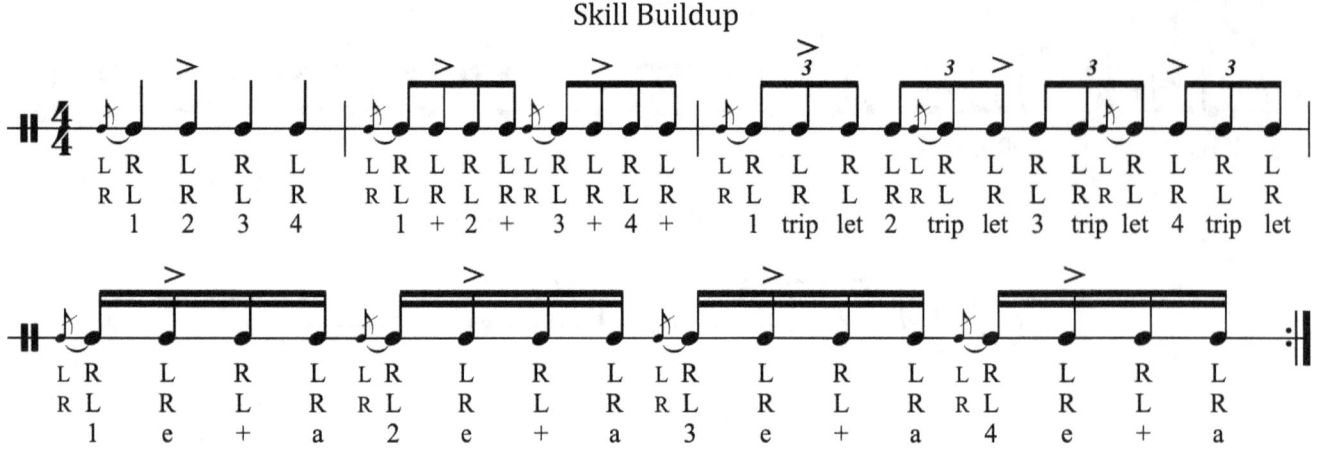

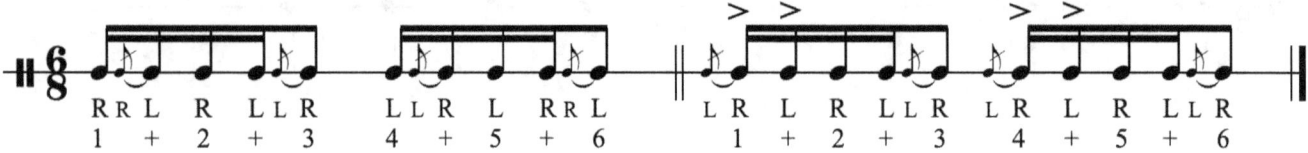

## Other Flamacues –
## Open Double and Single Flam Drag Beat and double accented Flamamacue

# 38. Flam Paradiddle

**PAS:** *#24*
**NARD:** *#6*
**Other Names:** *Flamadidle, Flamadiddle, Flam Perididdle*
**Alternation:** *yes*
**Origin:** *USA*

The Flam Paradiddle is a Single Paradiddle (20) with a grace note preceding the first primary note. Although it is a combination of other rudiments, it is not considered a hybrid rudiment, because it was invented before the concept of a hybrid rudiment existed. It is first found in an American book by Benjamin Clark, around 1797-1800, under the name Flamadidle. The NARD and PAS sheets agree on the name Flam Paradiddle, but Flamadiddle is much easier to say and play, making it a very effective alternative.

Although it seems simple, the Flam Paradiddle actually contains a hidden quadruple stroke, formed from the "Diddle," or final two strokes, of one iteration, plus the grace note and "Ra," or second primary note, of the next iteration. The quadruple stroke makes it hard to play quickly without significant practice and it is perhaps the only common American rudiment to contain a quadruple stroke. At the time that this rudiment first appeared, marching tempos were generally slower than rudimental music is performed today, meaning this rudiment would not have been as challenging, at the time.

### PAS Notation

### PAS Counted and Using the Name

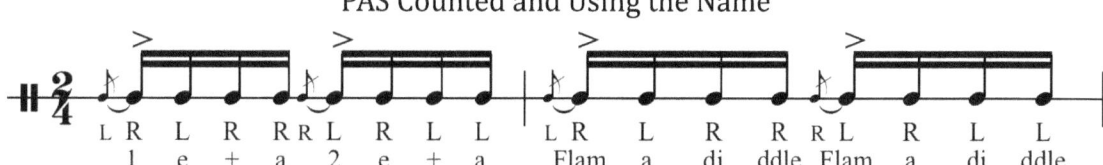

### NARD Notation

### Basic Strokes

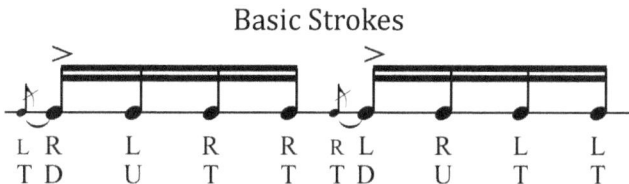

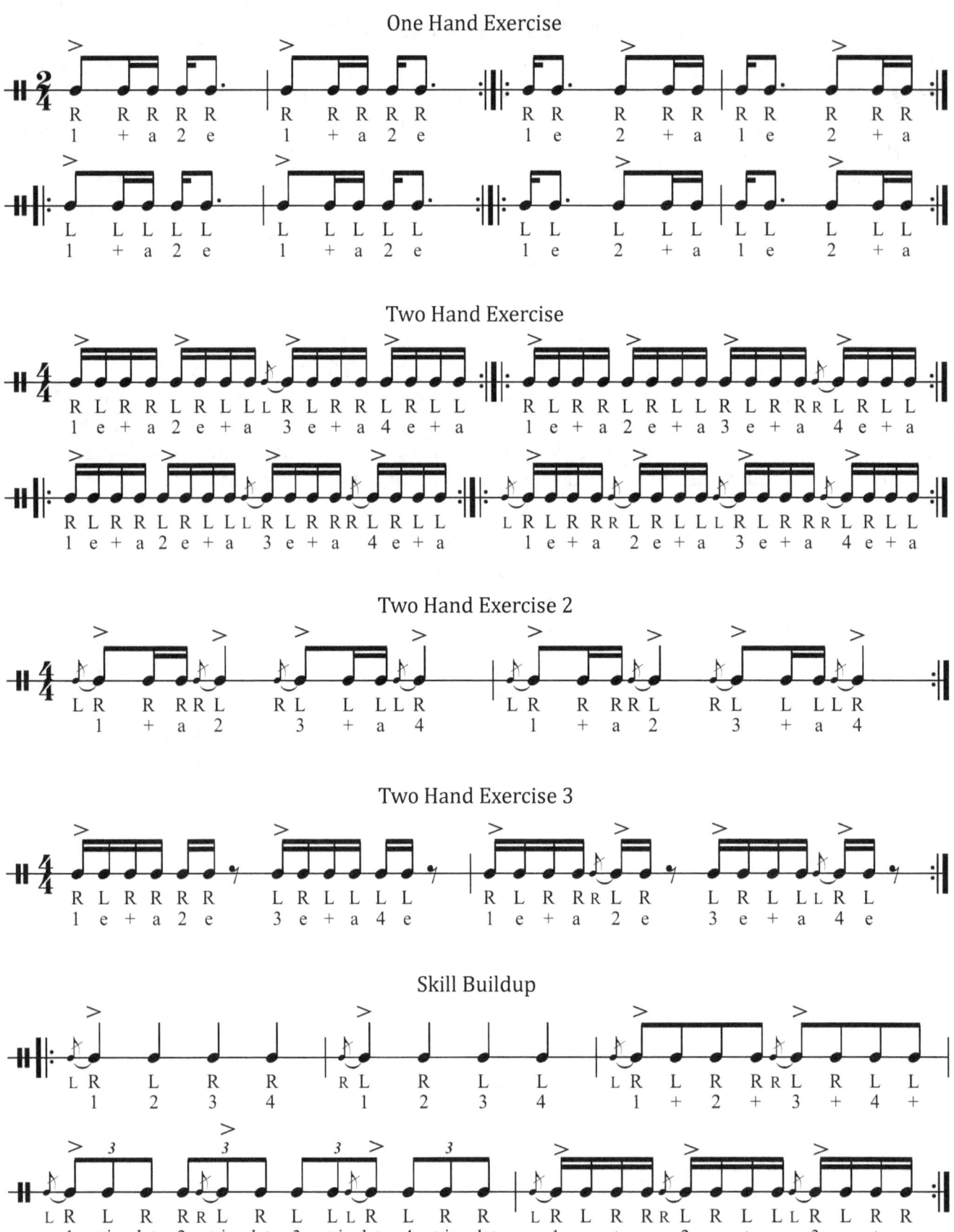

# 39. Single Flammed Mill

**PAS:** *#25*
**NARD:** *n/a*
**Other Names:** *Flam Mill, Schleppmühle*
**Alternation:** *yes*
**Origin:** *Switzerland*

The Single Flammed Mill is essentially a Reverse Flam Paradiddle (38), where a grace note precedes the "Diddle" portion of a Paradiddle (20), in the "Reverse" or "Mill" orientation. In other terms, the Single Flammed Mill is a Flam Tap (36) plus two further single strokes.

The Single Flammed Mill was first published as a rudiment in the USA in 1972, though it may have been in casual American use earlier in the 20th century. It is one of the more recent additions to the American rudimental repertoire, and is an acknowledged import from the Basel drumming system of Switzerland, where it was called the Schleppmühle, or Flam Mill. It was invented sometime after 1870, when the Basel drummers imported the Paradiddle-like sticking from the French, who called it Le Moulin, or The Mill. The French do not seem to have played this exact variation prior to the Swiss, however. Although Americans think of many rudiments as being of Swiss origin, the Single Flammed Mill is one of just a few that were taken recently, and directly, from the Basel system.

Despite the obvious similarity to the sticking pattern of the Flam Paradiddle, the Flammed Mill is actually much easier to execute at higher tempos. The Flammed Mill uses only single and double strokes, in contrast to the quadruple stroke required for the Flam Paradiddle. This is a simple function of where the grace note falls in the Paradiddle sticking pattern.

### PAS Notation

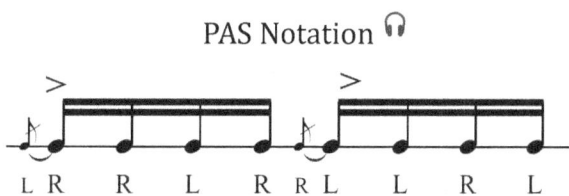

### PAS Notation Counted and Using the Name

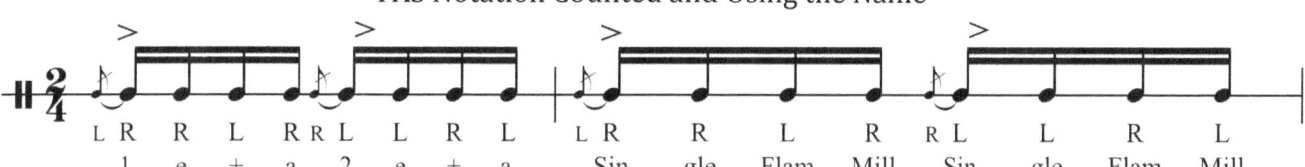

### Basic Strokes

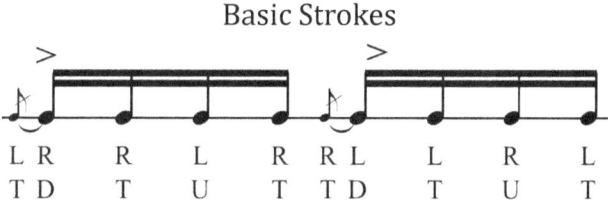

## Single Hand Exercise

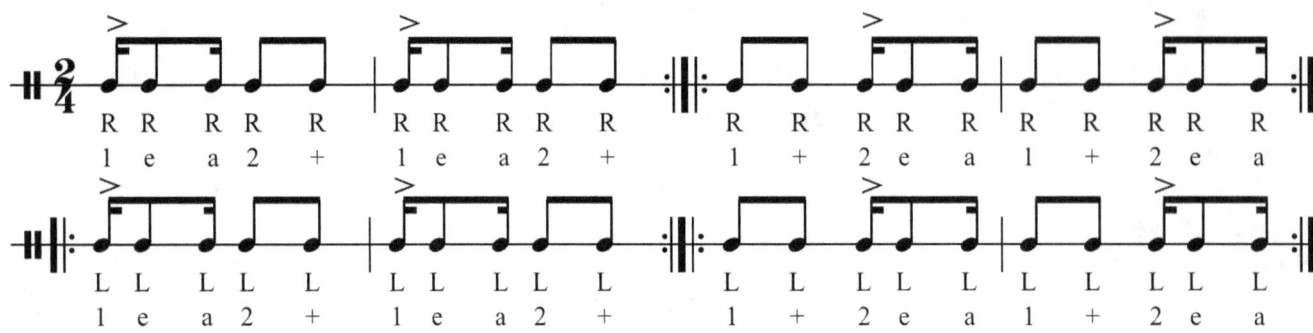

## Two Hand Exercise

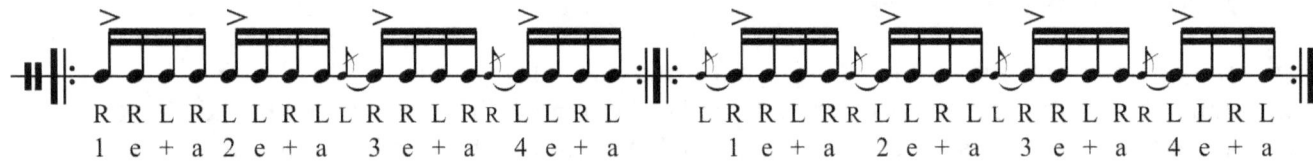

## Skill Buildup

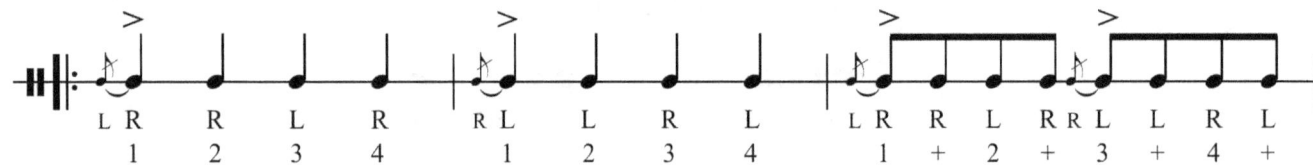

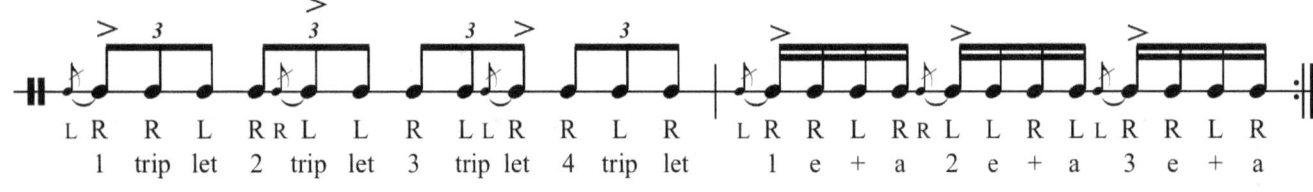

# 40. Flam Paradiddle-diddle

**PAS:** *#26*
**NARD:** *#24*
**Other Names:** *n/a*
**Alternation:** *yes*
**Origin:** *USA*

The Flam Paradiddle-diddle is a Single Paradiddle-diddle (22) with a grace note before the first full note. Described another way, it is a Flam Paradiddle (38) with an additional double stroke at the end. It could also be thought of as an Inverted Flam Tap (36) with two double strokes at the end. Unlike the Single Paradiddle-diddle, the Flam Paradiddle-diddle is played alternately between the hands. Continuing on the same hand, with the Flammed version would result in a quadruple stroke, while alternating requires only a triple stroke.

The Flam Paradiddle-diddle was likely invented in the USA, with its first appearance in a rudiment list dating to Charles Stewart Ashworth's 1812 book. In contrast to the progression of many rudiments, the Single Paradiddle-diddle, without the Flam (32), was only popularized as a variation of the Flam Paradiddle-diddle in the mid-20th century. The seemingly more complicated Flam version predates the non-Flam version by around 150 years.

### PAS Notation

### PAS Counted and Using the Name

### NARD Notation

### Basic Strokes

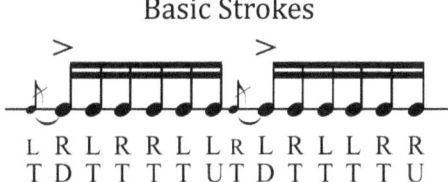

## Single Hand Exercise

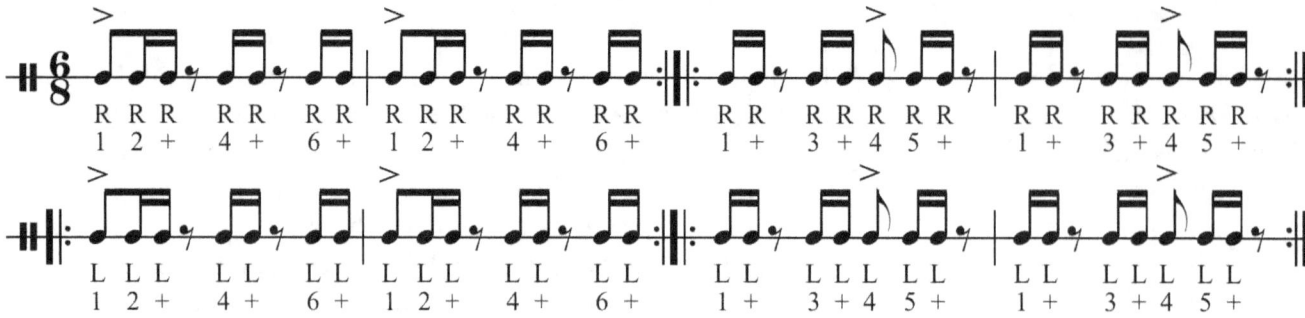

## Two Hand Exercise

## Skill Buildup

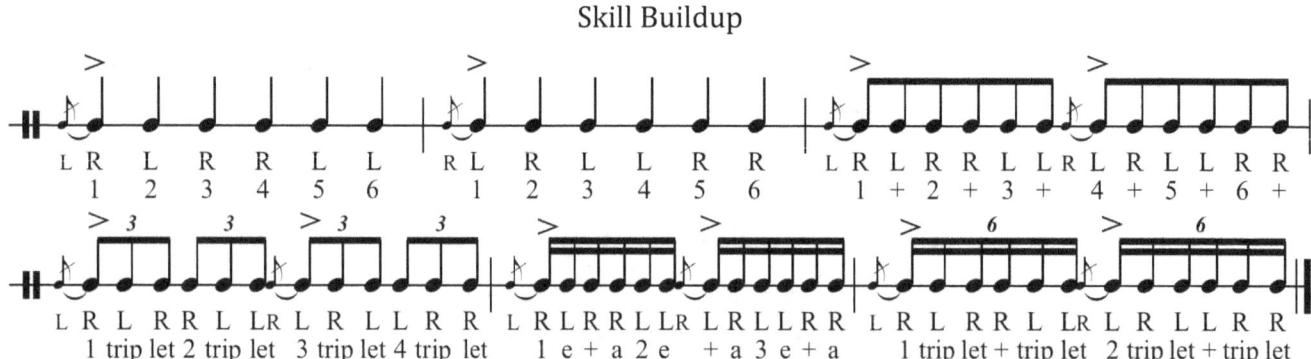

# 41. Pataflafla

**PAS:** *#27*
**NARD:** *n/a*
**Other Names:** *Patafla-fla, Cataflafla, Bataflafla, Flapataflaflla*
**Alternation:** *no*
**Origin:** *France*

The Pataflafla contains four alternating primary notes, the first and last of which are both preceded by a grace note – making the pattern: Flam-tap-tap-flam. It can also be described as a Flam Accent (35) with an additional Flam (32) at the end. It is thought to have originated in France, where it was called either the Pataflafla or Cataflafla, and is shown in manuals from 1863 and later. In Switzerland, it is known as the Bataflafla, and was imported from France around 1870. It appears in the USA in the 20th century, possibly for the first time in a solo in the *NARD Book of Solos* by Swiss composer Fritz Berger – though it is not named in this book. The first named instance in the USA may have been as late as 1957 by Vince Mott in his *Evolution of Drumming*.

American drummers often refer to the Pataflafla as a Swiss rudiment, despite its French origin and the fact that we normally use the French spelling. In both France and Switzerland, the Pataflafla or Bataflafla starts with the two single strokes and ends with two Flams, hence the name. Pa-ta indicates two single strokes, and Fla-Fla indicates two Flams, under the normal French syllabic rules. The PAS 40 notation starts with a Flam, as if it was Flapataflaflla (which can lead to some confusion). The notation and naming convention do not match on the rudiment sheet. Also of note, a left-handed version is rarely used and it is one of very few rudiments that are predominately played from just one hand.

A similar rudiment was listed in 1818 in the USA, called the Flam a Two and One Flam. It is not usually considered the same rudiment, because it was played in a slightly different rhythm. This is perhaps a precursor to the American convention of starting the normal Pataflafla pattern with a Flam, though it could just be a coincidence.

PAS Notation

L R L R R L L R L R R L

PAS Counted and Using the Name

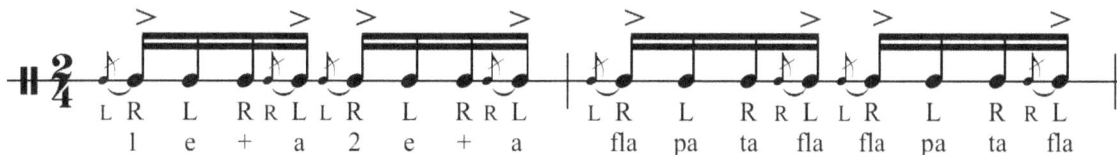

L R L R R L L R L R R L     L R L R R L L R L R R L
1 e + a 2 e + a     fla pa ta fla fla pa ta fla

Basic Strokes

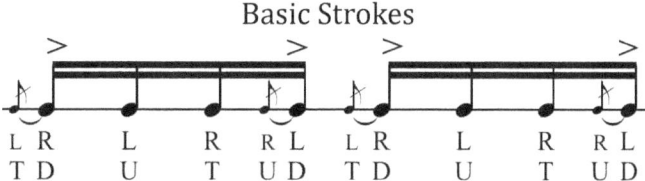

L R L R R L L R L R R L
T D U T U D T D U T U D

While this notation below is functionally the same as the American version, it is more obvious how the name fits the notation in this Swiss/French format.

European Presentation

Single Hand Exercise

Two Hand Exercise

Skill Buildup

# 42. Swiss Army Triplet

**PAS:** *#28*
**NARD:** *n/a*
**Other Names:** *Swiss Triplet, Modified Triplet, Ordonnanz Triole, Catapletes, Trioler med Slip, Wirbelschlag*
**Alternation:** *no*
**Origin:** *Switzerland*

The Swiss Army Triplet consists of a Flam (32) followed by two taps (one with the hand that played the primary note of the Flam, followed by one from the hand that played the grace note). It can also be described as a standard Flam Tap (36) followed by another tap (on the opposite hand). It originated in Switzerland, where it is called the Ordonnanz Triole, which very loosely translates to military triplet. Our American name for the pattern is actually pretty accurate, and it is one of the few rudiments that are correctly attributed to the Swiss by American drummers.

The Swiss Army Triplet first appeared as a snare drum rudiment in the USA sometime around the middle of the 20th century. John Pratt used them in some of his solos in the 1950s, which brought them to the attention of many other drummers. The same sticking was actually published in 1911 by Harry Bower, but he called it an Open Triple Roll, and it was supposed to be used for classical music. Since he did not refer to it as a rudiment, and because it was a roll and not a triplet (in the sense we know it today), it is hard to credit Bower for its popularity. His assessment of the sticking as a roll is somewhat accurate, as the Swiss Army Triplet is a series of slightly overlapped double strokes. Sanford Moeller similarly published a version of the Swiss Army Triplet called the Flam Tap Tap in 1925. But, just as with Bower, he cannot be fully credited with the modern concept of the rudiment that we use today.

In Europe, this pattern is almost exclusively played from the right hand. In American drumming, it is presented as being played with both hands, however in practice, the great majority of Swiss Army Triplets are still right handed. Very few examples actually fall on the left hand.

PAS Notation

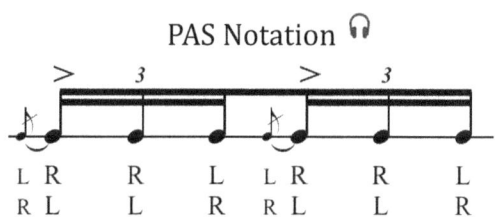

PAS Notation Counted and Using the Name

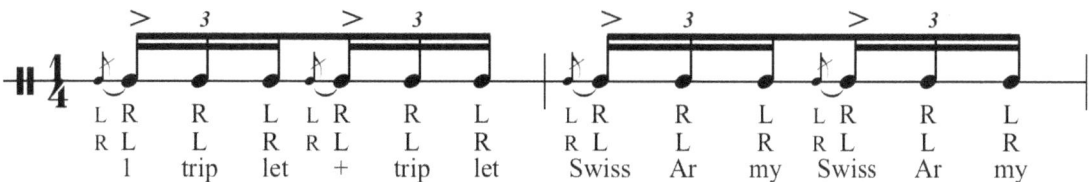

Basic Strokes

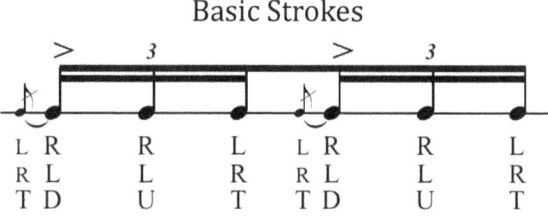

## Single Hand Exercise

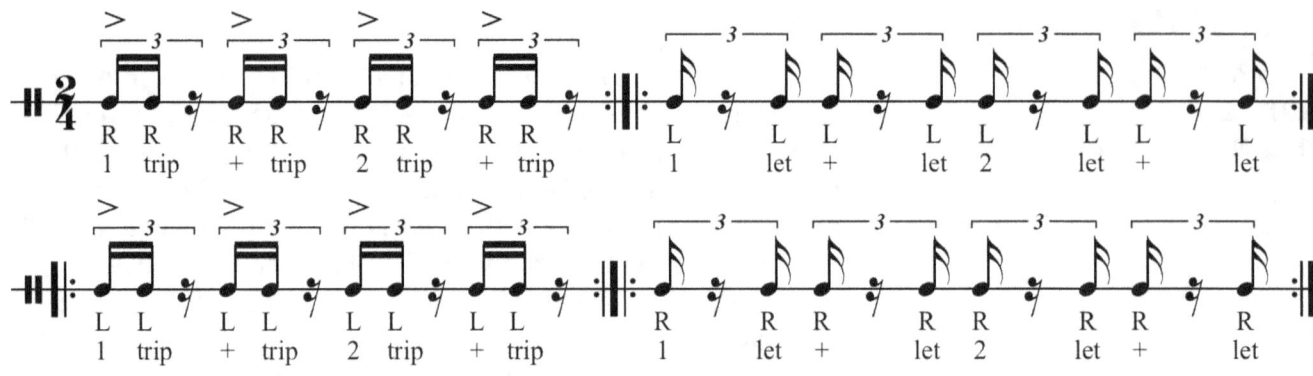

## Two Hand Exercise

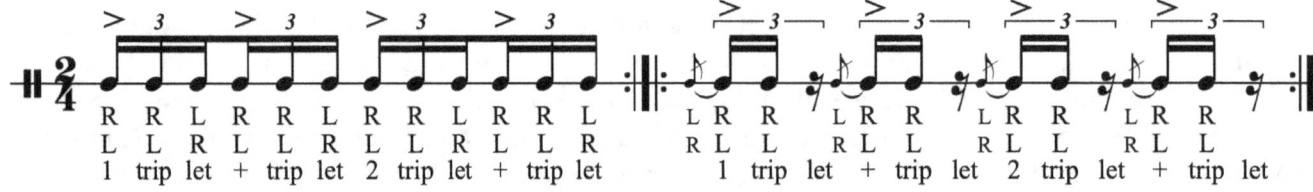

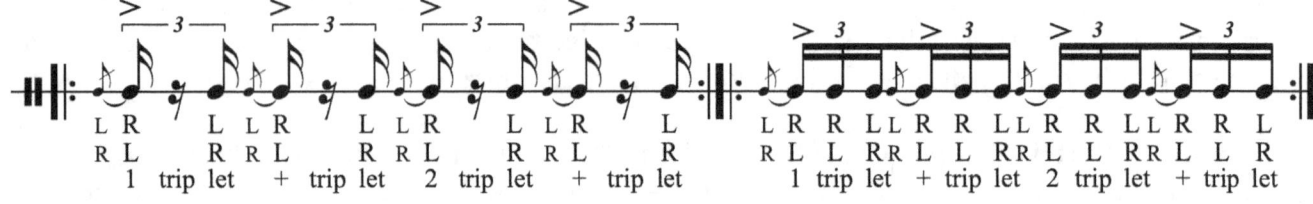

## Skill Buildup

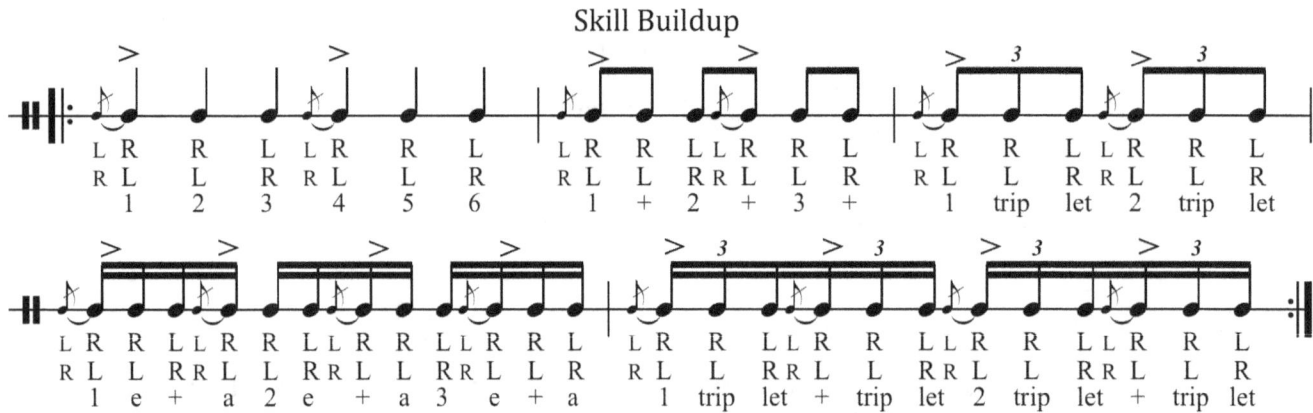

## Suggested Drum Kit Application

# 43. Inverted Flam Tap

**PAS:** *#29*
**NARD:** *n/a*
**Other Names:** *Flam and Stroke, Feint and Flam, Full Flam and Blow, Full Flam and Half Blow, Flam and Feint, Coup Lenglet, Coup Anglais, Doublé, Doppelstriech, Langt Forslag, Da Flam, Tap Flam, Swiss Tap Flam*
**Alternation:** *yes*
**Origin:** *England*

The Inverted Flam Tap consists of a Flam (32) followed by a tap (with the hand that played the grace note of the Flam). For example, a left grace note on a right primary note followed by a left tap. The rhythm may vary, and it can be found straight or dotted in the USA, and in other more syncopated or uneven rhythms, in Europe. The sticking is the important factor that separates this rudiment from the standard Flam Tap (36), which features a tap from the opposite hand.

The Inverted Flam Tap is generally harder to execute at speed than the standard Flam Tap, because it requires a much quicker up stroke to achieve the correct Flam position on each repetition. Both are essentially overlapping triple strokes, with the Inverted Flam Tap requiring an accent on the third note of the triple stroke.

American drummers often label the Inverted Flam Tap as a "Swiss rudiment." Indeed, Swiss drummers do play this pattern, though they adopted it from the French in the late 19th century. Americans actually implemented it earlier than the Swiss or French, having named iterations as far back as 1812. It ultimately traces its invention back to the British, who were definitely playing it by the 18th century, and possibly as far back as the 17th century, or even earlier. From this brief history, it's clear that the rudiment isn't especially Swiss, nor did Americans first learn it from the Swiss, and it should likely be referred to as a British or English rudiment, if anything.

PAS Notation 🎧

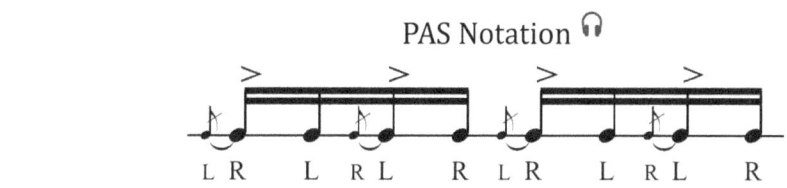

PAS Counted and Using the Name

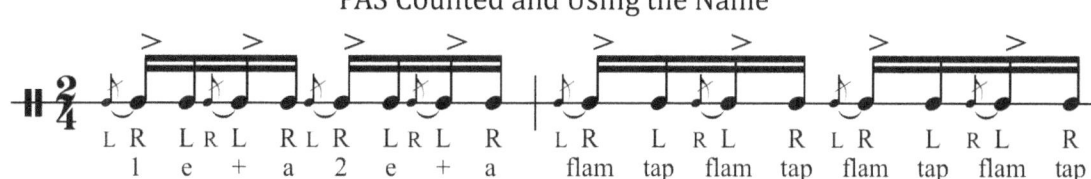

Basic Strokes

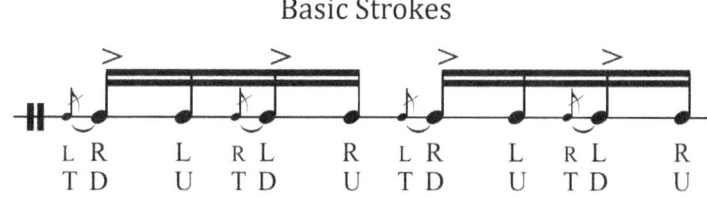

## Tap Flam Variation, Flam and Feint Variation, Feint and Flam Variation

## Single Hand Exercise

## Two Hand Exercise

## Skill Buildup

# Hybrid Rudiments

The term Hybrid Rudiment is somewhat flexible, but normally refers to a relatively recently created rudimental sticking pattern from the 20th or 21st centuries that contains elements from more than one standard rudiment. A rudiment that includes both Flams (32) and Drags (23), for example, would normally be considered a Hybrid – made from two existing rudimental elements. In practice, there are so-called Hybrid Rudiments that are not specifically mixtures of other existing rudiments, but simply new sticking patterns, altogether. There are also Hybrids that are just normal rudiments with a new name, such as Inverts, which is a new Hybrid name for the existing PAS Inverted Flam Tap (43). Further, some Hybrids exist on the PAS and NARD sheets already, such as the Flam Paradiddle (38) or Drag Paradiddle No. 1 (28), but they are not referred to as Hybrids, because they were used in traditional American drumming. Essentially, they are too old for the Hybrid concept. Some very recently created rudiments, such as the Single Paradiddle-diddle (22), are not considered Hybrids. The Paradiddle-diddle looks like a traditional rudiment, and is not a combination of two or more existing rudiment types, but was first printed as a rudiment in the 1960s. It is from the Hybrid age, but doesn't hybridize anything. This is, of course, all very confusing.

Hybrid Rudiments come mainly from drum corps, and specifically, Drum Corps International (DCI) arrangers. Starting in the middle of the 20th century, civilian and military drum corps began writing patterns that were either completely different from the standard NARD rudiments of the time, or were an intentional mixture of elements from the normal rudimental repertoire. From the 1950s into the 1980s, rudimental experts, and rank and file drummers, conflated these new and interesting patterns with Swiss rudiments. American innovations were becoming commonly used at the same time as newly imported rudiments from Basel drumming. Most drummers could not tell where the traditionally Swiss rudiments ended and the modern American inventions began. So, many "Swiss Rudiments" cited by Americans, especially rudiments with the word "Swiss" in the name, are actually Hybrids (with an erroneous origin story). The Swiss Army Triplet (42) is one of the exceptions to this confusion. It really is Swiss.

From the outset of DCI, it was common to use these newer patterns, and many were given names and treated as necessary practice material, along with traditional rudiments. Variations on variations built up over time, and there were already a large number of named Hybrids by the time anyone made a serious attempt to write them down. In 1992, James Campbell was able to identify 30 Hybrids in a *Percussive Notes* article. The very next year, in 1993, Ed Freytag listed 43 named Hybrids in his *Rudimental Cookbook*. Not all of Campbell's 30 made it into Freytag's 43, as there were many to choose from already. In the 21st century, there are many hundreds of named Hybrids, with over 550 of the most common included in the 2019 book *Encyclopedia Rudimentia*.

Unfortunately, some Hybrids have up to five different names, and in some cases, the same name will refer to multiple different patterns. In this book so far, we have noted the inconsistency and confusing nature of the many "normal" rudiments, but Hybrids are even less standardized, and much more variable. There is no official list, and nothing is codified with any authority. It is an ever-evolving organic field of study.

It is not reasonable for any single drummer to memorize every hybrid rudiment. Only seven have been explained in detail in the Hybrid section of this book, as an introduction to the concept. These have been selected because of their relative popularity and their interesting combinations of rudiments that are pedagogically useful. If the basic elements of rudimental drumming (and a bit of common Hybrid terminology) are understood, learning any new Hybrid is not terribly difficult. They should be treated as less important and taught later than most or all of the standard rudiments, since they are, at least nominally, built from those standards.

In the context of high school marching band, college marching band, DCI, DCA, WGI or other competitive marching ensembles, some understanding of Hybrids is absolutely essential. It is nearly impossible to play modern marching music without encountering some hybrid concepts. For drum kit players or classical musicians, a brief overview of the topic is all that is necessary. There are, however, some patterns that are beneficial for learning pure technique, such as the Eggbeaters (49) or Shirley Murphy (50). Others have direct applications beyond marching arts, like the Herta (48), which is a common sticking in many genres.

# 44. Flam Drag

**PAS:** *#30*
**NARD:** *n/a*
**Other Names:** *n/a*
**Alternation:** *yes*
**Origin:** *USA*

The Flam Drag consists of a grace note preceding a single stroke (a Flam (32)) followed by a double stroke and another single stroke (a Drag (23)). As the name suggests, it is simply a Flam and a Drag, usually notated as a triplet or group of three equal 8ths (with the middle note doubled). Other ways to think about it include: as a Flam Accent (35), with a double stroke on the middle note – or, a Single Drag, with an added Flam.

On the PAS sheet, the Flam Drag is placed within the Flam rudiments. Unlike any other PAS Flam rudiment, it also contains a Drag. None of the PAS Drag rudiments contain a Flam. This combination of the two skills is best described as a Hybrid Rudiment and placed here (not with the normal Flam rudiments). It is also a non-traditional rudiment, in the sense that it was rarely played (and never named) in American drumming before the 1970s. The sticking pattern has some precedent in official French military drumming – but even there, it is not a named rudiment. Dan Spalding listed it in an article in 1974, which may have been the first named appearance. It is almost certainly an invention of American drum corps arrangers, who likely had no prior knowledge of the French military duty.

### PAS Notation 🎧

L R L L R R L R R L

### PAS Notation Interpreted

### Basic Strokes

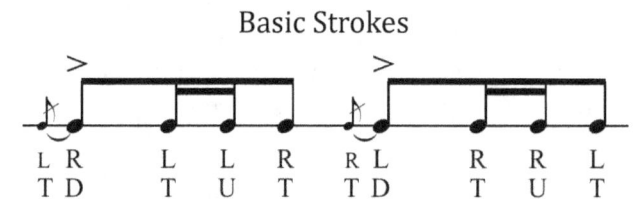

## Single Hand Exercise

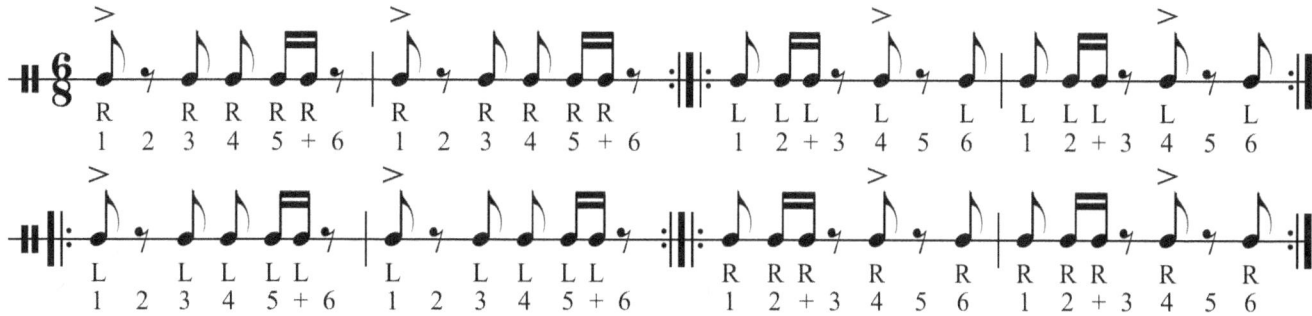

## Two Hand Exercise

## Skill Buildup

The Blushda is a popular drum set rudiment that is very similar to the Flam Drag, though it is often played with a non-alternating sticking. Below are two commonly used sticking patterns for the Blushda concept.

## Blushda Sticking Options

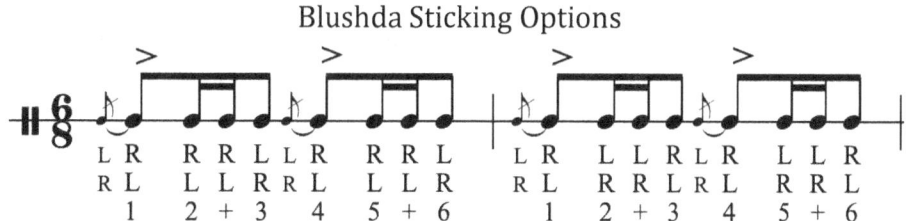

# 45. Cheese and Fuzz

**PAS:** *n/a*
**NARD:** *n/a*
**Other names for Cheese:** *Fluff (Flammed Ruff), Dram (Dragged Flam), Flag (Flammed Drag), Studders, Flagada, Verwisselslagen, 3er Streich, Pladada, Slip-Ruff*
**Other names for Fuzz:** *Flammed Buzz, Cheese Buzz, Tra*
**Alternation:** *yes*
**Origin:** *USA (as Hybrid rudiments), likely France or Switzerland (cheese-like traditional rudiments), Spain (fuzz-like traditional rudiment)*

The Cheese is a Hybrid Rudiment that mixes the Flam (32) and the Drag (23), or more simply, a Flam and a double stroke. It consists of a grace note preceding a double stroke (which may or may not be followed by one or more single strokes). Any note that already has a grace note, a Flam, can then be double stroked, which would result in a Cheese. Any notes already double stroked, as in a Drag, can be preceded by a grace note, which would result in a Cheese. Any single stroke can have both a grace note, and a double stroke added, to also become a Cheese. This is one of the most popular Hybrid Rudiment ideas, and a Cheesed iteration of essentially every other rudiment probably exists, somewhere.

The Hybrid Cheese may have its origins in the Air Force Drum Corps, where it was first used in a Flammed Dragadiddle or Flammed Ruffadiddle context in around 1954. Several iterations of the name were common from the 1960s through the early 1980s. Tom Float is usually credited with the name Cheese, claiming it was good on everything, like cheese. Cheese eventually overcame all other attempts at a name, despite being the least descriptive name for the pattern.

A Cheese-like rudiment is not a new idea. Flammed Drags exist in Swiss drumming and date to the 18th century, called Pladada or Dreierstreich. They are not quite the same as the modern Cheese, however, in that they were usually played as a Flam onto two 16th notes, followed by an 8th note – which is like a slightly compressed Swiss Army Triplet (42). The Danish-Norwegians had a similar idea called the Slip Ruff, and the Dutch called this concept the Verwisselslag. The French also had a similar rudiment called a Flagada in the 19th century. The French version was sometimes notated as a single grace note, tied to a set of two grace notes, tied to a primary note, or three grace notes of uneven spacing. Essentially, this was a Cheese on the pickup to the beat. None of these seem likely to have directly influenced the Hybrid Cheese as we know it today, but show that drummers think alike across time and space.

The Cheese Buzz or Fuzz (Flammed Buzz) has also been grouped in here, because any flammed double stroke, in any Hybrid Rudiment context, can be interchanged 1:1 with a Flammed Multiple Bounce Stroke (17). The timing and concept are the same; the difference is only the number of bounces after the grace note. The modern Fuzz also seems to be a recent Hybrid invention, though there is a similar traditional concept in Valencia, called a Tra. It is not likely to be directly related, but is very similar in execution.

There are two main practice variations for the basic Cheese. The first is a group of four, a Cheese Dragteenth or Cheeseteenth. The other is a group of three, a Cheeselet or Cheese Accent. Both begin with a Cheese followed by single strokes.

## Cheese Practice Patterns

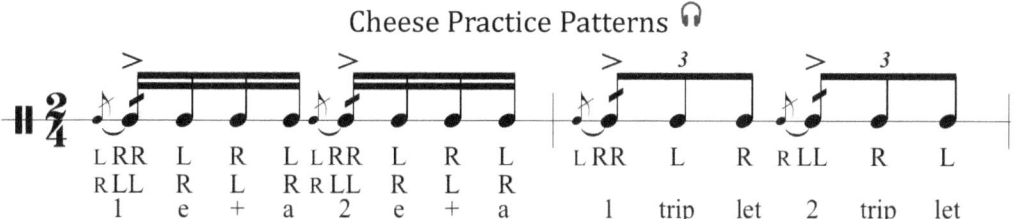

3
L RR L R L L RR L R L L RR L R R LL R L
R LL R L R R LL R L R
1 e + a 2 e + a 1 trip let 2 trip let

## Fuzz Practice Patterns – same as above but with a Multiple Bounce stroke

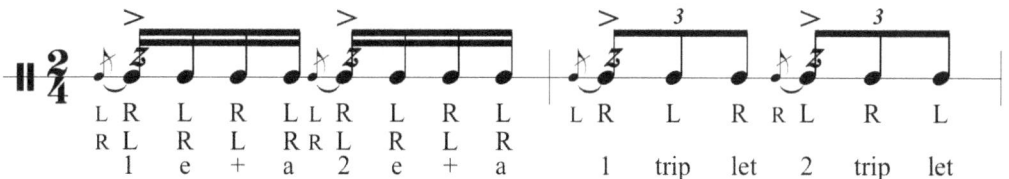

3
L R L R L L R L R L L R L R R L R L
R L R L R R L R L R
1 e + a 2 e + a 1 trip let 2 trip let

The following exercises will all feature the Cheeselet or Cheese Accent pattern, because it conveniently alternates hands. Practice each exercise with Cheeses and Fuzzes to work on both concepts.

## Single Hand Exercise

3
RR R R R RR R R R L L LL L L L LL L
1 trip let 2 trip let 1 trip let 2 trip let 1 trip let 2 trip let 1 trip let 2 trip let
LL L L L LL L L L R R RR R R R RR R
1 trip let 2 trip let 1 trip let 2 trip let 1 trip let 2 trip let 1 trip let 2 trip let

## Two Hand Exercise

3
R L R L R L R L R L R L L R L R R L R L L R L R R L R L
1 trip let 2 trip let 1 trip let 2 trip let 1 trip let 2 trip let 1 trip let 2 trip let
RR L R LL R L RR L R LL R L L RR L R R LL R L L RR L R R LL R L
1 trip let 2 trip let 1 trip let 2 trip let 1 trip let 2 trip let 1 trip let 2 trip let

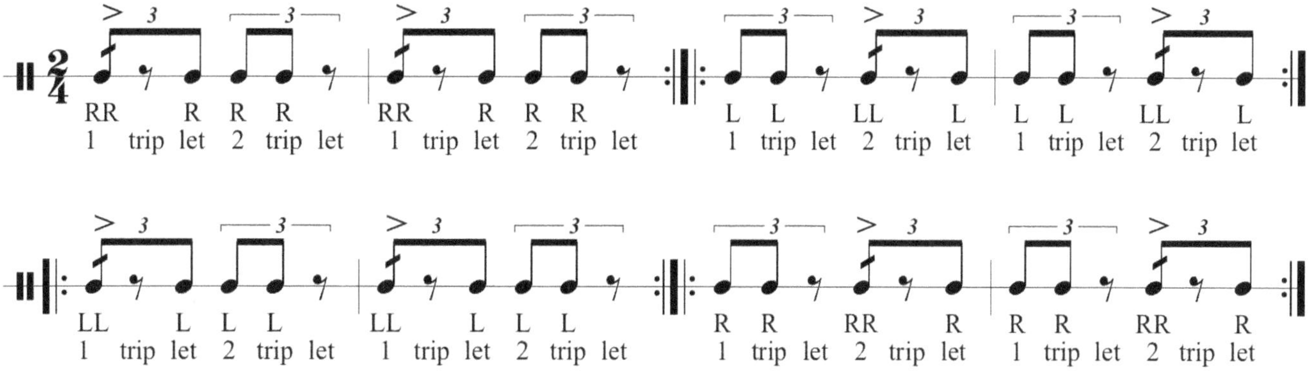

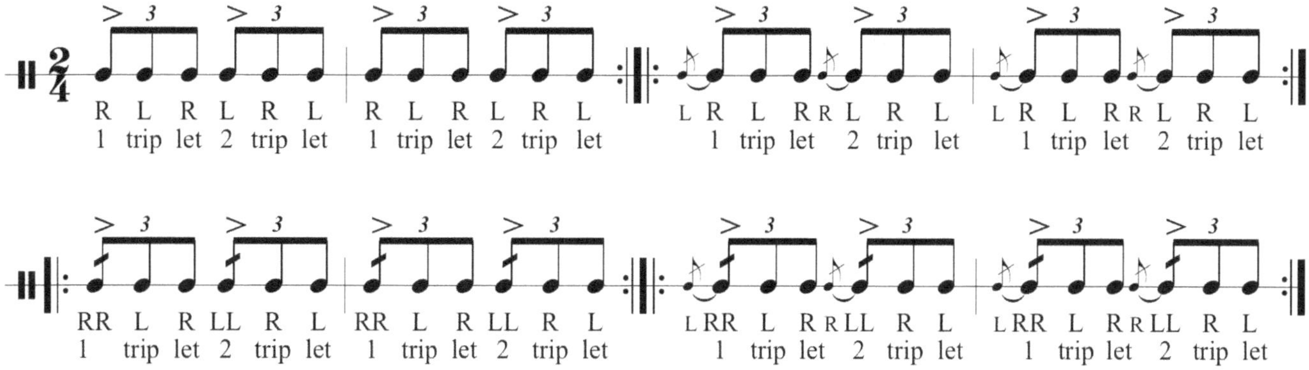

## Skill Buildup

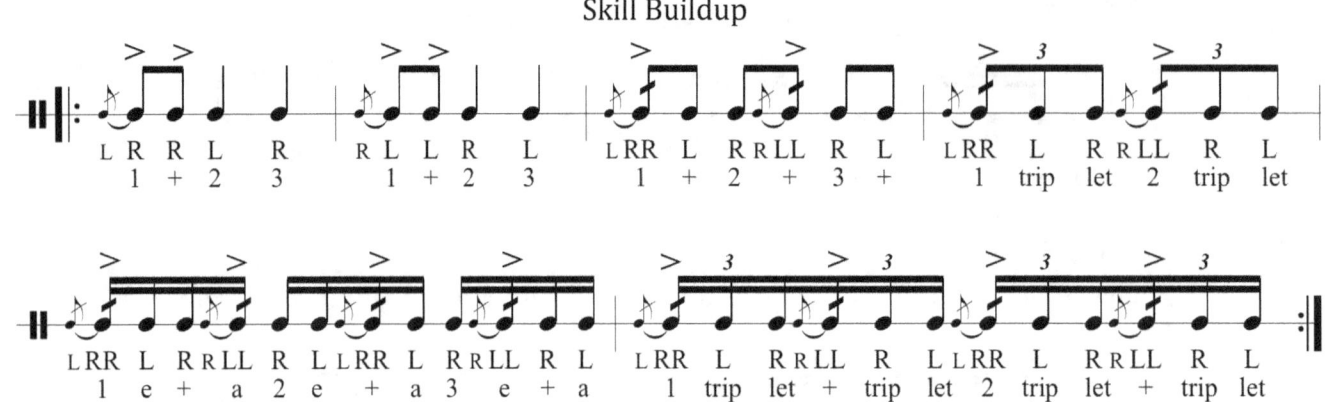

Below are three other rudiments with a Cheese component: Cheese Paradiddle, Cheese Inverts, and Cheese Back Flip.

## Other Cheese Rudiments

Below are three other rudiments with a Fuzz component: Fuzz Tap, Fuzzadiddle, Fuzz Chuchudda (or Fuzz-a-Chu)

## Other Fuzz Rudiments

# 46. Flammed 5 Stroke Roll

**PAS:** *n/a*
**NARD:** *n/a*
**Other Names:** *Flam 5 Stroke Roll, Flam 5, Flam Five, Flam Accent 5 Stroke Roll, Flam Fivelet, Swiss Roll, Vijfslag, Funfer Ruf, Deutsche Ruf, Ra de Six, Ran de 6, Rau da 6*
**Alternation:** *yes*
**Origin:** *unknown, possibly Switzerland*

The Flammed 5 Stroke Roll is a standard 5 Stroke Roll (6) preceded by a single grace note. It can also be thought of as a Flam (32) plus 4 additional notes. Because the first primary note after the grace note is actually part of a double stroke, it could be considered a Cheese (45) (see the previous Cheese rudiment page), but it is almost never described that way. A right-handed Flammed 5 Stroked Roll would consist of a left grace note onto a right double stroke, followed by a left double stroke, and then a right accented single stroke. While this section details the Flammed 5 Stroke specifically, any rudimental roll can begin with a Flam in the same manner.

The Flam 5 is one of the most common rudiments worldwide, despite being a Hybrid novelty in American usage. The first printed mention of Flammed Rolls in the USA was in the 1970s, and like many more advanced concepts, they were attributed to the Swiss and primarily used in drum corps settings. American drummers may have started playing them slightly earlier, but were very late to adopt the concept, compared to some other rudimental traditions. The Swiss explicitly mention Flammed Rolls starting in 1845, though the concept is likely much older. Beginning a 5 Stroke Roll with a grace note is standard practice in Switzerland, today (with the non-Flammed version being possible, but less common). German and Prussian rudimental drumming uses Flammed Rolls almost exclusively, though they are rarely notated or discussed. It is just assumed that rolls will begin with a Flam. The French and Italians (and some other countries) label the Flammed 5 Stroke as a 6 Stroke Roll. This can be confusing, but in their defense, six notes are actually being played. Several other rudimental systems also feature at least some usage of Flammed Rolls in their historic or modern practice.

Some Possible Flam 5 Interpretations

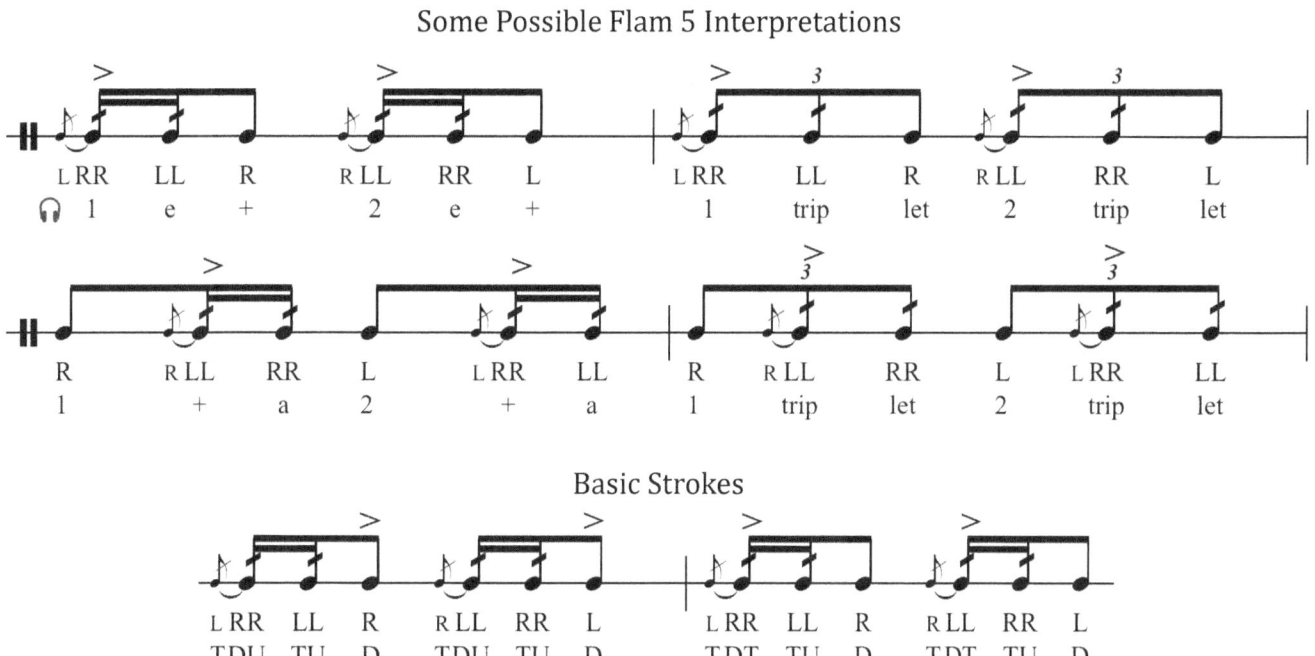

Basic Strokes

## Single Hand Exercise

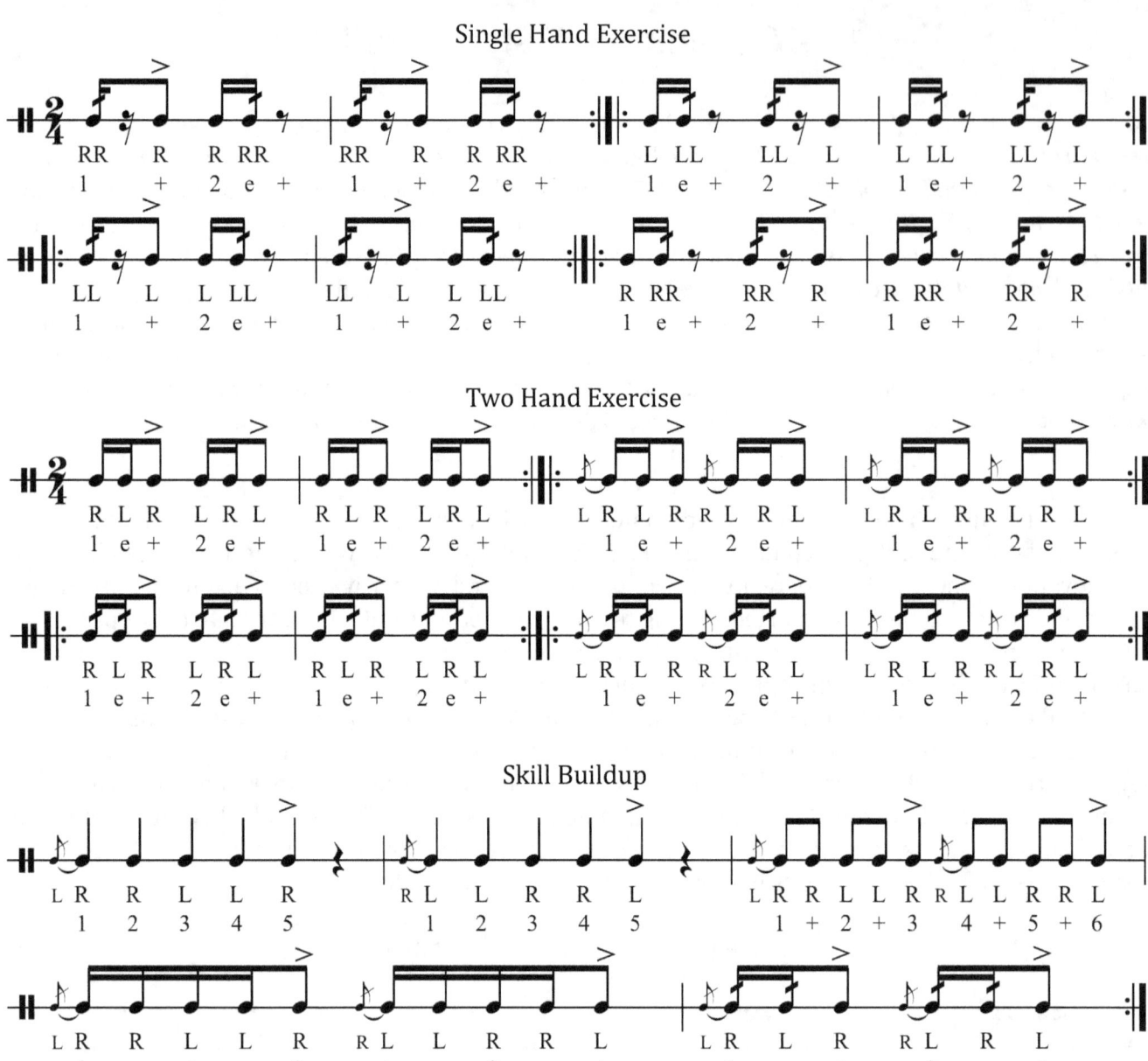

## Two Hand Exercise

## Skill Buildup

# 47. Single Dragadiddle

**PAS:** *35*
**NARD:** *n/a*
**Other Names:** *Diddly Diddle, Ruffadiddle*
**Alternation:** *yes*
**Origin:** *USA*

The Single Dragadiddle consists of a Single Paradiddle (20) with a double stroke on the first note. In other words, it is a double stroke, followed by a single stroke (as in a Drag (23)), and then another slower double stroke, like a diddle. A right-handed Dragadiddle would start with a right accented double stroke, a left single stroke, and two additional right strokes. It is the standard PAS rudiment #35, but is most accurately described as a Hybrid rudiment. It uses both the Drag and the Paradiddle, much like the Drag Paradiddles #1 and #2 (28, 29), but its recent invention, and its application of the Drag on top of the notes of the Single Paradiddle, make it dissimilar from the other Drag or Paradiddle rudiments.

One of the first published instances comes from a *Percussive Notes* article in 1972 where, like most mid-20th century rudiment lists, it was comingled with a selection of Swiss rudiments and other Hybrids. Oddly for a Hybrid rudiment, it was specifically attributed to a single person, John Davidson of the Buccaneers Drum Corps. A similar concept may have been used by the Air Force as early as the 1950s. Either way, it is still a very modern invention by rudimental standards, and one of the five or six newest rudiments on the PAS 40 list. Its use of a fast (32nd note), and slow (16th note) double stroke, in quick succession on the same hand, makes it especially difficult to play, once the tempo reaches a point where bouncing both sets of doubles is required.

## PAS Notation 🎧

R L R R L R L L

## Counted and Using the Name

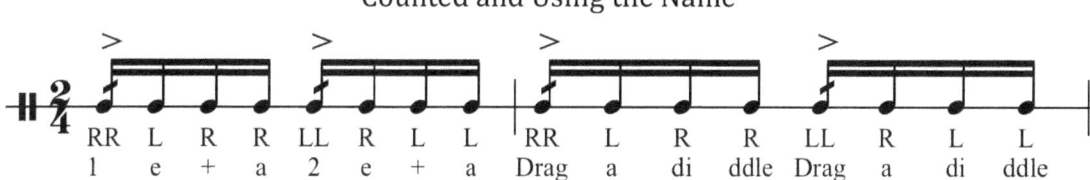

## Basic Strokes

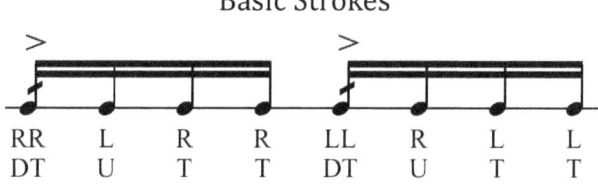

## Single Hand Exercise

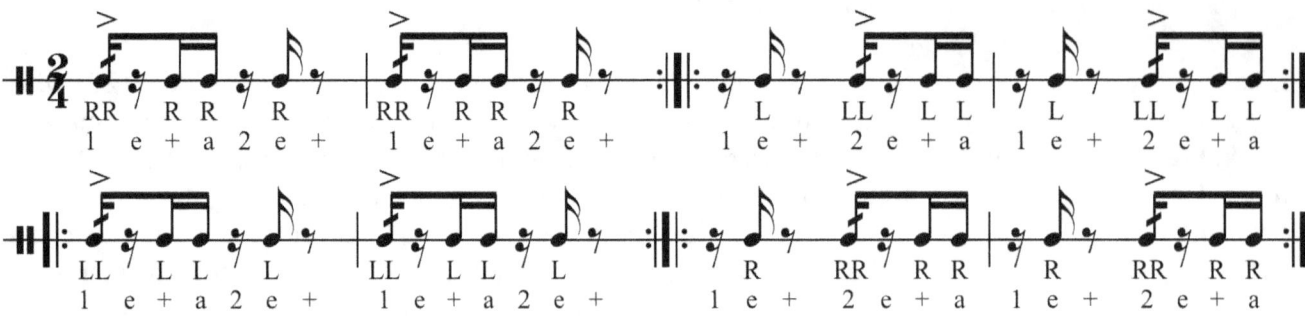

## Two Hand Exercise

## Skill Buildup

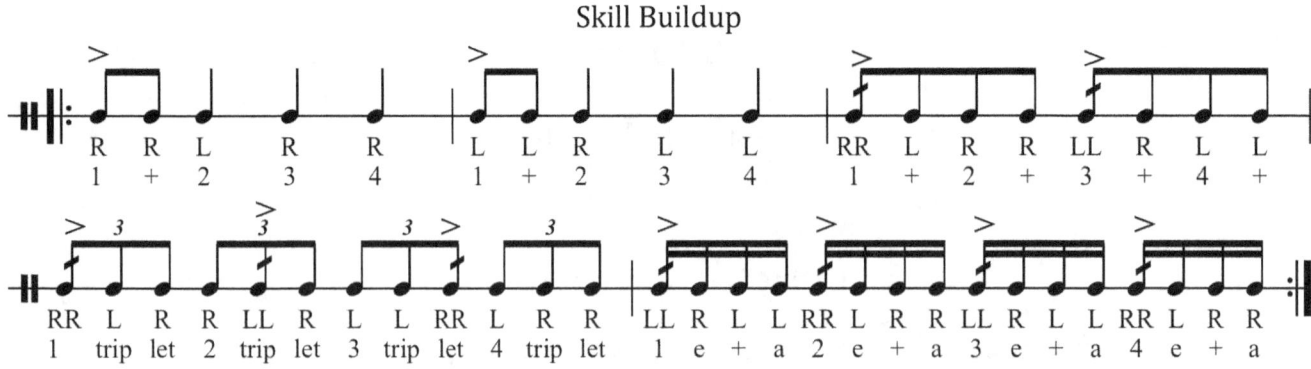

# 48. Herta

**PAS:** *n/a*
**NARD:** *n/a*
**Other Names:** *Hurta, Hairta,*
*Single Stroke Drag, Biddle-Up-Bup*
**Alternation:** *no*
**Origin:** *USA*

The Herta consists of four single strokes, the first two played twice as fast as the last two. It has a similar rhythm and sound to a Single Drag Tap (26), but played only with single strokes, instead of a Drag (23). A right-handed Herta typically starts with two 16th notes (right and left single strokes), and then follows with two 8th notes (right and left single strokes again, and the last note is often accented). Hertas are normally used in triple meter, or as triplets.

The Herta was originally referred to as the onomatopoetic Biddle-Up-Bup, in the 1970s. The name Single Stroke Drag was later postulated for it, though it would be more correct to call it a Single Stroke Drag Tap, or Single Stroke Single Drag. The name Herta (or a spelling variation thereof) became the standard by the mid-1990s and continues in common use, today. Herta is a much more succinct onomatopoetic name than Biddle-Up-Bup, although it requires the R to be slightly rolled to make sense.

Herta is considered a Hybrid mostly because of its recent origin. It could also be thought of as a combination of a 3 Stroke Ruff (2) and a Single Drag Tap.

Notation 🎧

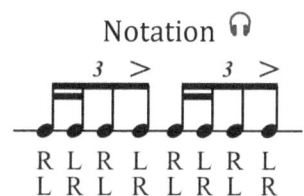

Counted and Using the Name (roll the R)

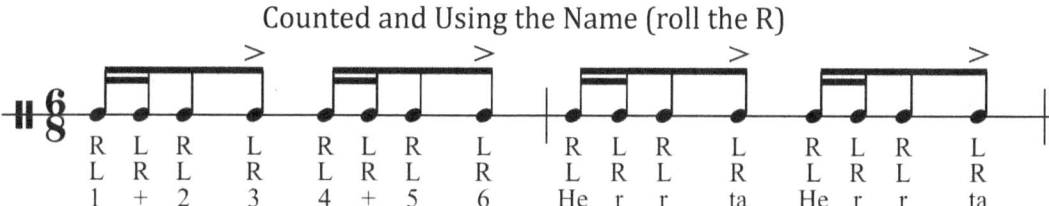

Basic Strokes

## Single Hand Exercise

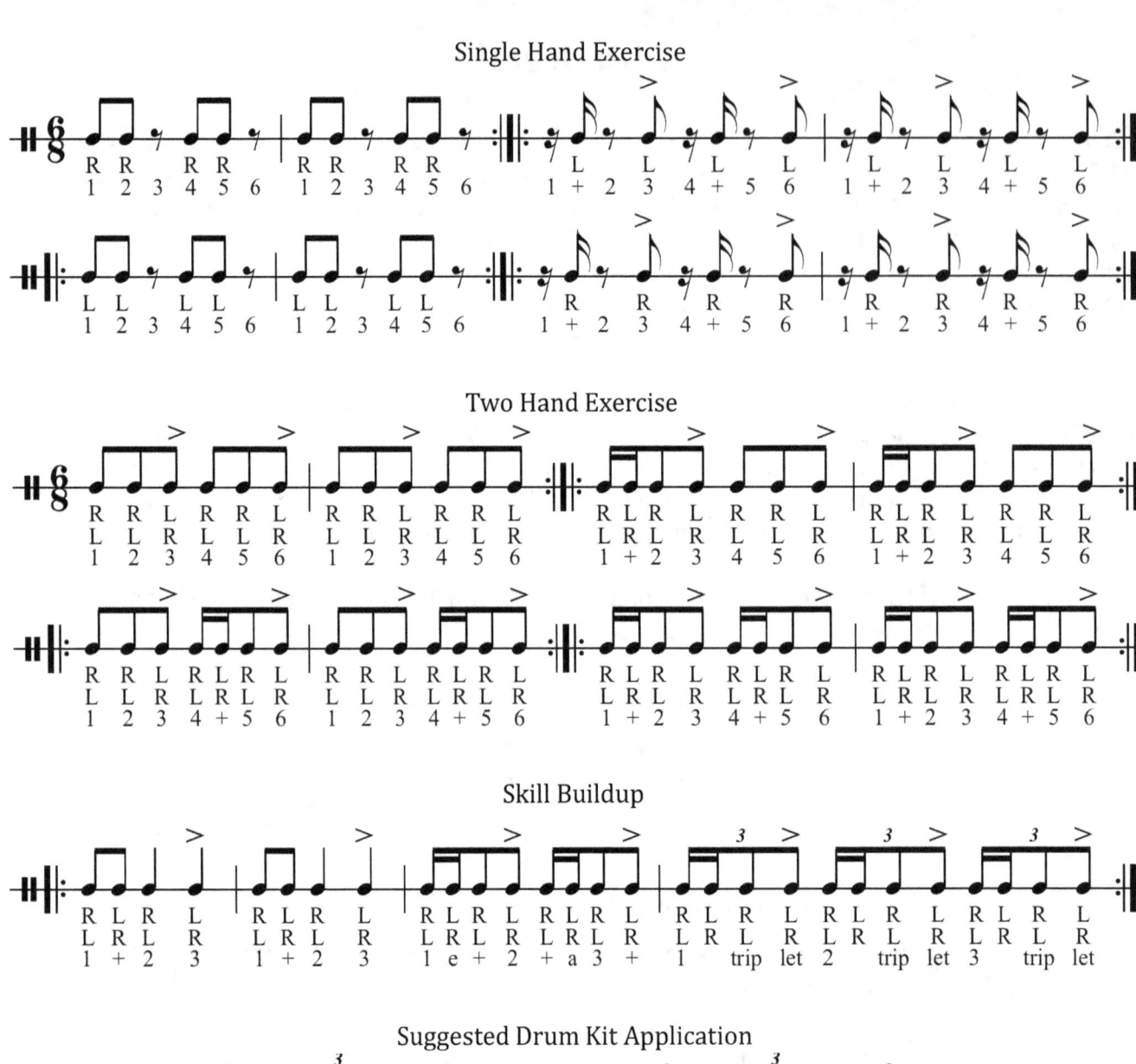

## Two Hand Exercise

## Skill Buildup

## Suggested Drum Kit Application

# 49. Eggbeater

**PAS:** *n/a*
**NARD:** *n/a*
**Other Names:** *Chinese Fives, Fyvie Five, Egg Beaters*
**Alternation:** *no*
**Origin:** *USA*

Eggbeaters consist of five notes played as a triple stroke followed by a double stroke. A right-handed Eggbeater starts with three right hands and then two immediate left hands. These can be grouped in several different ways. The most common pattern is a quintuplet, or five evenly spaced notes. Other interpretations include a 16th note triplet followed by two regular 16th notes (sometimes called Chinese Fives), or a 16th note triplet followed by two 32nd notes. All three of the rhythms can be considered versions of a basic Eggbeater. None of these variations is normally presented with an accent; all five notes must be played at the same height and dynamic.

The first published listing for an Eggbeater was in a 1992 article by James Campbell. There were a few variations listed together, implying that it had been in use for some time prior, with anecdotal evidence going back as far as 1978. Eggbeaters are considered a Hybrid, because they mix the Triple Stroke Roll (19) with the Double Stroke Roll (5). Using two different numbers of bounces (in close proximity) makes them challenging, but worthwhile, to practice rebound control.

These first three notation styles are easily counted, because the patterns start from downbeats. This is the modern Eggbeater, the Chinese Five, and an older version of the Eggbeater concept.

These next two versions of the notation are more challenging to count, because some do not start from a downbeat. In both of these measures, the second iteration of the pattern starts on the 'a' of beat 1. In the first measure, the notes are not evenly spaced, being a triplet, and then two 32nd notes. In the second measure, the notes are all evenly spaced, with a quintuplet over three 16th notes; the second set of upside down notes show where normal dotted 8th notes fall in the pattern (and are not to be played). These are uncommon variations of the rhythm, but possible.

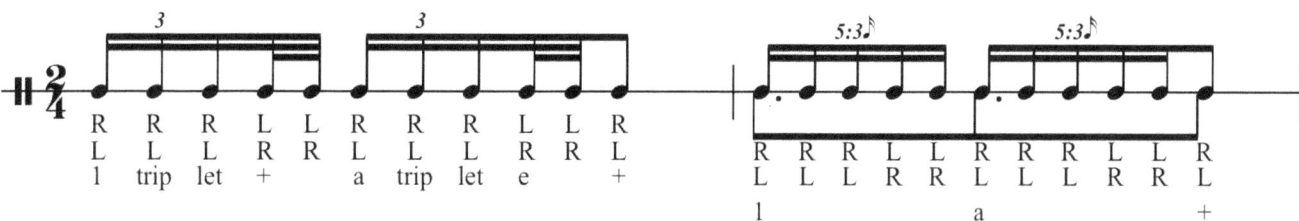

## Basic Strokes

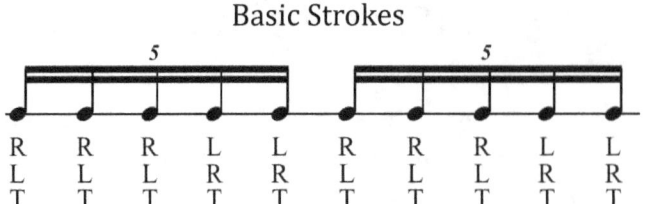

## Single Hand Exercise

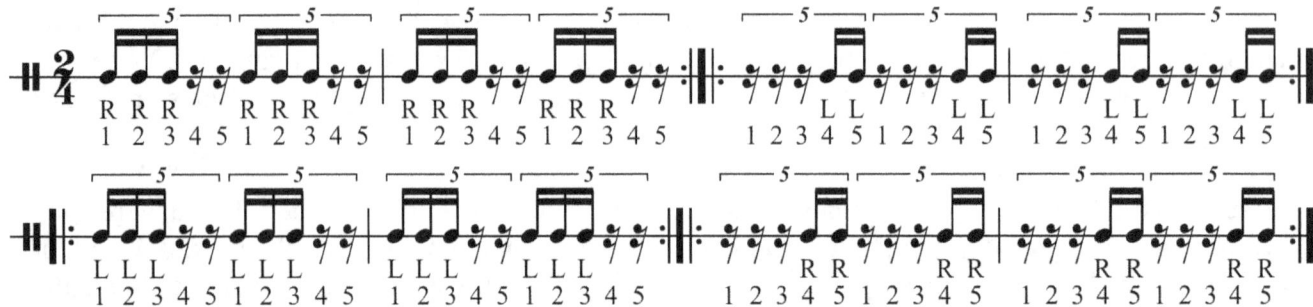

## Two Hand Exercise

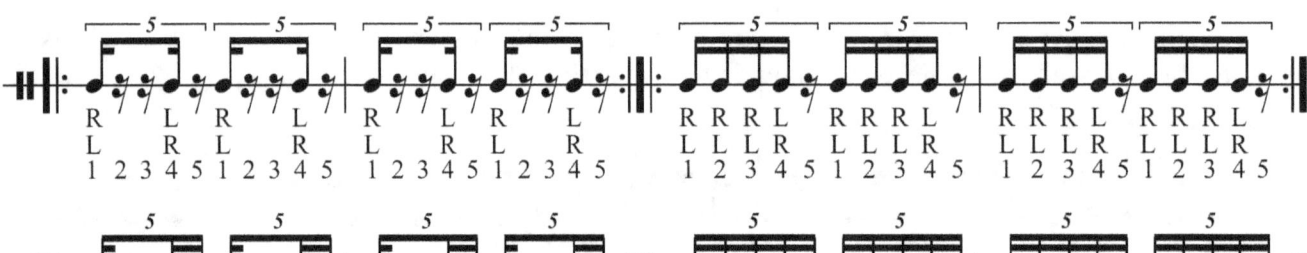

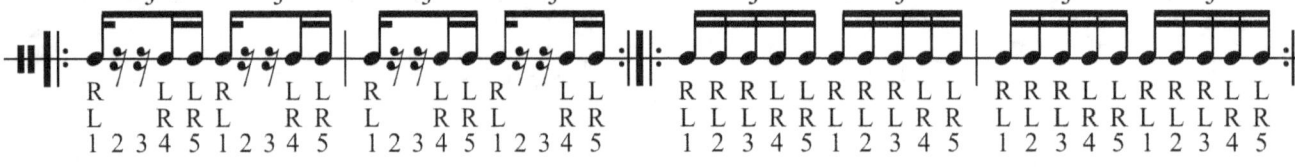

## Skill Buildup

# 50. Shirley Murphy

**PAS:** *n/a*
**NARD:** *n/a*
**Other Names:** *Shirley Murphey, 1-2-3, Murphs, Murfs, Murphies*
**Alternation:** *yes*
**Origin:** *USA*

The Shirley Murphy consists of a single stroke followed by a double stroke, followed by a triple stroke – all at the same note value. A right-handed Shirley Murphy starts with a right, then two lefts, and ends with three rights. These are usually grouped into two triplets, with one triplet containing the single stroke and double stroke, and the next being a triple stroke.

This is a Hybrid rudiment that combines the single, double, and triple strokes into a single pattern, and it is sometimes simply referred to as 1-2-3 (for the number of strokes on each hand). This combination of strokes can be quite difficult to achieve evenly, and that is why it is a valuable practice pattern. There is also a corresponding Reverse Shirley Murphy that is logically known as a 3-2-1. Shirley Murphy enters the published record in the 1990s – but, like many Hybrids, it is likely older. Shirley Murphy is normally notated with one accent, but can sometimes be found with two accents (as shown).

### Notation Options

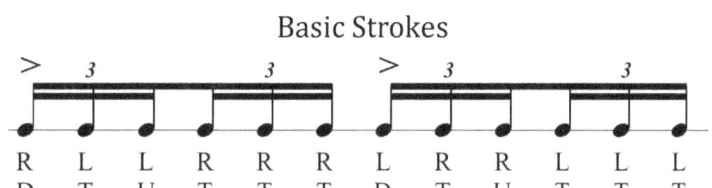

### Counted

### Basic Strokes

### Single Hand Exercise

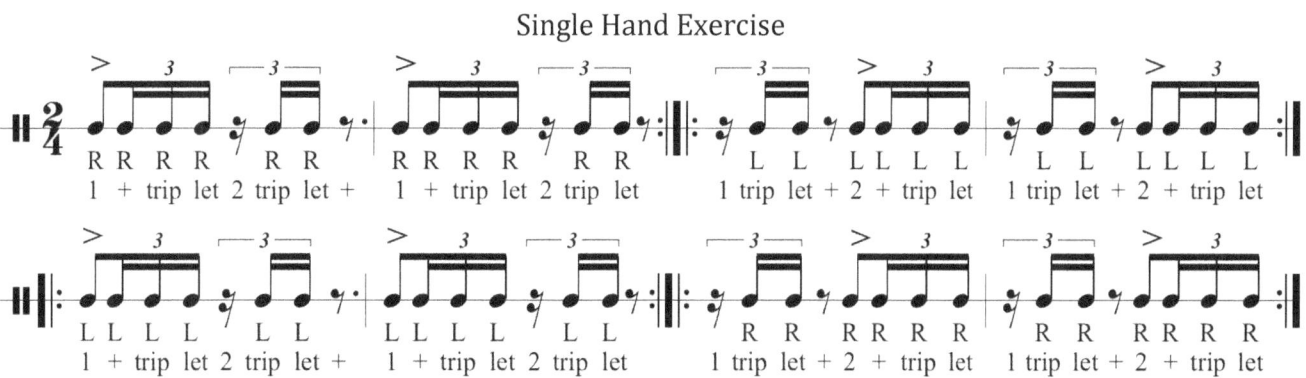

## Two Hand Exercise

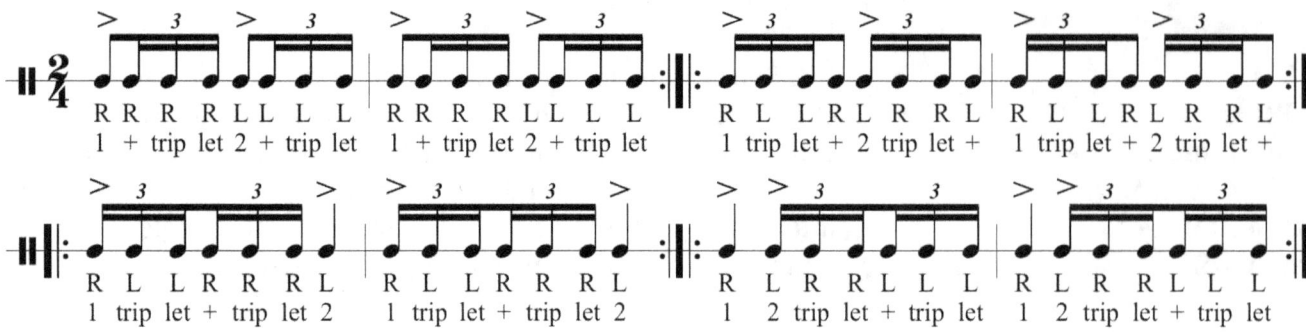

## Skill Buildup

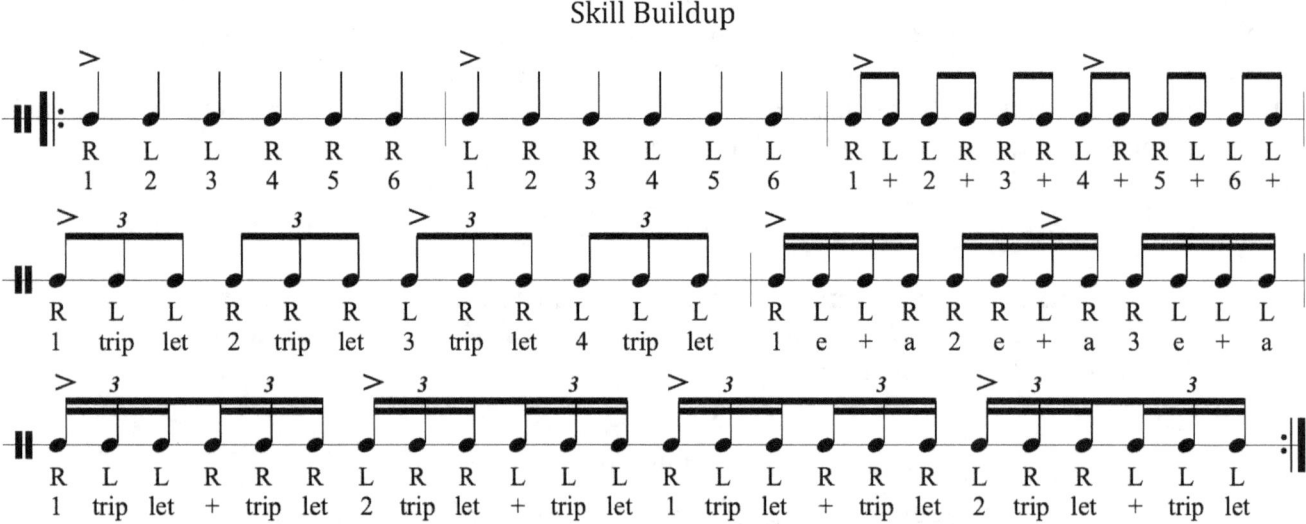

# Rudimental Glossary

*Accent:* a note played louder than unaccented notes, generally by lifting the stick and playing from a greater height.

*Backstick:* a note played with the butt end, or the back, of the drum stick for mostly visual appeal, but also some timbre difference. Some Hybrids require back sticking as a part of the pattern, but traditional rudiments do not specify. It can be added to any pattern at the player's or ensemble's discretion.

*Bounce:* when the stick is rebounded from the drumhead through the elastic property of the head itself.

*Charge Stroke:* two single strokes played close together, but not as close as a Flam. Also called an Open Flam. See the Charge Stroke (34) rudiment section for more.

*Dead Stroke:* a note that does not bounce or rebound from the drum head, but instead stays in contact with the surface of the drum.

*Diddle:* type of Double Stroke. Not a very precise term.
Possible definitions, not agreed upon universally:
  1. A Double Stroke played at the same note value as the adjacent notes of the passage, rather than doubling the note value or playing at any other subdivision – as in the rudiment Paradiddle (20).
  2. A Double Stroke played by bouncing the stick twice, using the rebound of the head for each single wrist motion. A bounced or rebound double.
  3. A Double Stroke played exactly twice the note value as the adjacent notes of the passage, often notated with a tremelo slash. As in the PAS rudiment Dragadiddle (47).
  4. Synonymous with Double Stroke, used interchangeably with no specificity to the technique.

*Double Stop:* two single strokes played simultaneously, one on each hand – together. See the Double Stop (33) rudiment section for more.

*Double Stroke:* two notes played by the same hand. These can occur in groups of any number, so long as each successive group of two is alternated between the right and left hands – two notes per hand. See the Double Stroke Open Roll (5) rudiment section for more.

*Drag:* three successive notes, normally played as a double stroke and a single stroke, or two grace notes on the same hand preceding a primary note on the opposite hand. See the Drag (23) rudiment section for more.

*Flam:* two single strokes played nearly simultaneously, but not quite. A grace note, and then a primary note, played very closely together in time. See the Flam (32) rudiment section for more.

*Fulcrum:* the point on the stick around which the stick rotates when playing a stroke. Much like the center of a seesaw or teeter-totter on a playground.

*Ghost Note:* an unaccented note that is even lower and quieter than a normal tap. Usually used in conjunction with drum kit playing, and not a common term for rudimental drumming.

*Gock Shot:* like a rimshot, a note played with the tip of the stick on the head and the shaft of the same stick on the rim, simultaneously. It differs from the rimshot in that it is played with the tip of the stick in the center of the drum, so that the rim contacts the shaft of the same stick about ½ of the way down the stick, closer to the player's hand. Produces a lower pitched and less cutting sound than a rimshot or a ping shot.

*Grace Note:* a note whose value is not precisely determined, nor counted. Written smaller than primary (normal) notes, and used for embellishment. See the grace note section for more.

*Guts:* alternative name for snare wires.

*Head:* the playing surface of a drum, made of a stretched membrane. Today they are made of Mylar (polyester) or Kevlar (aramid), but in the past they were typically natural hide, such as calf or goat, and were sometimes called skins.

*Hybrid Rudiment:* a rudiment that combines elements from different existing rudiments to form a novel pattern, and that was created relatively recently. See the Hybrid Rudiment section for more.

*Multiple Bounce Stroke:* any number of notes greater than two played by the same hand. Triple strokes are a specific variation of the Multiple Bounce, but groups of 4 or more are also considered to be Multiple. Sometimes described as a buzz, crush, or press. See the Multiple Bounce Roll (17) rudiment section for more.

*NARD:* acronym for National Association of Rudimental Drummers, formed in 1933, the official source for the standard 26 rudiments that predate the PAS 40.

*PAS:* acronym for Percussive Arts Society, formed in 1961, the official source for the 40 rudiments that have been the standard list since 1984, often referred to as the PAS 40.

*Ping Shot:* like a rimshot, a note played with the tip of the stick on the head and the shaft of the same stick on the rim, simultaneously. It differs from the rimshot in that it is played with the tip of the stick near the edge of the head, so that the rim contacts the shaft of the same stick very near the tip, less than 1/3 of the way down the stick, much closer to the tip. Produces a more overtone-laden sound than a rimshot or a gock shot.

*Rebound:* alternative to bounce, when the stick is rebounded from the drumhead through the elastic property of the head itself.

*Rimshot:* a note played with the tip of the stick striking the head and the shaft of the same stick striking the rim simultaneously. This produces a louder and more cutting sound than playing either the head or the rim independently. In rudimental drumming, a rimshot is specifically played with the tip of the stick about halfway between the center and the edge of the head, so that the rim contacts the shaft of the same stick about 1/3 of the way down the stick. Similar to a gock shot or a ping shot.

*Roll:* any sustained sound produced on the drum by any of several techniques. Single strokes, double strokes, triple strokes, or multiple bounce strokes can be used to create different types of rolls. Other combinations of strokes can also be considered a roll if the sounds are even and close enough together to be heard as a sustained sound.

*Ruff:* not a very precise term, and poorly defined. It generally means a short burst of sound and/or an embellishment prior to a downbeat, but has many connotations, and can contain differing numbers of strokes, stickings, and technical executions. The definition is often region or era dependent. See the 3 Stroke Ruff (2), 4 Stroke Ruff (3), Crushed Ruff (18), Drag (23), and Ruff (24) rudiment sections for more.

*Single Stroke:* an individual note played with one hand. These may occur in groups of any number, so long as each successive note is alternated between the right and left hands – one note per hand. See the Single Stroke Roll (1) rudiment section for more.

*Skin:* alternative name for a drum head.

*Snare Wires:* strands of various materials that cross the bottom or resonant head of a snare drum and provide the characteristic bright staccato sound. These can be made of coiled or flat wire, natural or synthetic gut, cord, cable, or other materials.

*Stick Click:* a note played with one stick upon the other wherein neither stick is touching the drum. It is purely the sound of the sticks contacting one another. Also referred to as stick-on-stick or stick beats.

*Stick Shot:* a note played with one stick upon the other, wherein the stick being played upon has its tip resting on the head of the drum.

*Stroke:* any motion of the fingers, wrist, or arm that results in the stick striking the head and producing a note. There are 4 Basic Stroke types, see the Basic Strokes section for more.

*Tap:* a note that is not accented, usually used in contrast to an accent. One of the Basic Strokes.

*Triple Stroke:* three notes played by the same hand. These can occur in groups of any number, so long as each successive group of three is alternated between the right and left hands – three notes per hand. See the Triple Stroke (19) rudiment section for more.

# Selected Bibliography

Anonymous. "Drum Beating." c. 1770-1790. Manuscript, University of Birmingham, Shaw Hellier Collection No. 287, Birmingham, England.

Anonymous. "Drummers Book of Music." c. 1778-1805. Manuscript, Massachusetts Historical Society, Boston, MA.

Ashworth, Charles Stewart. *A New, Useful, and Complete System of Drum Beating.* Boston: Graupner & Price, 1812.

Berger, F. R. *Instructor for Basle-Drumming.* Basle Drum-Editions, 1964.

Bower, Harry A. *The Harry A. Bower System for the Drums, Bells, Xylophone, and Tympani.* New York: Carl Fischer, 1911.

Bruce, G. and Emmett, D. *The Drummer's and Fifer's Guide.* New York: Wm. A. Pond & Co., 1862.

Campbell, James. *Rudiments in Rhythm.* Maryland: Meredith Music, 2002.

Clark, Benjamin. *Benjamin Clark Drum Book.* Boston: 1797.

Day, Isaac. "Isaac Day 1st Book." c. 1797-1808. Manuscript, Company of Fifers and Drummers, Ivoryton, Connecticut.

Diesenroth, Friedrich. *Der Spielmann Heft 6.* Wiesbaden: Rud. Erdmann, 1968.

Douce, Francis. "The Grounds of Beating the Drum." Francis Douce's Manuscript insert in Hawkinn's *History of Music* Volume III, c. 1600-1650. Bodleian Library, Oxford.

Echeverría Hermanos. *Reglamento e Instruccion de la Infanteria de Linea i Tiradores, para el Servicio de los Cuerpos de la Guardia Colombiana.* Bogatá: Echeverría Hermanos, 1862.

Espinosa, D. Manuel de. Joseph Grasch ed. *Toques de Guerra – Anyo 1769.* Barcelona: Iglesia de Santa Maria del Mar, 1788.

Eagle, Michael. "The Scottish Drumming Rudiments." Pearl Drums and Eagle Artist Management, 2014.

Freytag, Edward. *The Rudimental Cookbook.* Row-Loff Productions, 1993.

Fröhlich, Joseph. *Kurzgefaßte Practiche Anleitung zur Militær Musik.* München: Lith. Anat. v. J. Wild, 1861.

Fulling, Hans. *Øvelser for Marchtromme – Fløjte og Signalhorn.* 1963.

Guizzi, Febo et al. *Pifferi e Tamburi.* Libreria Musicale Italiano, 2006.

Hart, H. C., Colonel. *H.C. Hart's New and Improved Instructor for the Drum.* New York: William Hall & Son, 1862.

Hazeltine, David. *Instructor in Martial Music.* New York: C. Norris and Co., 1810.

Howe, Elias. *Howe's United States Regulation Drum and Fife Instructor for the Army and Navy.* Boston: Elias Howe, 1861.

Kastner, Georges. *Manuel Général de Musique Militaire a L'Usage des Armées Françaises.* Paris: Firmin Didot Fréres de l'Institute de France, 1848.

Keach, Burditt, and Cassidy, Eds. *The Army Drum and Fife Book.* Boston: Oliver Ditson and Co., 1861.

Krupa, Gene. *Drum Method.* Big Three, 1938.

Landberg, Rolf. *The Drumming Tradition of Sweden.* Rolf Landberg, 2024.

Lechat, Marcel. "Royaume de Belgique – Le Folklore de L'Entre-Sambre-et-Meuse – Cours du Tambour." 2005.

Lovering, Levi. *The Drummers Assistant or the Art of Drumming Made Easy.* Philadelphia: Bacon & Co., 1819.

Ludwig, William F. *Complete Drum Instructor.* Chicago: Ludwig Drum Co., 1942.

Mansilla, D. Lucio, Coronel. *Reglamento para el Ejercicio y Maniobras de la Infantería del Ejército Argentino.* Buenos Aires: Imprenta y Librerías de Mayo, 1875.

Moeller, Sanford A. *The Art of Snare Drumming.* Chicago: Ludwig, 1925.

Moore, J. Burns. *Art of Drumming.* Chicago: Ludwig, 1937.

Morello, Joe. *Rudimental Jazz.* Chicago: Jomor, 1967.

Mott, Vincent. *Evolution of Drumming.* New Jersey: Music Textbook Company, 1956.

National Association of Rudimental Drummers. *America's NARD Drum Solos.* Charles Dumont & Sons, 1943.

National Association of Rudimental Drummers. "The 13 Essential Rudiments." National Association of Rudimental Drummers, 1933.

National Association of Rudimental Drummers. "The 13 Rudiments to Complete the 26 Standard American Drum Rudiments." National Association of Rudimental Drummers, 1936.

Nemetz, Andreas. *Allgemeine Musikschule für MilitärMusik.* Wien: Ant. Diabelli & Comp., c. 1860.

Percussive Arts Society. "Percussive Arts Society International Drum Rudiments." Percussive Arts Society, 1984.

Percussion Creativ. "Rudimental Codex." Percussion Creativ, 2018.

Potter, Samuel. *The Art of Beating the Drum.* London: Henry Potter, 1815.

Rausher, J. *Marschen en Signalen voor de Tamboers en Pypers van de Armée.* S'Gravenhage, 1815.

Reale Epografia Militare. *Ordinanza di sua Maestá per gli Esercizj e le Evoluzioni delle Truppe di Fanteria.* Vol 1. Napoli: Reale Epografia Militare, 1846.

Rich, Buddy and Adler, Henry. *Modern Interpretation of Snare Drum Rudiments.* Embassy, 1942.

Robinson, Alvan. *Massachusetts Collection: Martial Musick.* Massachusetts: F. Goodale, 1818.

Rumrille, J. L. and Holton, H. *The Drummer's Instructor or Martial Musician.* Albany: Packard and Van Benthuyeer, 1817.

Secretaría de la Defensa Nacional. *Manual de Ademanes y Toques Militares.* DN M 522. Mexico: Secretaría de la Defensa Nacional, 2020.

Schweizer Armee. *Tambour-Ordonnanz.* Bern: Schweizer Armee, 2020.

Sousa, John P. *The Trumpet and Drum.* 1886.

Steuben, Friedrich Wilhelm de. *Regulations for the Order and Discipline of the Troops of the United States.* Philadelphia: Styner and Cist, 1779.

Stone, G. L. *Military Drum Beats for School and Drum Corps.* Massachusetts: George B. Stone & Son, 1931.

Strube, Gardiner A. *Drum and Fife Instructor.* New York: D. Appleton & Company, 1870.

Tourte, Robert. *Méthode de Tambour et Caisse-Claire d'Orchestre.* Paris: Editions Salabert, 1946

Ulano, Sam. *Practical Study Charts for Drummers.* Vol. 3. 1959.

U.S. Army. *United States Army Training Manual No. 6 – Musical Instruction for Army Bandsmen.* Washington: Government Printing Office, 1922.

Vasilyeiv, Alexander. *Практичекая школа для малаго барабана.* Юлій Генрихъ Циммерманъ, 1912.

Wilcoxon, Charles. *Modern Rudimental Swing Solos for the Advanced Drummer.* 1941.

Wilcoxon, Charles. *The All-American Drummer.* 1945.

# About the Authors

Ryan Alexander Bloom has studied rudimental drumming since 1996 and endorses Vater Percussion as an educator. He teaches marching and concert percussion in public schools, and teaches drum set and other percussion from his own studio. Ryan's original instructional drum books are published with Hudson Music and Mel Bay, including *Encyclopedia Rudimentia* and *Rudimental Grand Tour,* and his research has been featured in *Percussive Notes*. His other publications include translations of Swiss and French military rudimental manuals, and transcriptions of 19th century drum books into modern notation. Ryan holds a degree in percussion from the University of Colorado, has signed contracts with Candlelight Records and Redefining Darkness Records as a drum set player, and is continually refining his understanding of historical and modern international rudimental drumming. Learn more about Ryan and his other books at BloomDrums.com.

James Musser began on guitar in 1966, and added the drums in 1970, when his brother got a lightly used, 1967 blue sparkle Ludwig kit for Christmas. James was inspired by fusion drummers such as Bill Berg, Gary Husband, Billy Cobham, Lenny White, Narada Michael Walden, Furio Chirico, and so many others. He was fortunate to start his first fusion band in 1975. He is the owner and principal instructor at Peaceland Music in Torrance, CA since 1998, where he teaches private drum lessons as well as voice, guitar, violin, bass, and recording. His nominations include "Best Guitar" and "Best LA Band" at the *LA Music Awards*. His band was also awarded "Top 100 Unsigned Bands" from *Music Connection* magazine and "Best South Bay Band" from *Rock City News*. His patented Peaceland Guitar Ring slide innovations were twice awarded "Best In Show" at both the Winter and Summer NAMM Shows, consecutively. Peaceland Guitar Ring slides are currently available at MusiciansFriend.com, GuitarCenter.com, and PeacelandMusic.com, as well.

# Acknowledgements

Ryan would like to acknowledge and thank the following people for their support: his wife Rose, James (especially for his willingness to ask the tough questions), his private students (past and present), and his colleagues in the rudimental research community for their efforts in finding and distributing historical materials and knowledge.

James would like to sincerely acknowledge Ryan for his willingness to go the distance on this endeavor; to JoEllyn Musser for her eternal love and support in all ways; and to the students and colleagues at Peaceland Music for their inspiration and continued determination to learn and improve, each and every day.